ROBERT McGONIGLE

CASEBOOK OF MULTIMODAL THERAPY

Casebook of Multimodal Therapy

Edited by
ARNOLD A. LAZARUS
Graduate School of Applied and Professional Psychology
Rutgers—The State University of New Jersey

THE GUILFORD PRESS
New York   London

TO ANDREW SALTER,

for his inspiration and continued encouragement

© 1985 The Guilford Press
A Division of Guilford Publications, Inc.
200 Park Avenue South, New York, N.Y. 10003

Printed in the United States of America

Library of Congress Cataloging in Publication Data

Main entry under title:

Casebook of multimodal therapy.

  Includes bibliographies and index.
  1. Psychotherapy—Case studies. I. Lazarus,
Arnold A. [DNLM: 1. Psychotherapy—case studies.
WM 420 C337]
RC480.5.C366 1985   616.89'14   84-19835
ISBN 0-89862-647-1

CONTRIBUTORS

ALLEN P. BLASUCCI, PsyD, Co-Director, Multimodal Therapy Institute, P.A., Rocky Hill, New Jersey

LILLIAN F. BRUNELL, PsyD, private practice, West Orange, New Jersey; Consultant to the multidisciplinary teams, Essex County Hospital Center, Cedar Grove, New Jersey

HUGO J. DUIVENVOORDEN, MD, Department of Medical Psychology and Psychotherapy, Faculty of Medicine, Erasmus University, Rotterdam, The Netherlands

EDWIN R. GERLER, JR., PhD, Associate Professor of Counselor Education, North Carolina State University, Raleigh, North Carolina

SHARON L. GREENBURG, PhD, private practice, Chicago, Illinois; Adjunct Professor, Department of Counseling Psychology/Higher Education, Graduate School, Loyola University of Chicago, Chicago, Illinois

DONALD B. KEAT II, PhD, Professor–Director of Training, Counseling Psychology Program, and Coordinator, Child Counseling Program, The Pennsylvania State University, University Park, Pennsylvania; private practice, State College, Pennsylvania

MAURITS G. T. KWEE, MD, Senior Psychologist and Head, Inpatient Department of Behavior Therapy, "Het Sint Joris Gasthuis" mental hospital, Delft, The Netherlands

ARNOLD A. LAZARUS, PhD, Professor of Psychology, Graduate School of Applied and Professional Psychology, Rutgers—The State University of New Jersey, Piscataway, New Jersey; private practice, Princeton, New Jersey

LUIS R. NIEVES, PsyD, Co-Director, Multimodal Therapy Institute, P.A., Rocky Hill, New Jersey; Director, Self-Management Instruction Program, Educational Testing Service, Princeton, New Jersey

JAMES T. RICHARD, EdD, Professor of Psychology, Bucks County Community College, Newtown, Pennsylvania; Executive Director, Newtown Psychological Centre, Newtown, Pennsylvania; Assistant Clinical Professor, Hahnemann University Medical School, Philadelphia, Pennsylvania

MICHEL R. H. M. ROBORGH, MA, clinical psychologist/behavior therapist, Outpatient Department, "Sint Joris Nieuwe Plantage" of "Het Sint Joris Gasthuis" mental hospital, Delft, The Netherlands

JEFFREY A. RUDOLPH, PsyD, Director, Multimodal Therapy Institute, New York, New York; Adjunct Instructor, Adelphi University, Garden City, New York; Supervising Clinical Psychologist, Yeshiva University, New York, New York

JULIAN W. SLOWINSKI, PsyD, Director, Child and Family Outpatient Services, Pennsylvania Hospital, Hall–Mercer Center, Philadelphia, Pennsylvania; Department of Psychiatry, School of Medicine, University of Pennsylvania, Philadelphia, Pennsylvania

MARTIN YANIS, PhD, Principal Clinical Psychologist, New Jersey Department of Human Services, Trenton, New Jersey

PREFACE

Since the appearance of the first published account of multimodal (BASIC I.D.) assessment and therapy (Lazarus, 1973), several books (e.g., Lazarus, 1976; Keat, 1979; Lazarus, 1981; Brunell & Young, 1982) and numerous papers, articles, and chapters have appeared. First viewed as one of 66 *innovative psychotherapies* outside the mainstream of today's major treatment orientations (Corsini, 1981), multimodal therapy has subsequently been featured alongside psychoanalysis, Adlerian psychotherapy, rational–emotive therapy, behavior therapy, Gestalt therapy, and six other *current psychotherapies* (Corsini, 1984). Thus, multimodal therapy is now characterized as an integral part of the prevailing *Zeitgeist* of psychological treatments.

The present volume arose out of a need expressed by several colleagues and many students for additional "how to" and "when to" case material—that is, how and when to apply specific assessment–therapy procedures. Consequently, I wrote to several "multimodal therapists" and asked them if they would care to submit cogent case material. I rejected those cases that were presented in such a way that I did not learn something new. Thus, in my opinion, both novice therapists and seasoned veterans will find something of value in each chapter herein. Those readers already familiar with multimodal issues and the BASIC I.D. framework will find this book useful in placing "meat" on the theoretical "skeleton." For those who are unfamiliar with the multimodal format, Chapter 1 should provide the necessary background.

The discerning reader will note that in most instances, the techniques employed are drawn mainly from cognitive-behavior therapy and rational–emotive therapy. Multimodal therapy is predicated on technical eclecticism whereby its practitioners select those methods that are demonstrably effective; and the evidence (Rachman & Wilson, 1980) points to the efficacy of behvioral and cognitive–behavioral procedures over most other interventions. However, the multimodal framework facilitates the use of methods from family systems, communications training, Gestalt therapy, psychodrama, and many other orientations, when the situation demands it.

A recent survey of 100 patients who had not responded to at least three previous therapists before seeking multimodal therapy (thus excluding the "placebo reactors" and those common or garden-variety "neurotics" who require little more than a good listener, or a touch of empathy) revealed that 61 achieved objective and unequivocal benefits (i.e., quantifiable *decreases* in compulsive behaviors, depressive reactions, panic attacks, marital and family disputes, sexual inadequacy, avoidance behaviors; and corresponding *increases* in assertive responses, work-related achievements, and prosocial behaviors). As can be seen from the case descriptions in this book, the systematic and comprehensive scope of multimodal therapy tries to "leave no stone unturned" when ferreting out elusive problems and when designing effective remedies for each problem. Consequently, outcomes and follow-ups have been impressive.

Multimodal therapists constantly ask: What works, for whom, and under which particular circumstances? With many practitioners, clients seem to get only what the therapist practices—which may not necessarily be best for a particular client. In multimodal therapy there is a deliberate attempt to determine precisely what type of relationship, what type of interactive cadence, each particular client will respond to. We emphasize therapeutic flexibility and versatility above all else. There is no unitary way to approach peoples' problems. Some years back (Lazarus, 1977) I stressed that "I am opposed to the advancement of psychoanalysis, to the advancement of Gestalt therapy, to the advancement of existential therapy, to the advancement of behavior therapy, or to the advancement of any delimited school of thought. I would like to see an advancement in psychological knowledge, an advancement in the understanding of human interaction, in the alleviation of suffering, and in the know-how of therapeutic intervention" (p. 553). It is hoped that counselors and clinicians will find this book of value in attaining some of the forementioned goals.

REFERENCES

Brunell, L. F., & Young, W. T. (Eds.). (1982). *Multimodal handbook for a mental hospital.* New York: Springer.

Corsini, R. J. (Ed.). (1981). *Handbook of innovative psychotherapies.* New York: Wiley.

Corsini, R. J. (Ed.). (1984). *Current psychotherapies* (3rd ed.). Itasca, IL: F. E. Peacock.

Keat, D. B. (1979). *Multimodal therapy with children.* New York: Pergamon.

Lazarus, A. A. (1973). Multimodal behavior therapy: Treating the BASIC I.D. *Journal of Nervous and Mental Disease, 156,* 404–411.

Lazarus, A. A. (Ed.). (1976). *Multimodal behavior therapy.* New York: Springer.

Lazarus, A. A. (1977). Has behavior therapy outlived its usefulness? *American Psychologist, 32,* 550–554.

Lazarus, A. A. (1981). *The practice of multimodal therapy.* New York: McGraw-Hill.

Rachman, S. J., & Wilson, G. T. (1980). *The effects of psychological therapy* (2nd enlarged ed.). New York: Pergamon.

CONTENTS

1

A Brief Overview of Multimodal Therapy

ARNOLD A. LAZARUS

INTRODUCTION

While the need for psychological services is increasing rapidly, available financial resources are diminishing. In addition, the emphasis on accountability has become more compelling. Third-party payment agencies are far more stringent about treatment outcomes and cost-effectiveness. Protracted treatment procedures are difficult to justify in terms of cost–benefit analyses. Clearly, the overriding need is for psychotherapeutic methods that are both rapid *and* long-lasting. Multimodal therapy is the outgrowth of more than 20 years of clinical research into systematic, short-term, and yet comprehensive psychotherapeutic strategies. It provides an operational way of arriving at an answer to the question: What works, for whom, and under which conditions?

A fundamental premise of the multimodal approach is that patients are troubled by at least several specific problems that may require a wide range of specific treatments. Another basic assumption is that durability of results is a function of the effort expended by patient and therapist across seven dimensions of personality—behavior, affect, sensation, imagery, cognition, interpersonal relationships, and biological factors.

Most of our experiences comprise moving, feeling, sensing, imagining, thinking, and relating to one another. In the final analysis, we are biochemical/neurophysiological entities. Human life and conduct are products of ongoing *b*ehaviors, *a*ffective processes, *s*ensations, *i*mages, *c*ognitions, and *i*nterpersonal relationships, springing from a *b*iological matrix. BASIC IB is an acronym derived from this sequence, but for convenience and euphony, the letter D (for drugs) will stand for the biological modality, thus generating the more compelling acronym BASIC ID, or the preferred BASIC I.D. (I.D. as in "identity"). It is important to keep in mind that "D" stands for more than pharmacologic interven-

A brief version of this chapter was published in American Psychiatric Association: *Psychiatry Update: The American Psychiatric Association Annual Review* (Vol. III), edited by L. Grinspoon, 1984, Washington, DC: American Psychiatric Press. Used with permission.

tion, and includes all biological etiologies of "psychological" symptoms and dysfunctions, as well as the entire panoply of somatic interventions.

It is also essential to recognize and include factors that fall outside the BASIC I.D., such as political, sociocultural, and other macroenvironmental events. There are obviously crucial differences in adaptive interpersonal styles between people raised and living in Tennessee and Tibet, but regardless of an individual's background, detailed descriptions of salient behaviors, affective responses, sensory reactions, images, cognitions, interpersonal dealings, and biological diatheses will provide the principal ingredients of one's psychological make-up. It is assumed that BASIC I.D. comprises the entire range of human personality; that there is no problem, no feeling, no accomplishment, no dream or fantasy that cannot be subsumed by this schema. Multimodal therapy attends to specific problems or difficulties within a given modality as well as the interaction between this modality and each of the six others. For example, to assess how certain behaviors influence and are influenced by affects, sensations, images, cognitions, and significant relationships, is to know a great deal about individuals and their social networks.

BASIC I.D. is not an arbitrary division created *sui generis*. Since the publication of Brentano's *Psychologie vom empirischen Standpunkte* in 1874, the subject matter of general psychology (the scientific study of human behavior) has been concerned with sensation, imagery, perception, cognition, emotion, and interpersonal relationships. "If we examine psychotherapeutic processes in the light of each of these basic modalities, seemingly disparate systems are brought into clearer focus, and the necessary and sufficient conditions for long-lasting therapeutic change might readily be discerned" (Lazarus, 1973, p. 406).

TECHNICAL VERSUS THEORETICAL ECLECTICISM

Multimodal therapy is pluralistic and personalistic. It emphasizes that human disquietude is multileveled and multilayered and that few, if any, problems have a single cause or unitary "cure." A sensitivity to individual differences and exceptions to general rules and principles obviates the need to apply preconceived treatments to patients with similar "diagnoses." Rather, the multimodal clinician searches for appropriate interventions for each patient. Clinical effectiveness is predicated on the therapist's flexibility, versatility, and *technical* eclecticism.

The *theoretical* eclectic may subscribe to theories or disciplines that are epistemologically incompatible. The limitations of orthodoxy have become apparent, and many clinicians embrace multidimensional and multifaceted assessment and treatment procedures. Yet those who endeavor to unite the morass of competing systems, models, vocabularies, and personal idiosyncracies into a unified whole, tend to end up with an agglomerate of incompatible and contradictory notions (Lazarus, 1981; Messer & Winokur, 1980). The *technical* eclectic uses many techniques drawn from different sources without adhering to the theories or systems that spawned them. One need not believe in Gestalt principles to use Gestalt techniques; one may employ behavioral methods without subscribing to the tenets of social learning theory.

While a recent survey (Smith, 1982) indicated that the majority of therapists are eclectic and multimodal in outlook, in our view, only a few are multimodal therapists. The distinction is important. Multimodal therapy has a well-defined history, a systematic theoretical base, a coherent framework, and a wide range of specific techniques (Lazarus, 1976, 1981, 1984). Multimodal principles are expressed in terms that can be tested, and its procedures are consonant with current scientific findings. Multimodal therapists constantly adjust to the patient in terms of that mode of interaction most likely to achieve the desired aims of the therapy. The essential and distinguishing features of multimodal therapy are its comprehensive scope and its systematic methodology. Whereas some therapies are multifaceted and espouse "multimodalism" in principle, Multimodal Therapy alone uses the exhaustive BASIC I.D. schema.

> The aim of Multimodal Therapy (MMT) is to come up with the best methods for each client rather than force all clients to fit the same therapy. . . . Three depressed clients might be given very different treatments depending on their therapists' assessments and the methods they prefer. . . . The only goal is helping clients make desired changes as rapidly as possible. (Zilbergeld, 1982, p. 86)

MULTIMODAL DIAGNOSIS AND ASSESSMENT

The cliche "diagnosis must precede treatment" points to the obvious fact that when the real problems have been identified, effective remedies (if they exist) can be administered. Conventional diagnostic labels and nosological categories are less valuable for treatment planning than the construction of *Modality Profiles* (i.e., a chart that lists problems and proposed treatments across the BASIC I.D.). For illustrative purposes the Modality Profile of a 32-year-old woman diagnosed as suffering from "alcohol dependence" (DSM-III 303.9x) is presented in Table 1-1.

THE SELECTION OF TECHNIQUES

The Modality Profile in Table 1-1 clearly places the patient's alcoholism or excessive drinking in the context of a general series of specific and

TABLE 1-1. Modality Profile of a Woman with "Alcohol Dependence"

Modality	Problem	Proposed treatment
Behavior	Excessive drinking	Aversive imagery
	Avoids confronting most people	Assertiveness training
	Negative self-statements	Positive self-talk assignments
	Always drinks excessively when alone at home at night	Develop social outlets
	Screams at her children	Instruction in parenting skills
Affect	Holds back anger (except with her children)	Assertiveness training
		Anger expression exercises
	Anxiety reactions	Self-hypnosis and/or positive imagery
	Depression	Increase range of positive reinforcement
Sensation	Butterflies in stomach	Abdominal breathing exercises
	Tension headaches	Relaxation or biofeedback
Imagery	Vivid pictures of parents fighting	Desensitization
	Being locked in bedroom as a child	Images of escape and/or release of anger
Cognition	Irrational self-talk about low self-worth	Cognitive disputation
	Numerous regrets	Reduction of categorical imperatives (shoulds, oughts, musts, etc.)
Interpersonal relationships	Ambivalent responses to husband and children	Possible family therapy and specific training in use of positive reinforcement
		Support group to control alcohol abuse—Alcoholics Anonymous (AA)
	Secretive and suspicious	Self-disclosure training
Drugs/biology	Reliance on alcohol to alleviate depression, anxiety, tension	Possible use of disulfiram and antidepressant medication

interrelated problems. Seventeen problem areas are juxtaposed to 17 treatment recommendations. Typically, patient and therapist examine the profile and determine "treatment priorities." In the present case the following initial treatments were selected:

Relaxation Training

More than 45 years ago, Jacobson (1938) postulated that muscle tension is related to anxiety and demonstrated that the deliberate and progressive "letting go" of tense muscles can result in a significant reduction of subjective anxiety. Through alternate tension–relaxation contrasts (Bernstein & Borkovec, 1973) the patient was taught to identify her main tension foci. She was given a cassette recording for home use to augment the skills that were achieved in the consulting room.

Aversive Imagery

The patient was instructed to picture, most vividly and realistically, various aversive consequences that would accompany the ingestion of alcohol. For example, she was asked to imagine experiencing nausea and vomiting while pouring and tasting brandy, vodka, or beer (her three favorite drinks). This method is often referred to as *covert sensitization* (Cautela, 1967).

Assertiveness Training

In concert with relaxation training and aversive imagery, emphasis was placed on remedying the patient's interpersonal deficits—her inability to refuse unreasonable requests, her fear of making her own feelings known, her withdrawal tendencies, and her aggressive (rather than assertive) interactions with her children. This was dealt with by a combination of instruction, prescribed readings (e.g., Baer, 1976), and role playing (patient and therapist enacted several scenes until both agreed that they were well executed). Many studies have shown that these methods tend to promote social adeptness and result in decreased anxiety (e.g., Bellack, Hersen, & Turner, 1976; Goldsmith & McFall, 1975; Lewinsohn & Hoberman, 1982).

In addition to the foregoing procedures, the therapist had introduced methods of cognitive disputation (Ellis & Grieger, 1977) into the sessions, but they were postponed when it became clear that the patient felt overloaded. However, it was soon evident that therapy for her ambivalent feelings toward her husband and children could not be held in abeyance. Thus, one family session and one individual session per week were scheduled. Her depressed affect came into clearer focus, and a psychiatrist prescribed a tricyclic drug. The patient's excessive drinking was brought under control within 2½ months. (As therapy progressed additional problems came to the fore, certain proposed treatments were abandoned in favor of others, and a clearer understanding emerged of the patient as a wife, mother, daughter, and especially as a unique individual.)

In the present case the initial choice of techniques was commensurate with clinical behavior therapy (Goldfried & Davison, 1976), but as therapy continued, it seemed necessary to apply a series of techniques that transcended the typical range of methods employed by behavior therapists. Thus, "time regression images" transported the patient to early childhood encounters with her parents wherein she pictured herself retaliating for their alleged injustices (Lazarus, 1978). After several sessions she appeared to attain a fitting indifference to these real or imagined parental short-comings and reported feeling "freed up inside."

The art and science of multimodal therapy consist of administering *treatments of choice* whenever feasible, while tailoring their method of application to fit idiosyncratic requirements. Thus, lithium carbonate would generally be a treatment priority for patients with a bipolar affective disorder, but the way in which the subjects of medication, dosage, and blood level assay would be introduced, would depend on the patient's sensitivities, attitude toward drug taking, history of compliance, family pressures, and so forth. Moreover, it would be rare to treat only the "D modality"—assessment of the BASIC I. is often deemed necessary even when gratifying benefits follow the use of medical interventions. Thus, in reference to the treatment of schizophrenia and manic–depressive disorders, Fay (1976) stated that "in such cases, medication can be considered as a necessary though not always sufficient condition for the satisfactory resolution of the difficulty" (p. 66).

Other "treatments of choice" include the use of *in vivo* exposure for most phobic conditions and particularly in the treatment of agoraphobia (Mathews, Gelder, & Johnston, 1981). Moreover, the combined use of flooding and response prevention is often a *sine qua non* in the treatment of obsessive–compulsive disorders (Barlow & Wolfe, 1981). A comprehensive review of specific treatment outcomes and indications across the range of psychological problems is provided by Rachman and Wilson (1980). Multimodal therapists take cognizance of the scientific literature while simultaneously addressing the personalistic needs of the individual patient, couple, family, or group.

THE PROBLEM IDENTIFICATION SEQUENCE

The multimodal approach to diagnosis and treatment is similar to "the problem-oriented record approach." The emphasis upon problem specification in psychiatry was underscored by Hayes-Roth, Longabaugh, and Ryback (1972). This approach to record keeping and treatment had been introduced to medicine somewhat earlier, being best illustrated by Weed's (1968) work.

We will now describe the typical anamnestic procedures that enable a therapist to construct Modality Profiles. (The present chapter addresses adult outpatients. For the multimodal therapy approach to children, see Keat, 1979, and for its use with inpatients see Brunell & Young, 1982.)

The initial interview, as in most psychotherapeutic approaches, is devoted to eliciting and evaluating presenting complaints, establishing rapport, and formulating the optimal treatment. The multimodal therapist remains alert to dysfunctions across the entire BASIC I.D. Immediate antecedent events and the presymptomatic environment are carefully evaluated. In examining the postsymptomatic environment, a key question is, "Who or what appears to be maintaining the problems?" At the end of the initial interview, patients are usually given the 12-page Multimodal Life History Questionnaire (Lazarus, 1981), which they complete at home and then bring to their next session. The questionnaire, in addition to reviewing the patient's early development, family interactions, educational, sexual, occupational, and marital experiences, specifically assesses the most salient aspects of the BASIC I.D. Ambiguous or incomplete answers are usually discussed with the patient during the second session. Thereafter, with notes from the first two meetings, and responses on the Life History Questionnaire, it is relatively straightforward to construct a Modality Profile. Generally patients are asked to do their own Modality Profiles; it is often particularly valuable for therapist and patient to perform this exercise independently and then compare notes.

PATIENTS' INSTRUCTIONS FOR CONSTRUCTING MODALITY PROFILES

Before being asked to draw up their profiles, patients are provided with a brief explanation of each term in the BASIC I.D. A typewritten instruction sheet with the following information usually suffices:

Behavior: This refers mainly to overt behaviors: to acts, habits, gestures, responses, and reactions that are observable and measurable. Make a list of those acts, habits, etc., that you want to increase and those you would like to decrease. What would you like to start doing? What would you like to stop doing?

Affect: This refers to emotions, moods, and strong feelings. What emotions do you experience most often? Write down your unwanted emotions (e.g., anxiety, guilt, anger, depression, etc.). Note under "behavior" what you tend to *do* when you feel a certain way.

Sensation: Touching, tasting, smelling, seeing, and hearing are our five basic senses. Make a list of any negative sensations (tension, dizzyness, pain, blushing, sweating, butterflies in stomach, etc.) that apply to you. If any of these sensations cause you to act or feel in certain ways, make sure you note them under "behavior" or "affect."

Imagery: Write down any bothersome recurring dreams and vivid memories. Include any negative features about the way you see yourself—your "self-image." Make a list of any "mental pictures"—past, present, or future—that may be troubling you. If any "auditory images"—tunes or sounds that you keep hearing—constitute a problem, jot them down. If your images arouse any significant actions, feelings, or sensations, make sure these items are added to "behavior," "affect," and "sensation."

Cognition: What types of attitudes, values, opinions, and ideas get in the way of your happiness? Make a list of negative things you often say to yourself (e.g., "I am a failure," or "I am stupid," or "Others dislike me," or "I am no good"). Write down some of your most irrational ideas. Be sure to note down how these ideas and thoughts influence your behaviors, feelings, sensations, and images.

Interpersonal Relationships: Write down any bothersome interactions with other people (relatives, friends, lovers, employers, acquaintances, etc.). Any concerns you have about the way other people treat you should appear here. Check through the items under "behavior," "affect," "sensation," "imagery," and "cognition," and try to determine how they influence, and are influenced by, your interpersonal relationships. (Note that there is some overlap between the modalities, but don't hesitate to list the same problem more than once, e.g., under "behavior" and "interpersonal relationships.")

Drugs/biology: Make a list of all drugs you are taking, whether prescribed by a doctor or not. Include any health problems, medical concerns, and illnesses that you have or have had.

It is not assumed that patients are capable of identifying or articulating all problem areas throughout the BASIC I.D. It is obvious that different people display different degrees of awareness and disclosure, so that many thoughts, beliefs, wishes, feelings, impulses, and actions may not be immediately ascertained from the initial profile. During the course of multimodal therapy, *nonconscious processes* and *defensive reactions* are addressed whenever indicated (Lazarus, 1981). Indeed, part of the purpose of therapy is to discover certain hitherto unrecognized factors that fit into one or more categories of the BASIC I.D. (one form of "insight"). Assessment and therapy are both reciprocal and continuous. The technique of second-order BASIC I.D. assessment often uncovers material that has been inaccessible to other avenues of inquiry.

SECOND-ORDER BASIC I.D. ASSESSMENTS

The initial BASIC I.D. or Modality Profile provides a *macroscopic* overview of "personality." A complete diagnosis calls for an accurate and thorough assessment of each modality and the interactions among and between the seven modalities. A *second-order* BASIC I.D. consists of subjecting any item on the initial Modality Profile to a more detailed inquiry in terms of behavior, affect, sensation, imagery, cognition, interpersonal factors, and drugs or biological considerations. This recursive application of the BASIC I.D. to itself is usually conducted when problematic items result in treatment impasses.

For example, a patient being treated for generalized anxiety listed four areas of discomfort in his sensory modality—tension headaches, tightness in the chest, sweaty palms, and pain in the jaws (temporomandibular joint [TMJ] syndrome). He showed improvement in the first three complaints as his general anxiety level decreased and as he grew proficient at relaxation and diaphragmatic breathing exercises. His TMJ problem, however, persisted despite the use of special biofeedback procedures to alleviate the pain. He kept careful notes of specific times of day, places, situations, thoughts, and activities that preceded and followed those occasions when his jaws felt especially tight or painful. No discernible pattern could be traced. A second-order BASIC I.D. was conducted:

Therapist: What do you *do* when your jaws become extremely painful?

Patient: Well, it depends. When it's not too bad, I get by with extra-strength Excedrin® and perhaps 2 mg of Valium, but sometimes I take some pills my doctor gave me—they contain codeine. I rarely use the codeine pills more than once a week, but sometimes I take Excedrin® two or three times a day.

Therapist: Do you do anything else?

Patient: Sometimes it helps if I catnap.

Therapist: How would you describe your mood or feelings when your jaws ache so badly?

Patient: I get damn despondent!

Therapist: Depressed?

Patient: Yes, and angry. I feel, why me? But mainly I feel sort of discouraged.

Therapist: You have told me exactly how and where you get the pains. Have you observed any other sensations that accompany the tightness in the jaws and the pain—"like hot spikes being driven in"— that's what you said.

Patient: That's right. The shooting pains go right into my ears.

Therapist: Any other sensations?

Patient: Yes, nausea. That's probably more from the pills than anything else.

Therapist: OK, now try to imagine that your jaws are feeling very tight and painful. (*5-second pause.*) What picture comes to mind?

Patient: I don't know why, but my grandfather came to mind.

Therapist: Your grandfather. Maternal or paternal? Was there something distinctive about him?

Patient: Yes, my dad's dad. He was very British. (*Affecting an accent.*) Stiff upper lip and all that sort of thing!

Therapist: Stiff upper lip. How about a tight lower jaw?

Patient: (*Laughs.*) Actually my dad's expression was "grit your teeth men!" I haven't thought about that in years. He used to coach our track team when I was in sixth grade. I remember him saying, "Grit your teeth and put in that extra effort!"

Therapist: Well, here's the obvious question. I wonder if there's some connection between being a man, gritting your teeth, putting in that extra effort, and your aching jaws?

Patient: Well, as I mentioned when I first came to see you, I'm always sizing myself up, seeing where I rank on the pecking order.

Therapist: And where would you rate in your grandfather's eyes and in your father's estimation?

Patient: Well, my grandfather died more than 10 years ago. . . .

Therapist: But if he were alive today, what would he think of you?

Patient: Gee. That's hard. (*Pause.*) I guess he wouldn't think too much of me. The truth is I've never been much of an athlete. I guess I make up for it by earning more money in a year than my dad and his dad both made in 10 years.

Therapist: I think we have to cool your head before we can loosen your jaw.

Patient: What does that mean?

Therapist: I don't want to read too much into it, but it is my guess that your fiercely overcompetitive strivings are tied into proving your manliness or adequacy. You are less anxious than you were 3 months ago, and this is reflected by the fact that your tension headaches are less frequent; your chest pains and sweaty palms are no longer a problem. But the tension in your jaws still bothers you. This is the last frontier, and you may need to achieve a relaxed frame of mind before your jaw muscles will let up.

Patient: And how do we do that?

Therapist: Well, for now, I want to put the sensory mode on "hold"—although I want to be sure that you will continue doing your relaxation and breathing exercises. I want to take a closer look at some of your assumptions, and also at the images that tie into your thought processes.

Second-order BASIC I.D. of TMJ syndrome
  B Takes medication
    Catnaps
  A Despondent
    Angry
    Discouraged
  S Shooting pains into ears
    Nausea
  I Paternal grandfather (stiff upper lip)

C Grit your teeth men (from father)
I. Fiercely overcompetitive
D. Analgesic and antianxiety drugs, self-prescribed
and physician prescribed

Commentary

When selecting techniques, a multimodal axiom is: *Begin with the most obvious and logical procedures.* It is important to eschew simplistic panaceas, but it is also important to avoid the penchant for making straightforward problems needlessly complicated. Thus, in the foregoing case, the best established methods of anxiety reduction were administered —relaxation training, biofeedback, self-monitoring—but when an impasse was reached, a second-order BASIC I.D. underscored fundamental identifications and an adversarial interpersonal stance, which called for correction. While the initial Modality Profile had reflected overcompetitive strivings, it did not reveal the patient's concerns about his manhood and his attempts to meet real or imagined standards set by his father and grandfather. Accordingly, the treatment focused on the "scripts" that he had abstracted from his male models. With guidance from the therapist, he enacted several imaginary dialogues with his father and grandfather in which he persuaded them (and thus convinced himself) that their standards of manliness were irrational and obsolete. Subsequently, a second course of biofeedback successfully mitigated his TMJ discomfort.

THE USE OF STRUCTURAL PROFILES

Whereas Modality Profiles list specific problems in each dimension of the BASIC I.D., Structural Profiles provide a quantitative self-rating of the patient's proclivities in each of the seven modalities. In everyday terms some people are primarily "doers," whereas others are "thinkers," or "feelers," or people-oriented "relaters," and so forth. By using a ten-point scale for each modality, patients may be asked to rate the extent to which they perceive themselves as doing, feeling, sensing, imagining, thinking, and relating. They are also requested to rate the extent to which they observe and practice "health habits"—regular exercise, good nutrition, abstinence from cigarettes, and the like. A high D score on the Structural Profile indicates a healthy and health-minded individual. Structural Profiles may readily be drawn up from the instructions given in Table 1-2.

Simple bar diagrams or graphs may be constructed. Structural Profiles are especially useful in marriage therapy. Spouses may be asked to draw up their own profiles, their estimate of how their mate might perceive them, and a Profile of how they see their spouse. This frequently

TABLE 1-2. Drawing Up Structural Profiles

Here are seven rating scales that pertain to various tendencies that people have. Using a scale of 0 to 10 ("10" is high—it characterizes you, or you rely on it greatly; "0" means that it does not describe you, or you rarely rely on it), please rate yourself in each of the seven areas.

1. Behavior: How active are you? How much of a "doer" are you? Do you like to keep busy?
   Rating: 0 1 2 3 4 5 6 7 8 9 10
2. Affect: How emotional are you? How deeply do you feel things? Are you inclined to impassioned, or soul-stirring inner reactions?
   Rating: 0 1 2 3 4 5 6 7 8 9 10
3. Sensation: How much do you focus on the pleasures and pains derived from your senses? How "tuned in" are you to your bodily sensations—to sex, food, music, art, etc.?
   Rating: 0 1 2 3 4 5 6 7 8 9 10
4. Imagery: Do you have a vivid imagination? Do you engage in fantasy and daydreaming a great deal? Do you "think in pictures"?
   Rating: 0 1 2 3 4 5 6 7 8 9 10
5. Cognition: How much of a "thinker" are you? Do you like to analyze things, make plans, reason things through?
   Rating: 0 1 2 3 4 5 6 7 8 9 10
6. Interpersonal relationships: How much of a "social being" are you? How important are other people to you? Do you gravitate to people? Do you desire intimacy with others?
   Rating: 0 1 2 3 4 5 6 7 8 9 10
7. Drugs/biology: Are you healthy and health conscious? Do you take good care of your body and physical health? Do you avoid overeating, ingestion of unnecessary drugs, excessive amounts of alcohol, and exposure to other substances that may be harmful?
   Rating: 0 1 2 3 4 5 6 7 8 9 10

provides a springboard for a fruitful discussion of specific areas of incompatibility and precise measures for remedying particular discrepancies (see Lazarus, 1981). Moreover, when therapist and patient explore the meanings and relevance behind each rating, important insights are often gained. In addition to global self-ratings, Structural Profiles may be obtained for specific areas of functioning (akin to second-order Modality Profiles). For example, in the realm of *sexuality*, the degree of activity, emotionality, sensuality, imagery or fantasy may be rated on separate scales, together with questions about how highly valued sexual participation is (cognition), its specific interpersonal importance, and the patient's biological adequacy.

BRIDGING AND TRACKING

"Bridging" refers to a procedure in which the therapist deliberately responds to the patient in his or her dominant modality before branching off into other dimensions that seem likely to be more productive. This is in contrast to therapists who challenge or confront patients whose style is to avoid the expression of feelings and present an intellectual facade. Labeling these patients "resistant" or exhorting them to produce "gut feelings" (as we have seen some Gestalt therapists do) is seldom as fruitful as "bridging," and often has disturbing if not painful consequences (Lazarus & Fay, 1982). Here is a brief example:

Therapist: I want to know how you felt when your mother compared you to Sue.

Patient: I think she was only trying to be impartial. Let me tell you how her mind works . . .

Instead of truncating the patient's intellectualizations and emphasizing that the therapist was interested in her feelings, not her *post hoc* rationalizations, the therapist allowed her to complete her explanation. This took about 5 minutes. The therapist then continued to address her preferred modality—cognition—for awhile.

Therapist: So your mother sometimes bends over backwards to be fair. I guess she thinks that Sue is particularly vulnerable. She sees you as the stronger of the two so you sometimes get dumped on.

Patient: Well, its not that I get dumped on exactly.

Therapist: Of course, your mother's reasoning is that to be fair-minded, she must not take sides, but she does sometimes make comparisons.

Patient: (*Laughs.*) And sometimes I don't come out smelling like a rose.

Therapist: You're laughing, but do you really find it amusing?

Patient: Well, I understand her.

Therapist: Nevertheless . . . are you in touch with any feelings or sensations right now?

Patient: (*Rubbing her neck.*) I've got a slight headache.

Therapist: Let's focus on the headache. What can you tell me about it?

Patient: Nothing much. It's just throbbing a bit.

Therapist: Where is it throbbing?

Patient: (*Touches her temples and runs her fingers down the back of her neck.*) Sort of here and here.

Therapist: Can you get in touch with any feelings, any emotions?

Patient: (*Pause.*) I don't know. (*She covers her eyes, puts her head down, and begins to cry. She takes a handkerchief from her pocketbook and dries her tears.*) It makes me sad. I understand it, but it still upsets me.

Therapist: Let's talk about the sadness.

The bridging maneuver commenced when the therapist switched from the cognitive emphasis and inquired "Are you in touch with any feelings or sensations right now?" This elicited a sensory response from the patient—"I've got a slight headache." The therapist then focused on the sensory modality, which rapidly elicited affective reactions. Thus, a six- or seven-minute "detour" avoided unnecessary confrontations, permitted the patient to be "heard," and brought forth the feeling states that the therapist was initially interested in pursuing.

Similarly, in treating a man who was highly "visual" and who created vivid images that preceded and accompanied virtually every encounter, it was necessary first to discuss his mental pictures before bridging to his thoughts and feelings. By referring to "a sensory reactor," "an imagery reactor," or "a cognitive reactor," we do not mean to imply that a person will always respond in a given modality. Clinically, however, we have noted a tendency for people to favor one or two modalities (which often correlates with their quantitative ratings on a Structural Profile). By joining the patient in his or her preferred modality, it is usually simple to guide him or her into other areas of discourse.

"Tracking" refers to a careful scrutinizing of the "firing order" of the different modalities. For example, some patients tend to generate negative emotions by dwelling first on catastrophic ideas (cognitions), immediately followed by unpleasant mental pictures (images), that lead to tension and heart palpitations (sensations), culminating in avoidance or withdrawal (behavior). The foregoing cognitions–images–sensations–behavior (C-I-S-B) pattern may call for different treatment strategies than, say, a sensations–cognitions–images–behavior (S-C-I-B) pattern.

Clinically, we have found that it is usually more productive to administer techniques in the same sequence as the patient's firing order. Thus, relaxation and biofeedback would be favored as initial treatments for a patient with an S-C-I-B order (i.e., predominantly sensory techniques to meet the patient's sensory trigger), whereas patients with a C-I-S-B pattern would be expected to respond less well to sensory techniques, until some improvement was evident in cognitive and imagery areas. Some experimental support for these observations has recently been presented (Öst, Jerrelmalm, & Johansson, 1981; Öst, Johansson, & Jerrelmalm, 1982).

CONCLUDING COMMENTS

A brief overview of multimodal therapy has been presented. It is hoped that the BASIC I.D. framework will appeal to those who are interested in multidimensional and multifaceted interventions, while remaining cognizant of the limitations of unsystematic eclecticism. Above all, the multimodal approach permits the clinician to identify idiosyncratic variables and thereby avoids molding patients to preconceived treatments. Halleck (1982), commenting on the multimodal orientation, stated that "it should cause us to ponder the limits of our current practices and convince us that the goal of rational multidimensional practice is achievable" (p. 24).

REFERENCES

Baer, J. (1976). *How to be an assertive (not aggressive) woman*. New York: New American Library.

Barlow, D. H., & Wolfe, B. (1981). Behavioral approaches to anxiety disorders: A report on the NIMH-SUNY research conference. *Journal of Consulting and Clinical Psychology, 49*, 448–454.

Bellack, A. S., Hersen, M., & Turner, S. M. (1976). Generalization effects of social skills training in chronic schizophrenics: An experimental analysis. *Behaviour Research and Therapy, 14*, 391–398.

Bernstein, D. A., & Borkovec, T. D. (1973). *Progressive relaxation training: Manual for the helping professions*. Champaign, IL: Research Press.

Brentano, F. (1972). *Psychology from an empirical standpoint*. New York: Humanities Press. (Originally published, 1874.)

Brunell, L. F., & Young, W. T. (1982). *Multimodal handbook for a mental hospital*. New York: Springer.

Cautela, J. R. (1967). Covert sensitization. *Psychological Reports, 20*, 459–468.

Ellis, A., & Grieger, R. (1977). *Handbook of rational-emotive therapy*. New York: Springer.

Fay, A. (1976). The drug modality. In A. A. Lazarus (Ed.), *Multimodal behavior therapy*. New York: Springer.

Goldfried, M. R., & Davison, G. C. (1976). *Clinical behavior therapy*. New York: Holt, Rinehart & Winston.

Goldsmith, J. B., & McFall, R. M. (1975). Development and evaluation of an interpersonal skill training program for psychiatric inpatients. *Journal of Abnormal Psychology, 84*, 51–58.

Halleck, S. L. (1982). The search for competent eclecticism. *Contemporary Psychiatry, 1*, 22–24.

Hayes-Roth, F., Longabaugh, R., & Ryback, R. (1972). The problem-oriented medical record and psychiatry. *British Journal of Psychiatry, 121*, 27–34.

Jacobson, E. (1938). *Progressive relaxation*. Chicago: University of Chicago Press.

Keat, D. B. (1979). *Multimodal therapy with children*. New York: Pergamon.

Lazarus, A. A. (1973). Multimodal behavior therapy: Treating the BASIC I.D. *Journal of Nervous and Mental Disease, 156*, 404–411.

Lazarus, A. A. (1976). *Multimodal behavior therapy*. New York: Springer.

Lazarus, A. A. (1978). *In the mind's eye*. New York: Rawson. (Reissued 1984, Guilford.)

Lazarus, A. A. (1981). *The practice of multimodal therapy*. New York: McGraw-Hill.

Lazarus, A. A. (1984). Multimodal therapy. In R. J. Corsini (Ed.), *Current psychotherapies* (3rd ed.). Itasca, IL: Peacock.

Lazarus, A. A., & Fay, A. (1982). Resistance or rationalization? A cognitive-behavioral perspective. In P. L. Wachtel (Ed.), *Resistance: Psychodynamic and behavioral approaches*. New York: Plenum.

Lewinsohn, P. M., & Hoberman, H. M. (1982). Depression. In A. S. Bellack, M. Hersen, & A. E. Kazdin. (Eds.), *International handbook of behavior modification and therapy*. New York: Plenum.

Mathews, A. M., Gelder, M. G., & Johnston, D. W. (1981). *Agoraphobia: Nature and treatment.* New York: Guilford.

Messer, S. B., & Winokur, M. (1980). Some limits to the integration of psychoanalytic and behavior therapy. *American Psychologist, 35,* 818–827.

Öst, L. G., Jerrelmalm, A., & Johansson, J. (1981). Individual response patterns and the effects of different behavioral methods in the treatment of social phobia. *Behaviour Research and Therapy, 19,* 1–16.

Öst, L. G., Johansson, J., & Jerrelmalm, A. (1982). Individual response patterns and the effects of different behavioral methods in the treatment of claustrophobia. *Behaviour Research and Therapy, 20,* 445–460.

Rachman, S. J., & Wilson, G. T. (1980). *The effects of psychological therapy* (2nd ed.). New York: Pergamon.

Smith, D. (1982). Trends in counseling and psychotherapy. *American Psychologist, 37,* 802–809.

Weed, L. L. (1968). Medical records that guide and teach. *New England Journal of Medicine, 278,* 593–600.

Zilbergeld, B. (1982). Bespoke therapy. *Psychology Today, 16,* 85–86.

2

The Case of P

SHARON L. GREENBURG

This chapter shows how a creative and flexible therapist can draw upon the multimodal framework to assure a comprehensive and systematic assessment–therapy context. In presenting a fairly "typical" client seen by most private practitioners, Sharon Greenburg provides the opportunity for the reader to determine whether or not the multimodal orientation provides clear-cut advantages over other formal or eclectic approaches. We have here, in my view, an excellent illustration of multimodal therapy in action. In treating "P," who presented with three or four major problems, the BASIC I.D. assessment brought to light more than 20 specific and interrelated problems that called for a wide array of particular interventions. Apart from the technical aspects, this chapter shows how the therapeutic relationship provides the soil that enables the techniques to take root. It also shows how the selection of techniques is not a capricious affair but follows a logical sequence, often based on the "firing order" of the various modalities.

INTRODUCTION

One of the strengths of the multimodal approach is its adaptability to both the style of the therapist and the needs of the client. It allows for flexibility in the degree of structure and the nature of the client–therapist relationship, as well as the synthesis of both the cognitive and affective elements necessary for therapeutic change.

This case illustrates my emphasis on the client–therapist relationship as a primary source of interpersonal data and a means of new learning. I apply the multimodal approach in a relatively unstructured style, but in both assessment and treatment use the interactions across the BASIC I.D. as my conceptual model. The case also demonstrates how I link past and present events to use this insight as a means of cognitive restructuring. Finally, it shows how the multimodal approach uses the client's strengths to determine therapeutic interventions.

DESCRIPTION

P was an attractive 27-year-old woman of average height and weight. She was well-groomed and casually yet fashionably dressed. Most salient about her were intense blue eyes, which expressed both intelligence and weariness. Her facial expression was listless and her voice flat with a dryly humorous quality.

PRESENTING PROBLEMS

P sought therapy to determine direction in her life and to increase her self-confidence in order to be able to make important decisions. She had been depressed and anxious intermittently over the past 8 years. Recently, she had become concerned over increasing periods of withdrawal, which she feared might develop into psychotic behavior. She described her problems as "moderately severe."

HISTORY

P came from an upper-middle-class family living in another region of the country. The youngest of three children, she had an older sister and brother. P described her mother, a housewife, as loving and supportive but manipulative. From her previous therapy P believed that her mother needed her to be dependent. As the youngest child, P was always considered the "baby." She described her father, an executive in a large corporation, as intelligent, honest, opinionated, and hardworking but not involved with his children. P had always been close with her brother and very close with her sister. P's family moved to a different town three times during her school years. Each time P found it harder to make friends. She remembered feeling very lonely and hating herself, especially in her junior and senior years in high school.

P traced the beginning of her problems to the second semester of her freshman year in college. At that time she was feeling insecure in a relationship with a boyfriend and unsure about her career goals. She began feeling anxious and depressed. When feeling tense her eyelid would twitch. To avoid embarrassment P would restrict her activities so that others would not see her twitching. She sought therapy for help with her problems, consulting with a psychiatrist and psychologist. For a period of several months she took tranquilizers. The twitching gradually subsided, according to P, because she forced herself to function despite it. Her father's advice to ignore it seemed to help.

P now worked as an administrative assistant in an optical supply company, a job that bored her and paid poorly. Though she liked some aspects of her job (e.g., contact with customers), she felt that she wasn't working up to her capacity. She had a Bachelor of Science degree in teaching from a respected state university. After teaching for a year, she decided that she had no interest in making it her career. Prior to her present job, she had worked as an optometrist's assistant but found the work menial. At one time she had wanted to be an optometrist but found the science requirements too difficult.

For the last 3 years P had been involved in an ambivalent relationship with a man. Though she had close women friends in the past, she had none at the time she began therapy.

STRENGTHS

P's intelligence was evidenced by her quickness of perception, college grades, and previous testing. She had well-developed powers of logic and reasoning, which she enjoyed using. She applied her dry sense of humor to herself and others easily. Though reserved, she was warm and likeable. She had the capacity to make and keep friends. She felt confident and comfortable in her sexuality.

MULTIMODAL ASSESSMENT

As in behavioral analysis, the first step was to break down P's presenting problems of low self-esteem, lack of direction, depression, and anxiety into operational terms. This was done by exploring the manifestations of the problems across all modalities. Unique to the multimodal approach, the BASIC I.D. provides a guideline that ensures a thorough and systematic analysis of both overt and covert material. I gather information clinically and from the Multimodal Life History Questionnaire, which I give to the client at the first session. I try not to structure the sessions too much in order to avoid a question and answer format. A looser structure allows me to observe the client's interpersonal style first-hand and assess his or her priorities and degree of initiative. As therapy proceeds I continue to assess new problems across modalities and look for repetitive patterns.

In the first few sessions I asked P to talk about how she experienced her problems. As she discussed each I would inquire about manifestations in any modality she omitted. I observed that P's style was sincere, reflective, and relatively passive. She was slow to respond and somewhat guarded.

BEHAVIOR

P's most salient behavioral deficit was her passivity in both work and interpersonal areas of her life. Though working below her capacity at a low-paying job, she avoided looking for a better one or seeking further training. More specifically, she avoided getting into a job-interview situation, because she anticipated that she would twitch and be unable to answer questions. In the past she would twitch when anxious, but more recently this behavior had not occurred. Nevertheless, she avoided tense situations. In her personal life P remained in a 3-year relationship with a man about whom she had mixed feelings. She wanted the affection and unconditional acceptance he gave her, but was unwilling to commit herself to marry him because he lacked "polish." She was dissatisfied with the relationship and had been avoiding making a decision about resolving it. She also avoided getting into situations where she would meet new people, especially attractive, eligible men. An exploration of past decision making revealed a pattern of responding to the expectations of others.

P wanted to develop and implement a plan of action for finding more satisfaction in her career and for resolving the relationship with her boyfriend. She wanted to stop avoiding decision making and start taking action. An analysis of past behaviors indicated that P derived the most satisfaction from facing and mastering challenging situations, whether physical or emotional.

AFFECT

P's primary negative feelings were depression and anxiety. The depression came from her hopelessness about eliminating the immobilizing anxiety that led to her avoidance behavior. She felt conflicted, both wanting and fearing change. Her anxiety stemmed from inferiority feelings and negative expectations maintained by negative cognitions and images. P was worried about what she feared were "schizophrenic tendencies." At times she would withdraw and feel distant from others, as if she were "behind a plastic shield." She also feared being alone at night. In general, P was distrustful of the validity of her feelings. She would tend to rationalize when trying to make a decision rather than trust her intuitive feelings. Her affect was generally flat, evidenced by the even tone of her voice and the lack of vivacity in her facial expressions. She often felt inhibited and guarded with others. She wanted to feel more self-confident and trusting of her feelings. She wanted to be more spontaneous and relaxed in interpersonal situations and more involved and challenged at work.

SENSATION

P's withdrawal behavior was accompanied at times by a distortion of depth perception. She felt further away from others than the actual distance, as if she were looking at the scene from the outside. Sometimes when feeling this way she also felt nauseous. She tended to get headaches when tense and suffered from fatigue at times. Pleasant sensations for P were sensual and sexual. She enjoyed having sex and usually experienced orgasm when having sex with her boyfriend. P wanted to eliminate her disturbing sensations. She wanted to feel alert, involved, and generally more relaxed.

IMAGERY

Imagery played an important role in triggering P's anxiety and fears. She would picture herself twitching in situations in which she felt evaluated, such as a job interview or an encounter with an attractive new man. She had fearful images of waking up to find a man standing over her about to attack her with a knife or gun. She had vague images of ghostlike spirits. When asked to picture herself, she saw no well-defined self-image but immediately saw large hips. She tended to see herself as boring and less attractive than other more confident women. A pleasant image for P was making love to someone she loved. P wanted to rid herself of debilitating images and develop a more positive self-image.

COGNITION

P held numerous dysfunctional beliefs that were primary precipitants of her problems. She believed that any objectionable behavior or mistake would cause others to reject her completely. At the same time she believed it catastrophic if others did not like or approve of her. P's general belief about mistakes being catastrophic appeared more specifically in decision making. She believed that all decisions were final and that it would be terrible if she made the wrong one. She told herself that with stakes that high she could not trust herself to make important decisions and that others could make better ones. At the same time she believed that she should be decisive and confident. Her specific fear of twitching was related to her belief that others would see that she was insecure and would reject her. Conversely, she believed that she should look calm and in control at all times. P had several negative beliefs about herself, which maintained her low self-esteem. She believed that she was inferior, and compared unfavorably to confident, attractive people. She thought of herself as a boring person, and one not to be taken seriously.

P wanted to think more positively about herself and develop coping thoughts that would allow her to take more risks and act spontaneously. She wanted to believe in herself. In these endeavors P's strong cognitive powers and reasoning capacity would prove to be assets.

INTERPERSONAL RELATIONSHIPS

P was generally unassertive and guarded with people whom she admired. Her voice had a flat quality and would vary only slightly in volume and pitch. She seemed to expect that others would find her boring. She also expected that others would not trust her. These interpersonal characteristics were clearly evident in the interaction between therapist and client.

P's current interpersonal relationship of central importance involved her boyfriend of 3 years. He wished to marry her, but she avoided any commitment because of her mixed feelings about him. She vacillated between wanting to break up with him and fearing that she'd lose him. He was passive in the relationship, accepting her on whatever terms she wished. At one point during therapy when not seeing him, P had a brief affair with a younger man. It ended several weeks later when P saw that her new lover's feelings about her were inconsistent. Though P had several close women friends in the past, at the time she began therapy she had lost touch with them. Her work situation was fairly isolated socially. She interacted with only one woman, the manager. P missed having close women friends. At the same time P felt competitive with women, including her sister and friends. P still remained close to her sister, yet didn't see her too often because they lived a considerable driving distance away. Her relationship with her parents (particularly with her mother) was dissatisfying. She neither saw nor spoke to them often.

P wanted to resolve her relationship with her boyfriend. She wanted to either accept him or find someone else whom she could love. She wanted to develop close friendships with women again without envying them. She wanted a more authentic relationship with her mother. In general, she wanted to be more spontaneous and assertive with others.

DRUGS/BIOLOGY

P was in good health both in childhood and adolescence. During her adolescent years she did suffer from migraine headaches. Occasional colds were her only other health problems. Several years ago, when treated by a psychiatrist for her anxiety attacks, she had used tranquilizers.

Her current health was excellent. She took no medication, generally slept well and ate properly. She did not smoke and drank only occasionally. Her weight was normal and she enjoyed physical activities. Occasionally, she would get a headache or bowel disturbance and sometimes felt fatigue.

DETERMINING THE FIRING ORDER

Distinctive to the multimodal approach is determining the "firing order," that is, how the modalities interact to cause the client's problems. P had two repetitive firing orders. They were: cognition–affect–behavior and imagery–cognition–affect–behavior. An example of the first firing order involved decision making. When P faced an important decision, she would think, "I can't trust myself to make this decision. If I made the wrong one, it would be irrevocable and terrible. Others would disapprove of me." Thoughts such as these would make P anxious (affect) and she would either ask others to make the decision or avoid it (behavior). These consequences would lead to further cognitions that she was weak and incompetent. These negative self-statements lowered her self-esteem and created feelings of failure and depression. Feeling worse about herself, P would feel even less trusting of herself to make future decisions, thus creating a vicious cycle. P's inhibition in social situations and avoidance of meeting new attractive men were also precipitated by dysfunctional cognitions. They included the following: "If I say or do even one wrong thing, others won't like me. If a person I admire doesn't like me, it would be terrible. I am a boring person." Thoughts like these and their resultant anxiety led to self-conscious, stilted behavior when around attractive, confident people, or to avoidance of these situations altogether. Her guarded behavior did in fact make her less interesting to others, and their lack of interest reinforced her belief that she was a boring person, again a vicious cycle. Her withdrawal behavior resulted from the same firing order with a sensations component. She was able to identify thoughts of being trapped or unable to change a painfully boring work situation that preceded these occurrences. She would then feel depressed (affect) and psychologically withdraw (behavior). Accompanying physical symptoms were distortion of depth perception and nausea (sensation).

Though P's predominant firing order was cognition–affect–behavior, at times imagery was the precipitating factor. For example, P feared being alone at night. Her fear was triggered by the frightening image of awakening to find a man standing over her with a knife or gun intending to attack her. Another example of the imagery–cognition–affect–behavior firing order operated in her avoidance of job interviews. She would picture herself twitching in the interview (imagery) and think, "I will totally lose control in the situation. The interviewer will see that I am insecure and reject me" (cognition). P would then become so highly anxious (affect) that she would avoid applying for a new position (behavior). Consequently, she felt depressed and trapped (affect) and would deride herself for her cowardice (cognition).

Attending to both cognitions and imagery as eliciting factors in P's problems maximized the likelihood of the effectiveness of treatment and durability of results.

TREATMENT INTERVENTIONS

The overall plan was to identify and eliminate negative thoughts and images as they emerged during P's efforts to initiate change. My style is to address the firing order as it comes up naturally in the therapy sessions, either in processing outside material or here-and-now interactions. P first of all needed some hope that she could overcome her passivity. I pointed out that starting therapy was a positive step that she had initiated. This action was contradictory to her belief that she was incapable of change. She wanted to find direction in her life, so we began with some information seeking and data gathering. P took the Strong–Campbell Interest Inventory, a career counseling instrument that measures basic interest areas and compares them with those of people in a wide range of occupations. P also completed the Multimodal Life History Questionnaire, which required that she focus on her goals.

Shortly after therapy began P was faced with the decision of whether she was going to live with her boyfriend. Her dysfunctional cognition was that she could not be trusted to make this important decision. P tended not to trust her feelings and would rationalize instead. I helped her to make a decision not to live with him by merely reflecting what clearly was her sense that it did not feel right. Because I accepted her feelings as a valid data source, P was able to do the same. I also positively reinforced P's making a decision.

P's dysfunctional belief that other people didn't trust her came out early in the therapeutic relationship. She declined to take home the Strong–Campbell Interest Inventory because she didn't have enough money with her and assumed that I wouldn't trust her. When I assured her that she could pay at the following session, she was surprised and pleased. This incident provided the opportunity to identify the belief, "I don't expect to be trusted," and to provide contrary evidence.

P was worried about what she saw as "schizophrenic tendencies," a feeling of distance from others as if a "plastic shield" separated her from them. I reassured P that on the basis of her past history and level of functioning that she was not likely to become psychotic. I instructed her to carry a small notebook and chart these detached periods, including: when they happened; how long they lasted; triggering events; and what feelings directly preceded them. P was able to pinpoint her withdrawal behavior as occurring either on the way to work or on the job, which she found boring and depersonalized. We reframed her cognition of this withdrawal as a means of avoiding her feelings about her job rather than psychotic behavior. Seeing its function changed her self-perception from the belief that she was going crazy to the awareness that she was merely avoiding negative feelings.

Another fear P raised was of being alone at night. In this instance an image rather than a cognition initiated the firing order. She would picture herself awakening to a man standing over her with a knife or gun about to attack her. I used associated imagery, which elicited other frightening images of ghostlike spirits. When I asked when she first began to have these fears, she remembered her sister scaring her when she was quite young by making spooky sounds outside of her door. I helped her see the relationship of her fear to these images. We then explored the rationality of her belief that she was in danger, that is, the likelihood of a man getting into her apartment. She in fact had adequate security devices and was living on a high floor. P later reported that since our discussion of her fears of being attacked at night, they had evaporated. She felt reassured that others also had irrational fears and that they came from frightening images and memories. Here again, P responded positively to my inference that she was sane and that her fears were understandable.

I observed that P seemed anxious in our sessions at times, and I helped her to explore this. P associated feeling similarly with her mother and sister. With me as well as her mother and sister, the anxious feelings were caused by her belief that if she said or did something wrong or "crazy," she would be rejected. Once we identified this dysfunctional belief, I used rational-emotive therapy (RET) in the context of the therapeutic relationship to challenge it. One of P's strengths was a good sense of humor. She found the exaggerations of RET funny, laughed frequently, and was able to see the irrationality of her belief.

When P's Strong-Campbell Interest Inventory profile arrived, she was disappointed to see no strong overall theme. P felt depressed when completing the inventory and suggested that this might account for her lack of defined interests. I agreed that this might be true and also suggested that her low scores indicated a need for further exploration and information gathering about possible career choices. Furthermore, the inventory did provide some surprising and useful information. It suggested that she preferred limited contacts with people; she had previously thought the opposite but now realized that what she liked about dealing with customers was solving their problems rather than the interactions themselves. The inventory also indicated a preference for an occupation that wouldn't require prolonged graduate training. With this new information, which upon consideration felt accurate, she could begin to narrow her career focus. Her next step was to browse through the *Occupational Outlook Handbook* for occupations that seemed to subjectively appeal to her and to read about them.

P was feeling increasingly depressed at work and more motivated to change her situation. Therapy focused on further data gathering to help her make a career change. The broad goal was broken down into several steps in a shaping process. I had P list her ten most satisfying accomplishments, her reasons for feeling proud of them, and the skills and personal qualities involved. This exercise revealed P's pride in physical endurance, solitary pursuits, traveling in foreign countries, getting her last job, and being first in a sales training class. In general, P was proud of facing and mastering challenging situations.

A fantasy exercise, in which P pictured herself in an ideal career, revealed how her dysfunctional beliefs hindered her. She pictured herself fashionably dressed, getting on the train with her briefcase. The image stopped there when she pictured the downtown area with all the "sharp" people there. She began to feel anxious, and connected this with the thought, "I can't compete with attractive, confident women." She had a second fantasy of herself managing a sports equipment store. The fantasy stopped when she pictured herself having to do some selling. P decided that she didn't like selling things that she didn't believe in and identified herself as one of them. She realized that her inability to change jobs came from her belief that she would be unable to sell herself in an interview. She identified the underlying negative self-statement, "I am an inferior product."

When I asked her where she got this idea, P traced the belief that she couldn't compete to her mother's negative comparisons. Her mother would frequently compare her negatively to friends, and P always felt that her sister was her mother's favorite. We frequently traced her low self-esteem to the internalized messages she gleaned from interactions with her family while growing up. When she would express negative thoughts and feelings about herself, I often asked where she learned them and whether she had ever felt that way before. The purpose of this insight-oriented strategy was to help P see the origins of her present negative feelings and beliefs in past interactions, that is, as faulty learning experiences subject to relearning. Thus, P was able to change her thought from "I am inferior," an attribute, to "I have learned to think negatively about myself and can change that." In reviewing the past P realized that she had always believed that it was her fault that her parents weren't more loving and accepting. By viewing their behaviors more objectively from an adult perspective, she was able to challenge that belief. As was the case with her fears of being alone at night, P found reassurance in understanding the link between her negative thoughts and feelings about herself and her parents' behaviors. The exploration of past family interactions were also useful in helping P to recognize and accept her feelings. She avoided either experiencing or expressing strong feelings. I focused on eliciting feelings of hurt and anger, which had not been previously expressed.

A visit home provided P with fresh material to process in therapy. During the visit her mother got angry with her over a trivial incident and didn't talk to her for the rest of the day. This extreme response, P noted, was very typical of her mother's past and present behavior. I elicited her feelings of guilt about her mother's anger and her resentment over having to watch every word. My acceptance of her anger as valid reinforced P's growing belief that she had a right to her feelings. She also experienced a sense of safety in expressing strong feelings in an open spontaneous way. To further experience and express her anger, I suggested that she try the empty-chair technique developed in the Gestalt approach. P was to imagine her mother actually sitting in the room and tell her how angry she felt about her manipulations. P had trouble carrying this out. She felt silly, similar to how she felt when giving a serious opinion in a social situation or practicing a sales talk in front of a mirror. She identified the negative self-statement, "I am not a person to be taken seriously." Once identified, P was able to successfully challenge it.

The therapeutic strategy towards P's determining a career direction was a behavioral shaping process continuing throughout the course of therapy. It began with the data-gathering steps: the Strong–Campbell Interest Inventory and exercises designed to examine past accomplishments and future aspirations. It continued with P's reading the *Occupational Outlook Handbook* and picking out three interesting occupations. P became interested in a new position and agreed to call for further information. I positively reinforced her following through on this contact the following week. Her call provided her with some basic information, but she realized she needed to meet with someone for more practical information about getting the position. She agreed to call for an interview.

Concurrently, there were several interpersonal developments as therapy proceeded. P had decided that she would no longer have or expect an exclusive relationship with her boyfriend. She had also started dating a man a few years younger than she. At first she felt quite passionately involved with him, but her feelings changed as she noted frequent vacillations in his feelings about her. She was pleased to find herself decisive in breaking off the relationship. She also renewed friendships with two former women friends. She found herself more assertive with them, and believed that her new behavior came from accepting the validity of her feelings and her right to express them. I reflected P's good feelings about herself when she was assertive.

P's progress toward a new career was not without its setbacks. She felt disgusted with herself for not making any further phone calls for an informational interview. We were able to identify several dysfunctional thoughts that created enough anxiety to prevent her calling. They were: "I will be refused," "I'll look foolish," and "I probably won't find this job interesting either." I helped P challenge these thoughts using RET methods.

P was feeling vulnerable and sad following the break-up of her new romance. P realized that except for her relationship with S, her former boyfriend, she felt insecure with men. She traced these feelings to her father's coldness and lack of involvement with her as a child. In her relationships with men she admired, as with her father, P felt unlovable, overly eager for approval, and inhibited. Therapy focused on ventilating her feelings of hurt and anger toward her father as well as identifying and challenging negative self-statements about being unlovable and uninteresting. P began to see that her negative self-statements developed from her interpretation of her father's aloofness. I used RET methods to help P challenge and change these thoughts. At this point in therapy P reported feeling better about herself than ever before and more able to move.

She did inquire further about the new position. Though encouraged by this step, she still felt in a rut about having resumed her ambivalent relationship with S, her former boyfriend. She didn't want to commit herself to him, yet feared he would find someone else. She wanted both freedom and security and derided herself for her ambivalent feelings. I helped her experience and better accept these opposing sides by the Gestalt technique of dialoguing in which she spoke from each position. This technique helped her to challenge the dysfunctional belief, "I should always be clear and decisive." Consequently, this lessened her self-disgust when she wasn't always able to resolve things quickly.

After a depressing Christmas visit with her family, P resolved to make the new year one of change for her. She signed up for two noncredit courses. At the following session she suggested that she stop therapy for about a month. Her reasons were that she felt that she was making progress in her life and that she was short of money. I suggested that we explore other possible reasons and mentioned that deferred payments were an option. P admitted that she was feeling pressured by therapy to change the status quo regarding her job and her boyfriend. She saw herself going over the same material and failing to make substantial changes. She feared that I was becoming bored and disappointed. She was also feeling more distanced from me because of a 3-week lapse in sessions over the holidays. P was feeling anxious and responded by wanting to avoid the anxiety-arousing situation, therapy. I helped her to identify the irrational thought, "If I don't make enough progress, my therapist will disapprove of me." We used RET to challenge this belief. P felt relieved to acknowledge her fears and challenge her negative thinking. This avoidance pattern in interpersonal situations was typical. By processing it when it occurred in the therapeutic relationship, she was able to check out the inaccuracy of her thoughts. When P convinced herself that I was not going to reject or disapprove of her for her perceived lack of progress, she chose to continue weekly sessions.

In reviewing P's progress, we concurred that she was feeling more self-confident but needed additional work on asserting herself and taking risks. She was still unhappy with her reaction to her mother's unpredictable withdrawal of affection and wanted to behave more assertively with her. In examining all possible consequences, P realized that to be assertive with her mother, she would have to risk her disapproval. We worked on developing the belief that behaving assertively with her mother would make her feel better about herself and might even improve the relationship in the long run. P was able to generalize this belief to other relationships as well.

P seemed to rebound and resumed making information-seeking phone calls. She also planned to go on a business trip to another city and felt enthusiastic about going. The trip turned out to be a very positive experience. She was pleased with her ease at meeting people. She was especially glad to find herself comfortable with a former employer who knew her during her most anxious period. She had feared twitching in his presence but was in fact at ease during their lunch together. He told her that he was amazed by the change. This feedback bolstered her confidence. She also was pleased with a change she saw in herself. When P and her sister had dinner with her father, who was in town for business, she noticed that his eye contact was primarily with her sister. P became aware that this behavior was typical and directly related to her feeling of not being taken seriously. She resisted it and realized that her cognition about not being a person to be taken seriously had changed. At one point during the session, P's voice was especially flat and she seemed visibly depressed. I inquired what she was feeling and thinking. She was able to identify feeling bored when she ran out of things to say, just the way she felt at work. She connected the feeling to the negative self-statement, "I am a boring person," which she was able to successfully challenge. She was displeased with the flatness of her voice. I suggested that she try the Yes–No Exercise, often used in assertiveness training to experiment with different volumes, pitches, and inflections. I wanted to assess when she felt most comfortable and uncomfortable and to determine whether a full range of vocal expression was in her behavioral repertoire. In this exercise P was to say "No" to my "Yes," matching the volume, pitch, and inflection. She was able to do this but felt most discomfort with the highpitched exuberant tones. Sounding exuberant felt silly. She identified the thought, "It would be terrible if I made a fool of myself." She was able to use RET methods to challenge this belief.

P was forced to more actively look for another job since her company was relocating to another city and P didn't want to move. She began to work on a resume. With the pressing need for a new job, we began to focus on P's high anxiety about the interview situation. Her greatest and most concrete fear was that of twitching in the interview and not being able to answer questions. I reassured P that she could prepare for the interview by developing a supportive belief system and a combination of imagery for goal rehearsal and role playing. I used assertiveness training methods specifically applied to the interview situation. P remembered that in the past when troubled by twitching, she was successful in overcoming it by facing and remaining in the anxiety-arousing situation whether she would twitch or not.

Developing supportive beliefs for assertive behavior was the first step. I helped P to reframe the interview situation from a one-way evaluation of her to a mutual evaluation in which she was also evaluating the suitability of the position. I helped her to identify and accept her rights as an interviewee and to determine her goals both for the interview and the job situation. The next step was to use imagery for goal rehearsal to build her confidence and skill. I instructed P to picture various aspects of the interview situation in very concrete terms, such as being introduced, answering questions, and asking questions. I coached her in picturing herself confident, relaxed, and still. For homework she was to repeatedly practice picturing herself behaving confidently and competently in an interview situation. The last step was role playing the various steps involved. I used modeling, coaching, and positive reinforcement to shape desirable interview behaviors.

P had identified three career options for herself, including a more responsible position in her present field. She made several calls to all contacts she knew and applied for a job advertised in the newspaper. When her application didn't get her an interview, she felt depressed and lost confidence. We successfully challenged her belief that this would happen every time. Shortly afterward, P applied for and got a new job in her present field that offered more stimulation, money, and opportunity. Though she was not totally sure about taking it, and did consult with her parents and friends, she herself made the decision to try it out. An important cognitive change allowed her to see that the decision wasn't final.

P found her new job more interesting and challenging. Her coping skills had improved considerably. She was able to accept her own nervousness about functioning on the new job and to relax more. She was assertive with the somewhat aggressive woman training her. She was also becoming more assertive with her mother in phone conservations and with her insurance company who had quarreled with her last claim for reimbursement for therapy. P was no longer feeling depressed or unduly anxious. She continued to be enthusiastic about her job and more self-confident in general.

P had not resolved her relationship with S, continuing to see him, but not exclusively. She found that when she was feeling better about herself, she felt better about the relationship and conversely. P now saw the connections among her thoughts and images, behaviors, and feelings. She was able to identify and challenge negative thoughts and practice positive imagery. She knew that when assertive, she felt attractive and competent, and when passive, she felt unattractive and ineffectual. At this point in therapy, I raised the subject of termination and suggested she think about whether she reached her therapeutic goals.

P expressed fears of the old patterns returning. She noticed herself withdrawing at work in the morning when she felt pressured and anxious. When I reminded her to focus on any negative thoughts or images, she was able to identify thoughts about making mistakes or choosing the wrong priorities. She was quickly able to challenge them and substitute more coping thoughts. With the idea of termination coming, P expressed her sadness over ending the therapeutic relationship in which she now felt safe to let her guard down. She was aware of her need for a supportive, accepting relationship with a woman as she had developed with me.

Termination became the final therapeutic intervention. P wanted to continue therapy because she believed that she couldn't continue to grow by herself. Her dysfunctional belief, that she must look to an expert, the therapist, rather than trust herself created her anxiety about termination. Here I set up a paradoxical situation in which the expert was telling her that she was the "expert" on herself and that termination was appropriate. At the same time I told P that should she feel stuck or have difficulty coping in the future, she could always come back for a few sessions or even resume therapy. This idea countered P's dysfunctional belief that all decisions were final and it would be terrible if she made the wrong one. P felt considerably less anxious, believing that she could always change her mind. Termination occurred at this session as planned with a follow-up session scheduled 5 weeks later to monitor her progress. Therapy had consisted of 30 sessions over approximately 9 months.

At the follow-up session, P was feeling stimulated by her job and valued by her boss and coworkers. She still was bothered occasionally by self-consciousness and lapses in self-confidence but had been successful in applying the coping mechanisms she learned in therapy. Her periods of withdrawing at work when anxious had lessened. Though at times she continued to have negative thoughts, images, and feelings, she now felt that she had a way of changing them. No further sessions were scheduled, but P understood that she could come back whenever she felt stuck.

P did not call again for 1 year and 8 months. At that time she came in following the break-up of a romantic relationship. She was able to identify images and thoughts of herself twitching and looking insecure as the precipitants of her anxiety. In the session she was able to formulate more coping thoughts and practice positive imagery. She also felt particularly vulnerable because she was approaching her 30th birthday and believed that "time was running out." She had negative thoughts about not being

TABLE 2-1. Summary of BASIC I.D. Problem Assessment and Treatment Interventions

Modality	Problem	Intervention
Behavior	Avoids changing jobs	Cognitive restructuring, behavioral shaping, problem solving, contracting, goal rehearsal, modeling, coaching, behavior rehearsal, systematic exposure
	Avoids making decisions	Reflection of feelings, problem solving, dialoguing, positive reinforcement
Affect	Depressed and hopeless about changing avoidance behaviors	Cognitive restructuring, contracting
	Anxious over possible rejection or disapproval	Rational–emotive therapy, positive imagery
	Fearful of being alone at night	Associated imagery, rational–emotive therapy, cognitive restructuring
	Detached and distant	Recording and self-monitoring, tracking
	Flatness (i.e., feelings not owned or expressed)	Elicitation and reflection of feelings
	Hurt and anger toward parents	Anger expression, empty-chair technique
	Conflict over desire for change and fear of change	Dialoguing
	Distrust of feelings as valid data source	Reflection of feelings, cognitive restructuring
Sensation	Distortion of depth perception, at times accompanied by nausea	Recording and self monitoring, tracking, cognitive restructuring
Imagery	Pictures self awakening to man standing over her with weapon	Tracking to fear response, reality assessment of probability
	Pictures ghostlike spirits	Tracking, rational–emotive therapy, exploration of origin
	Pictures of self twitching in job interview	Positive imagery
	Unattractive self-image, large hips	Rational–emotive therapy, positive imagery
Cognition	Irrational beliefs about mistakes leading to total rejection, the necessity of others' approval, and decisions as irreversible	Rational–emotive therapy
	Negative thoughts of self as unlovable, boring, and not to be taken seriously	Exploration of origins, rational–emotive therapy, cognitive restructuring
	Belief that she can't be trusted	Therapist validation of perceptions, feelings and decisions; self-tracking; therapist demonstration of trust; paradox

TABLE 2-1. (*Continued*)

Modality	Problem	Intervention
Interpersonal relationships	Nonassertive with people she admires	Assertiveness training, that is, cognitive restructuring, modeling, coaching, role playing; positive reinforcement for assertion in therapy situation
	Inhibited in social situations	Positive imagery, Yes–No Exercise
	Vacillating about relationship with boyfriend	Dialoguing
	Envious of friends	Cognitive restructuring
Drugs/biology	No problems	

in a meaningful relationship with a man and not accomplishing much. I asked her to define her terms, "meaningful" and "accomplishment." In focusing on what the words meant, she was able to be more objective about herself, seeing her own achievements and relationships on a continuum. One more session was scheduled the following week. P was feeling better about ending her recent relationship and generally more confident about her capacity to handle things. No further sessions were scheduled.

DISCUSSION

Though many of the treatment interventions were either behavioral or cognitive (see Table 2-1), this case illustrated how the multimodal approach utilizes additional methods taken from various other theories. Treatment focused considerable attention on affect through continuing reflection of feelings, anger expression, the empty chair technique, and dialoguing. It was crucial that P experience and accept the validity of her feelings in order to channel them appropriately. Another important focus in this case was on the imagery modality in both assessment and treatment. I used associated imagery in assessment and goal rehearsal and positive imagery in treatment. Unlike cognitive–behavioral approaches, I focused on the past as well as the present when I felt that exploration of the origins of negative feelings, thoughts or behaviors would be useful for cognitive restructuring. For this client, insight into how her problems developed was an important step in changing her beliefs about herself and her capacity to change. Finally, the therapeutic relationship was extremely significant in this case. We often processed our relationship to gather data and offer an immediate opportunity for new interpersonal learning. I positively reinforced P's in-session expression of feelings and assertive behaviors. I demonstrated my trust in various ways. I shifted the "expert" role to her by having her make the connections in tracking her firing orders and challenging her dysfunctional beliefs. We developed a collaborative relationship in which P took an increasingly active role.

3

Multimodal Treatment of Agoraphobia: A Problem-Focused Approach

JEFFREY A. RUDOLPH

Multimodal therapy focuses on intraindividual *problems when indicated and immediately switches the emphasis to* interpersonal *difficulties when necessary. By attending to the individual and his or her parts, and then examining (and treating) the individual in his or her social setting, both personal and family (systems) considerations are covered. In this chapter Jeffrey Rudolph clearly demonstrates how the BASIC I.D. framework facilitates the clinician's awareness of when to dwell mainly on one or the other—the individual client, the spouse, the couple, and/or the family. Agoraphobia is anything but a unitary problem, and this chapter shows the interlocking mosaic of problems that requires specific correction. In many cases in* vivo *exposure plus the use of antidepressant medication (mainly to combat panic attacks) are considered essential. But as the present case so vividly illustrates, such a bimodal regimen would be likely to meet with limited success.*

INTRODUCTION

Over a hundred years have elapsed since Westphal (cited in Marks, 1969) first described the agoraphobic syndrome. Although much attention has currently been focused on the understanding and treatment of this disorder, therapeutic efforts all too often insufficiently address factors relevant to its onset and maintenance, for example, marital and social instability, high trait anxiety, negative cognitive expectancies, and deficient behavioral and interpersonal skills (Mathews, Gelder, & Johnston, 1981). Indeed, the polysymptomatic profile of the agoraphobic individual makes decision making for even the most astute clinician a difficult process. Furthermore, contemporary unimodal therapeutic methods (e.g., *in vivo* reinforced exposure, cognitive restructuring, and pharmacologic interventions) have been viewed as often necessary but insufficient in effecting significant and durable treatment results (Wilson, 1982). Clinicians cognizant of the "murky mosaic" of problems presented by the agoraphobic client—such as fear of loss of control, generalized anxiety, depression, and interpersonal isolation—often attempt to execute an amalgam of therapeutic strategies without a practical blueprint for outlining a hierarchy of prescriptive priorities. It is therefore this author's view that most contemporary treatment approaches to agoraphobia have compromised treatment efficacy by (1) emphasizing intraindividual variables at the expense of interpersonal factors, both in assessment and treatment, and (2) failing to attend to cognitive, interpersonal, behavioral, affective, and biological problem components in a systematic and comprehensive manner.

Multimodal therapy, by comparison, is particularly well suited to the multifaceted, complex nature of agoraphobia. Specifically it is designed to:

1. provide comprehension to interconnecting events, circumstances, and psychobiological processes;
2. identify and pinpoint precipitating and maintaining factors in the agoraphobic symptom matrix;
3. offer a comprehensible, educationally based framework emphasizing self-assessment and self-control;
4. permit ongoing assessment and prescriptive reformation as required through the course of treatment.

The following case study illustrates the successful application of the multimodal therapy approach in the treatment of a 35-year-old woman who, by her own admission, had been unsuccessfully treated for agoraphobia by several professionals utilizing traditional and unimodal approaches. The case illustrates a number of extramural complications which preempted a "frontal attack" on the client's presenting agoraphobic symptoms and further necessitated several strategic reformulations during the course of treatment.

PRESENTING CHIEF COMPLAINTS

Mrs. B was an attractive 35-year-old agoraphobic woman referred for multimodal therapy by her psychiatrist. At the outset Mrs. B described her condition as extremely severe, stating that her core fear was uncontrollable panic attacks. In her words:

> I can't handle anything by myself anymore; I feel like I'm being confined without any escape. It feels like I'm walking around in a clouded state of perpetual exhaustion not knowing when the next anxiety attack will hit; when it does I would hyperventilate, tremble and experience pins and needles, rubbery knees and a nauseating wave through my body.

Looking exasperated, Mrs. B asserted that the only way she would gain some relief would be to ingest 10 mg of Valium, prescribed by her family doctor, and then try to go to sleep.

She maintained that these attacks generated constant apprehension of losing control and severely restricted her daily activity. She would venture from her house only for what she deemed "essential reasons" and only while accompanied by her husband. Mrs. B expressed guilt, confusion, and despondency over these difficulties. Believing that her illness contributed to her failure as a wife and mother, she asserted her secret fear was that she would be viewed by her family as an emotional cripple and remanded to custodial care. This concern, she stated, was well grounded, as she and her husband communicated little and had been growing apart for years. Mrs. B further felt that she had lost total control in managing her two teenaged daughters who increasingly were belligerent to her and manifested behavioral problems she felt helpless to deal with.

FAMILY BACKGROUND AND HISTORY OF PRESENTING COMPLAINTS

Mrs. B was the mother of two daughters, aged 13 and 17. She and her husband met while both were in high school, and they had been married for 18 years. Mr. B was self-employed, owning a retail business. Mrs. B had been a working partner in this business, helping her husband with the management and bookkeeping, until her worsening condition necessitated relinquishing duties to her older daughter and a hired employee. Living with the family was Mr. B's elderly mother who was nonambulatory, suffering from intractible arthritis and arteriosclerosis.

Mrs. B described her relationship with her family as "at best strained," and expressed much trepidation over her ability to keep everyone together during the period of her illness. Relatedly, she recounted that her marriage had been progressively deteriorating for years, and her husband had recently threatened to leave her. She went on to exclaim, "The children are both fed up and scared with my craziness and either yell at me or ignore me; I feel like I've failed both as a mother and a wife." Mrs. B traced the genesis of her problems back 5½ years, when she experienced her first panic attack. The attack coincided with her parents and minister all moving out of the community. She stated that her anxiety gradually increased following the attack and she markedly curtailed her travel away from the house. Things worsened until, in her own words, "I fully collapsed, had a nervous breakdown, and became totally bedridden."

Mrs. B was born and raised in a small eastern city. She was the middle of three siblings, having a brother aged 31 and a sister aged 39.

Mrs. B portrayed her mother as supportive and gregarious, but extremely nervous and insecure, always feeling deprived of caring and contact from her husband. The client corroborated this view stating that she often felt like a husband to her mother, frequently staying up late hours to comfort her mother through long periods of her father's absence. Mrs. B considered family health problems as an additional contributing factor to what she viewed as an unstable childhood. She was told that her mother had had a nervous breakdown when she was 9 months old, which had rendered her mother incapable of properly caring for her for roughly 3 years. During this period she and her sister were primarily raised by a neighbor. When Mrs. B was 19 year old, her mother's health once again failed (she developed cancer of the uterus). The patient recalls that during this period she felt extremely stressed, obsessed that her mother would die and she would inherit the burden of family caretaking responsibilities.

In addition to family difficulties, Mrs. B reported that as a teenager she suffered from a pervasive sense of social apprehensiveness. Self-conscious of her appearance and her behavior, she considered herself an outsider with her peers, dated little, and longed for the security of a husband and family. Mrs. B met her husband when she was 16 years old. They dated for a year and married when Mrs. B became pregnant. When she was 23 years old, expecting their second child, the family bought a house close to Mrs. B's parents. Also, during this period the client's husband began a home repair business. This marked a time of relative security for the patient, which lasted until her father became chronically ill with an arterial embolism. His condition necessitated an early retirement, leading to protracted withdrawal and depression. Shortly after her father's illness, Mrs. B's parents moved out of the area. Also, at this juncture her husband's mother, whom the couple portray as a "difficult, demanding, and chronically ill woman," moved into their household. Feeling estranged from her parents and under pressure to manage a growing family and business, the client once again experienced herself buckling under stress. Mrs. B's marriage began to show progressive signs of deterioration, and she began to experience her husband as critical, explosive and emotionally removed from the family. Feeling angry and alienated, she reacted defensively, withdrew from him, and sought out her older daughter as a confidante and companion. Further complicating matters, Mr. B interpreted his wife's withdrawal and ambivalent behavior as disloyalty and indifference. Subsequently, expressions of anger and exasperation escalated between Mr. and Mrs. B. It was then that Mrs. B first entered psychotherapy. Her therapist interpreted her presenting problem as symbolic of repressed sexuality and the desire to emancipate herself from the marriage in order to seek an independent lifestyle. With her therapist's encouragement she secretly established a separate bank account and began soliciting attention from other men.

Although Mrs. B felt somewhat vindicated from her anger through these actions, feelings of guilt and apprehension increased. As the client experienced herself increasingly anxious and in conflict, she began to manifest appetitive disturbances, and within a 6-month interval, her weight dropped in excess of 35 pounds. This precipitated several visits to her family doctor who prescribed Valium as a sedative and referred her to an internist for endocrinologic testing. These tests revealed a glucose intolerance indicative of a sensitivity to sugar and elevated cortisol levels suggestive of an anxiety-based depression. She was placed on a high-protein, low-carbohydrate diet and monitored closely for subsequent cortisol fluctuations.

A religious woman, Mrs. B further sought relief through involvement with her church. Offering her services as a parish secretary, she developed a close friendship with her minister. Shortly thereafter the minister unexpectedly left, and Mrs. B was told by the church elders that his departure was precipitated by his inability to handle growing feelings toward her. It was while participating on a search committee for a new minister that Mrs. B experienced her first panic attack. She described the event as a "surging hot flash," "weakness in the knees," and "dizziness," followed by her "blacking out." Shortly thereafter, she experienced a second panic attack while driving with her daughter to keep an appointment with her former therapist. She described this episode as a "close call," stating that she just managed to pull the car off the road and avoided a head-on collision before she "lost control and blacked out." Following this incident, Mrs. B ceased driving and began to severely curtail her activities outside the home.

MULTIMODAL ASSESSMENT AND TREATMENT PLAN

Based on the synthesis of data gathered from the Life History Questionnaire (Lazarus, 1981) and the initial assessment interviews, a Multimodal Profile was constructed for Mrs. B (Table 3-1).

As the item "loss of control" is considered to be a focal variable in the agoraphobic symptom matrix, a second-order BASIC I.D. Modality Profile was conducted on this item to more specifically help target precipitating and maintaining factors (Table 3-2).

Perusal of the second-order BASIC I.D. Profile revealed the prominent role that marital difficulties played in the maintenance of this client's agoraphobic problems (e.g., anxiety-producing anger, and guilt related to communicating with her husband, as well as fear of ultimate rejection and separation from her family). The modality profiles further highlighted two important themes: (1) a deficit of "self-control strategies," vital in moderating negative sensory and physical experience associated

TABLE 3-1. Mrs. B's Multimodal Profile

Modality	Problem	Proposed treatment
Behavior	Phobic avoidance: Limits scope of movement to going to therapy and local grocery shopping; will not travel alone	Systematic *in vivo* exposure in conjunction with self-instructional training
	Withdraws to bedroom; spends much time in bed watching TV and talking on phone	Change in stimulus conditions via creation of increased exposure to family
	Avoids confrontation with husband and daughters	Assertiveness training; instruction in operant principles of child management
	Procrastination punctuated by spurts of diffuse, exhaustive activity	Structured activity assignments in conjunction with self-reinforcement
	Hyperventilation	Diaphragmatic breathing exercises
	Occasional drinking to steady nerves	Instruction in substitutive coping strategies
Affect	Pervasive anxiety punctuated by feelings of panic and loss of control	Autogenic training; relaxation imagery; diaphragmatic breathing
	Depression marked by acute feelings of helplessness and self-denigration	Increase "purposeful" activity; strengthening Mrs. B's role as mother, wife, and decision maker; anxiety-management training
	Boredom and feeling of lethargy	Prescription of pleasant activities
	Periodic outbursts of anger toward husband and children followed by guilt and remorse.	Instruction in directive self-disclosure of feelings
Sensation	Tension headaches (frontal area)	Differential relaxation training
	Dizziness, visual disturbances, numbness, and tingling in extremities	Diaphragmatic breathing exercise
	Tachycardia, rapid pulse, "hot flashes"	Autogenic relaxation phrases in conjunction with digital thermal biofeedback
	Fatigue, pent up tension	Physical exercise
Imagery	Images of gloom and rejection and guilt—for example, being left by husband and children; leaving husband and engaging in a "wild sexual affair with Mr. B's close friend"; being ridiculed and laughed at by family and friends; husband's mother dying due to her negligence	Relationship enhancement interventions focusing on reinforcing couple's strengths and areas of compatibility
Cognition	Anticipatory anxiety fueled by negative interference chaining	Use of "calming self-talk" and self-instructional dialogues
	Preoccupation with death of family and self	Cognitive restructuring and rational refutation of negative attribution and beliefs

TABLE 3-1. (*Continued*)

Modality	Problem	Proposed treatment
	(Internal dialogues replete with categorical imperatives, dichotomous reasoning and perfectionism —for example, "I am totally responsible for my family's happiness and must please them at all costs; I am a victim of circumstances and can't control what's happening to my body and mind; if I continue to show weakness I'll be rejected and abandoned by my family.")	
Interpersonal relationships	Alternates between child-like dependent behavior and angry retaliatory gestures with husband and children	Specific self-sufficiency assignments and training in direct and confrontative behaviors
	Overidentification with mother	Encouraging internal locus of control and self-esteem enhancement
	Avoidance of intimate sharing	Inner circle strategy; discussion and training in self-disclosure
	Sporadic flirtatiousness with other men	Encouraging elimination of all conflict-producing behavior
	Weak parent–child boundaries; inappropriate affiliative behavior with older daughter	Family problem-solving sessions reinforcing Mrs. B's parental authority; strengthening a sense of marital congruity with children
Drugs/biology	Valium use, 5 mg twice daily	Instruction in substitutive anxiety alleviation techniques
	Glucose intolerance	Physician-supervised high-protein, low-carbohydrate diet
	Elevated adrenal cortisol levels; rapid weight fluctuations; disequilibrium and dizziness	Referral to physician when organic problems are suspected or biological interventions are indicated; possible use of tricyclic antidepressants, or monoamine oxidase inhibitors to offset panic attacks

with autonomic arousal, and (2) a pervasive attitude of alienation and hopelessness reinforced by interpersonal and situational avoidance.

Since the viability of Mrs. B's marriage was a primary issue related to therapeutic planning for this client, the couple was initially given the Marital Satisfaction Questionnaire (Lazarus, 1981). While the data from these inventories underscored their dysfunctional communicative and behavioral patterns (which exacerbated Mrs. B's difficulties), it also re-

TABLE 3-2. Second-Order BASIC I.D.: "Loss of Control"

Modality	Problem
Behavior	Withdraws to room Avoids people (with the exception of older daughter) Rapid thoracic breathing
Affect	Anxious and panicky; fear of blacking out Guilt concerning hurting her husband with her actions and thoughts
Sensation	Rapid heart beat Dizziness Lightheadedness Weakness of legs and knees
Imagery	Imagines herself out "partying and living it up with other men" "Going crazy"; being separated from her family and "put away"
Cognition	Thoughts of criticism, rejection and embarrassment from others
Interpersonal relationships	Withdrawal; becomes silent and uncommunicative Angry and blameful of husband for not caring
Drugs/biology	Takes Valium Has cocktail to calm her nerves

vealed that the two were highly motivated to remain together and desired to work out their differences. A decision was therefore made to enhance Mrs. B's sense of familial security by integrally involving her husband in a systemic therapeutic approach.

Another initial therapeutic concern was Mrs. B's damaged attributional system that, among other things, resulted in her feeling that her previous actions and malintentions had resulted in her receiving her "just rewards." Failure to adequately address these views could have left Mrs. B open to tempering her constructive efforts and sabotaging her progress. Concerted focus was thus placed on building a psychoeducational framework that emphasized an understanding of how anxiety attacks evolve and are perpetuated and what one can do about them. Thus, instead of focusing on attacking agoraphobic symptoms (e.g., behavioral avoidance patterns), initial emphasis was placed on (1) teaching Mrs. B rational problem-analysis skills, (2) developing the family as a supportive resource, and (3) increasing empathy and support within the marriage.

TREATMENT: PHASE I

From the outset it was obvious that Mrs. B was significantly contributing to her problems through a litany of anxiety-engendering cognitions and the deployment of ineffective self-control strategies (e.g., Valium, isolation and avoidance behaviors, and inappropriate "therapeutic raps" with her daughter). Furthermore, when tracking the modality firing order of Mrs. B's anxiety attacks, interpersonal and cognitive factors were discovered to play a pivotal role. As a result, with her husband present, Mrs. B's difficulties were explained to be an outgrowth of faulty communication patterns, misperceptions concerning the nature and consequences of stress, and an overabsorption of maladaptive defensive anticipations. Relatedly, the role of "catastrophic expectations" was discussed, and Mrs. B was instructed to maintain a daily stress journal, which would serve as the foundation of a self-management guidance program. The journal was constructed to include stress-engendering situations, related thoughts, images, coping strategies, and outcome ratings. An entry taken from this diary (Figure 3-1) reveals how Mrs. B would typically generate anxiety through deficient interpersonal strategies.

Mrs. B was encouraged to explore the interconnectedness and sequence of such unfolding events and her reactions to them; thereby, through early detection, she could employ strategies that would "head problems off at the pass." With the help of thermal and electromyographic (EMG) biofeedback, she was instructed to rate and evaluate her physical

FIGURE 3-1. Entry from Mrs. B's daily stress journal.

Date/time	Situation	Anxiety level (0–100)	Thoughts, images, and feelings	What did you do to cope?	Result
4:15–4:45	Daughter requested to help prepare dinner	70 SUDs	I had dinner planned the way I wanted it. She was interfering, telling me what to do. I wanted it the way I planned it. I shut up and didn't make a scene. Felt anxious and angry. Why can't anything turn out the way I'd like it to?	Cleaned up kitchen and kept telling myself to clear my head. I let anger out by yelling at everybody else to get out of my way until I was done working in the kitchen.	Still felt tense during dinner. It took me 3 hours to calm down. Eventually I did. 30 SUDs

reactions to stress in a more objective fashion. To facilitate understanding the role of her internal dialogues and misattributional thinking, both the client and her husband were encouraged to read *I Can if I Want To* (Lazarus & Fay, 1975) and *Stop Running Scared* (Fensterheim & Baer, 1977).

Next, to help the client control hyperventilation and generalized anxiety, Mrs. B was instructed in diaphragmatic breathing and autogenic training. A "menu" of autogenic phrases was presented, and the client reported that several were particularly effective in inducing a calming state: "My stomach and the whole central portion of my body feel heavy, relaxed, and comfortable. I can feel warmth flowing down my arms into my hands. My thoughts are turned inward and I am at ease." A cassette relaxation tape employing these suggestions was made for home practice, and results were shared weekly in conjunction with self-monitered stress data.

By the fourth session Mrs. B's daughters were invited to share their perceptions of their mother's difficulties and its impact upon the family. This meeting set the stage for the client, with the help of her husband, to restore her role as a functioning mother and authority figure for the children. This was primarily accomplished by teaching the couple operant techniques (e.g., contingency contracting) to more effectively control the children's verbally abusive and manipulative behavior.

With Mr. and Mrs. B now aligned on issues related to the handling of their children, marital matters could be directly addressed. Multimodal Structural Profiles were constructed for the couple (Figure 3-2) whereby the two were asked to rate (on a scale of 1–10) the extent to which they perceived themselves as active, emotional, sensual, imaginative, intellectual, people-oriented, and health-minded.

When the results of these profiles were discussed with the couple, the two were pleasantly surprised to discover stylistic congruities that suggested distinct zones of compatibility. First, Mr. B, traditionally viewing his wife as an emotional, unreasonable woman, was pleased to learn how high she rated herself as a thinker. This awareness led to explorations as to how the two could bilaterally utilize their "intellectual" styles to resolve their problems and reason through their differences. Additionally, Mr. B's Structural Profile revealed that while he was disinclined to actually express his feelings, he nonetheless rated himself as a very emotional individual. This admission was extremely reassuring to Mrs. B, who often experienced her husband as cold and devoid of feeling. It further served as an impetus to discuss the importance of "emotional" expressions such as the use of "I feel" messages.

Following these "orientation" exchanges, the couple was instructed to regularly schedule time-limited communication periods as a forum

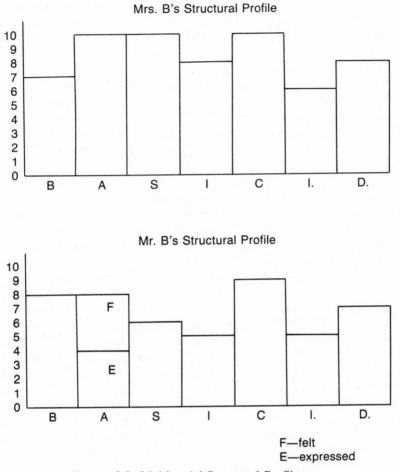

FIGURE 3-2. Multimodal Structural Profiles.

through which "gripes" could be ventilated and problems solved. These "therapeutic sessions" were geared to encourage Mrs. B to be more assertive and for the couple to explicitly exchange views, free from hidden agendas or metareferences. Finally, the two were instructed to identify and partake in at least three enjoyable activities a week.

Significant benefits were reported through the use of the foregoing procedures, and the couple admitted to an increased spirit of compatibility. Furthermore, during this period Mrs. B began to report a diminution of generalized anxiety and depression. She, however, still complained that her mother-in-law was "driving her crazy" with perpetual demands, and she felt too scared and guilty to set limits on her involvement.

With her husband's expressed support, a contingency program was constructed whereby Mr. B's mother would be jointly advised by the two as to what would and would not be done for her (e.g., meal preparation). In addition, a *quid pro quo* arrangement was devised, whereby the elderly Mrs. B could earn more "socialization time" with the two through cooperating with Mrs. B on household responsibilities. Although there was some initial testing of the limits by Mr. B's mother, these interventions were reported to be useful and appeared to further enhance Mrs. B's sense of "being in control."

By the 11th meeting sufficient progress had been made in the interpersonal and behavioral modalities to warrant a concerted focus on agoraphobic coping-skills training and *in vivo* exposure to anxiety-engendering situations. Mrs. B's scope of movement at this juncture was still limited to local marketing, occasional visits to her husband's business, and infrequent visits to her parents' home. A Client's Manual for Agoraphobia (Mathews *et al.*, 1981) was given to Mrs. B to facilitate programmatic practice and the mastery of anxiety-reduction principles. A Partner's Manual (Mathews *et al.*, 1981), designed to be an instructional guide for the spouse/helper, was similarly offered to Mr. B. Having familiarized themselves with these programs, and having discussed the rationale of systematic exposure, a travel hierarchy was constructed. It should be noted that at this time Mrs. B had been reporting a significant diminution of hyperventilation episodes due to regular practice of abdominal breathing exercises. However, she asserted that the thought of traveling any distance from her home, or to unfamiliar places, triggered off upsetting thoughts of "blacking out" or having a full-blown panic attack. As cognition was viewed as a prepotent modality in triggering anticipatory anxiety, a cognitively oriented self-instructional program adapted from Meichenbaum (1977) was designed and involved the selection, memorization, and prescripted recall of reassuring self-statements (e.g., "I can develop a plan to deal with this problem. This anxiety is to be expected. It is a reminder to use my coping exercises. Relax, I'm in control. Take a slow deep breath and count. Ah, good.").

Mrs. B reported that although fulfilling her behavioral assignments was far from easy, concerted use of these statements helped keep her "on target" and encouraged her to "hang in there and stick it out." In addition to using this menu of coping sentences, Mrs. B was encouraged to deal with anxiety-engendering "what ifs" by placing the word "so" before "what if," and then rationally generating behavioral options (e.g., "So what if I feel anxious at the restaurant . . . I could talk to J about it, he'll understand; if we have to we could always get up and leave.").

After initial successes with these endeavors, Mrs. B agreed to (1) spend more time at her husband's business, (2) resume driving, and (3) begin to travel alone.

TREATMENT SETBACKS AND THERAPEUTIC REFORMULATION: PHASE II

At or around this period Mrs. B experienced a significant setback, which was precipitated by three important stressors occurring closely in tandem.

First, the couple's business had steadily grown and the two had decided to sell the store and move to a larger location. This decision resulted in a spate of legal and financial difficulties, which significantly undermined Mrs. B's new found sense of confidence. As negotiations for the new store were being completed, Mrs. B developed a viral infection that developed into Meniere's disease. The resulting symptoms of dizziness, nausea, and imbalance, although effectively treated by antibiotics, rekindled Mrs. B's fears and she perceived herself as regressing back into an intractible agoraphobic state. To complete this chain of unfortunate circumstances, Mrs. B's father had a sudden heart attack, lapsed into a critical state, and died within a week. Mrs. B retreated to her home and lapsed into a state of apprehension and inactivity. *In vivo* coping-desensitization exercises were suspended, and several supportive sessions ensued where importance was placed on Mrs. B giving herself permission to react to real-life crises in natural ways. Some difficulty was engendered here in disabusing the client of notions that she should be able to handle these events with equanimity. In addition, as Mrs. B was quite concerned with the state of her health, still experiencing symptoms of dizziness and disequilibrium, a recommendation was made for a neurologic assessment. The examination and tests showed no organic pathology, and Mrs. B was thus encouraged to view her present physical difficulties as residual effects of her inner-ear infection compounded by the impact of situational stressors.

Within several weeks Mrs. B reported feeling some improvement, and *in vivo* desensitization excursions were resumed. Focus was now placed on time-limited nonworking visits to the couple's new business. During this period Mrs. B continued to accumulate positive experiences from her *in vivo* excursions. As she expressed increasing optimism she was encouraged to resume more responsibility in managerial and administrative business functions. Furthermore, during this period Mrs. B's avoidance of driving was once again targeted for intervention, and several sessions were devoted to short trips with the couple where I would instruct Mrs. B in the application of coping self-dialogues and breathing exercises. A cassette tape recording of both Mrs. B and her husband reassuringly talking the client through an anxious state in an actual driving episode was made, and Mrs. B was instructed to listen to it both before and during subsequent trips to minimize anticipatory anxiety.

Finally, a home-based physical fitness program was instituted whereby Mrs. B could healthfully stress her body and increase her aerobic capacity through the use of an exercise bicycle.

At this juncture Mrs. B asserted that she no longer felt she required Valium, and in concordance with her family internist, use of this drug was discontinued.

At the time of completion of this chapter, the client and her husband have been seen for 42 sessions. While markedly improved, Mrs. B cannot be said to be "cured" of her agoraphobic problems, nor is her need for further psychotherapy considered over. For one thing, Mrs. B's scope of movement is currently basically restricted to more familiar and local destinations, and she still expresses much trepidation over traveling alone. However, multimodal therapy has afforded Mrs. B a much enhanced sense of self-esteem, through providing this woman with an increased locus of control and an unshakable sense of family support. In addition, she now has an armamentarium of applied and proven coping skills at her disposal as she increasingly challenges defensive and avoidance behavioral patterns. Finally, motivation and spirit is high, and Mrs. B has developed a more directive role both in her therapy and in her life.

SUMMARY AND CONCLUSION

Because agoraphobia is a multifaceted disorder, it was essential to develop a therapy plan that assigned each of Mrs. B's presenting problems to its proper place in a treatment hierarchy. While initial emphasis is often ascribed to direct assault on panic attacks, a multimodal assessment revealed that anxieties concerning separation from her family, and protracted marital difficulties, were prominently fueling Mrs. B's problems. As a result, initial emphasis was placed on the development of a family-based treatment approach. The approach particularly focused on her behavioral deficits, as these lacunae potentiated both anxiety and avoidance patterns. In tracking the modality firing order that led to Mrs. B's anxiety attacks, *cognitive factors* were further discovered to play a pivotal role. Consequently, a self-instructional anxiety management program was constructed whereby Mrs. B was taught to monitor and evaluate both cognitive and situationally based stressors and deploy appropriate coping strategies (e.g., rational self-talk and diaphragmatic breathing). The rational, problem-focused flavor of this approach was, as Mrs. B corroborated, particularly well suited to her personality style and consequently enhanced treatment compliance and outcome expectancies.

Use of the multimodal schema was viewed as the key to providing a precise understanding of interrelated problem areas. Furthermore, the construction of a flexible and personalistic therapeutic program, which could be clearly understood and applied by this client, was considered to be the contributing factor to treatment success.

Despite marked progress, the client at this juncture cannot be considered "cured," nor is her need for psychotherapy over. Based on this client's current progress, however, a complete durable recovery is expected.

REFERENCES

Fensterheim, H., & Baer, J. (1977). *Stop running scared*. New York: Dell.

Lazarus, A. A. (1981). *The practice of multimodal therapy*. New York: McGraw-Hill.

Lazarus, A. A., & Fay, A. (1975). *I can if I want to*. New York: Morrow. (Paperback, Warner Books, 1977.)

Marks, I. M. (1969). *Fears and phobias*. London: Academic Press.

Mathews, A. M., Gelder, M. G., & Johnston, D. W. (1981). *Agoraphobia: Nature and treatment*. New York: Guilford.

Meichenbaum, D. (1977). *Cognitive-behavior modification: An integrative approach*. New York: Plenum.

Wilson, G. T. (1982). Fear reduction methods and the treatment of anxiety disorders. In C. M. Franks, G. T. Wilson, P. C. Kendall, & K. D. Brownell, *Annual review of behavioral therapy* (Vol. 8). New York: Guilford.

4

Multimodal Treatment of Depression and Obesity: The Case of Single Susan

LILLIAN F. BRUNELL

The art and science of psychotherapy find a harmonious blend in the multimodal tradition. Whenever feasible, the multimodal clinician draws on scientifically established treatment procedures, but their final execution calls for personal skill and experience. Lillian Brunell shows very clearly how the BASIC I.D. framework fosters a targeted yet comprehensive treatment plan that addresses virtually every significant facet of psychological disturbance in her client. This chapter underscores the necessity of first establishing particular relationship ingredients before proceeding with strategic maneuvers. It highlights specific tactics that generate a sense of control and a feeling of hopefulness in the client. Brunell also succeeds in demonstrating how the problem-focused emphasis, within the seven vectors of personality, unearths the interplay of both obvious and subtle intrapersonal and interpersonal considerations. The manner in which this leads logically to treatment planning and technique selection is an important feature of this important chapter. After perusing this chapter, I hope that the reader will agree that the multimodal approach provides a unique and systematic framework and a comprehensive "blueprint" for assessment and therapy. Brunell's detailed weight-loss rules and strategies are a bonus!

INTRODUCTION

Multimodal therapy contains many of the components of other therapy systems, but in its broad yet integrated approach is different from other systems. While other therapists may attempt to change the affect of a depressed patient through the use of techniques such as exploration and identification of precipitating factors, ventilation of suppressed affect, and alteration of negative self-image, the multimodal therapist utilizes a much more comprehensive approach, which attends systematically to each of seven personality modalities as described by Lazarus (1976, 1981). Multimodal therapy is rigorously geared to a carefully designed broad-

50

based assessment procedure that is linked to specific treatment interventions for the defined problems. It is a systematic approach to therapy that methodically employs a wide range of treatments to accomplish integrated, durable treatment (Brunell & Young, 1982).

The particular case I have chosen to demonstrate multimodal therapy is that of a 26-year-old depressed, unmarried woman, named Susan. When asked to begin by telling something about herself, Susan said, "I have the distinction of being the world's oldest living virgin." This was to be the first of many self-deprecating, "humorous" remarks to occur during the course of therapy.

Susan is the second child of an upper-middle-class family. She is 1 year younger than her sister. Both siblings are above average in intelligence. Susan was unable to find an academic goal for herself and dropped out of college after her sophomore year. She had entered therapy at that time (aged 19) and was given medication for depression. Susan described herself as having been "depressed" for a long time. She went to work in her father's business. After 3 years she undertook a course of study in a secretarial school and completed the program at the top of her class. She then found employment with a marketing company dealing with fashion accessories.

Susan started as a secretary, worked diligently, and displayed a great deal of ability and initiative. She described herself as a "workaholic." (She acknowledged, however, that this was largely due to her attempts to avoid confronting her empty social life.) Now, after 2 years, she had assumed considerable responsibility in the area of product advertising: placing ads in the media, arranging for product displays, and preparing the details for the company's participation in major marketing conventions. However, no official change in her job title or salary was forthcoming even though she was no longer functioning as a secretary. Despite all her efforts and prodding, no tangible recognition had been awarded. Since overtime payments had been eliminated throughout the company, she had actually suffered a considerable decrease in her earnings. Promises by her employer to "do something about it" bore no fruit.

When she first entered therapy, Susan's appearance could best be described as "dumpy." She was decidedly overweight although she had already lost some poundage via a weight-loss center. Her fear was that her weight would take the inevitable swing upwards as it had many times in the past in her "yo-yo" pattern. Her muscle tone appeared poor and contributed to a rather "lumpy" figure. Her choice of clothes was unremarkable and did nothing to improve her appearance. Frequently, when she wore knits, her outfits pointed glaringly to her worst figure flaws.

Susan's hair was quite long, wavy, and lustrous. She spoke with pride about it and regarded it as her most attractive feature. She generally pulled it back tightly into a chignon arrangement or wore it in another style suitable for very long hair. This gave her face a round, ageless appearance that was not particularly attractive. Her perception was that her hair was very pretty and made her look very young. She wore glasses that obscured her best feature. The general effect was of a youngish woman of uncertain age and undistinguished appearance.

Susan shared an apartment with a long-time female acquaintance whom she did not regard as a close friend. She accepted her roommate's promiscuous lifestyle but was not part of it and did not wish to be. The two young women tolerated each other fairly well but generally avoided intrusion into each other's lives. Susan kept busy socially with one or two old friends (female) who seemed to turn up from time to time, with her parents, and occasionally with her sister. Her sister lived at some distance and was fairly well established professionally. She had an active group of single professional friends and Susan would sometimes join them for some planned activity. There were also one or two older, married women friends at the office with whom she had a friendly relationship. Susan had no active social group of her own that she could participate in regularly.

At the time she started therapy, Susan had never had a real "date" that had been initiated through her own personal contact. She had never had a boyfriend although there had been numerous "crushes" on young men she had come into contact with in the past. No one had ever shown any sexual interest in her, and she regarded herself as totally unappealing to men. She was particularly uncomfortable in the presence of attractive young women of her age, since she felt this only emphasized her own shortcomings. She tried to avoid situations where she would anticipate unsuccessful competition with other young women. She saw her failure with men as a completely hopeless situation with no likelihood of change. In fact, she had the potential to be far more attractive than she realized, or perhaps would allow herself to be. Even more important was that her difficulties with men were undoubtedly due mainly to personality factors rather than to her unremarkable appearance.

One of the reasons Susan initiated therapy at this time was that she felt herself to be extremely attracted to a married man, Bob, at her office and the "affair" was totally frustrating to her. She felt time was running out for her and it was now or never. It was an approach–avoidance situation. He obviously enjoyed her attention, sought it out, encouraged her, and then pulled away just short of consummation. Susan single-mindedly sought to alter her "oldest-living-virgin" status while Bob just as earnestly cheered her on and then artfully engaged in fancy footwork to avoid a sexual confrontation.

As part of this push–pull manipulation, he would ask Susan to do personal errands for him and constantly engineered situations that required her to drop things off at his home. There, she would encounter an enraged wife who barely suppressed her animosity. She could not understand why Bob's wife was so hostile, since their relationship had never moved past the flirtatious stage; she thought his wife could not possibly be aware of what went on in the office. Susan was only too happy to do anything that would ingratiate her with this man in the hope that the relationship would then move toward the sexual conclusion she desired. He was equally intent on not allowing that to happen, even if he had to mobilize his wife's anger to stop it. Susan was oblivious to the fact that her motives were obvious to others, including Bob's wife, since she felt that she had valid "business" reasons for her many personal services. Yet as soon as she lost interest in Bob, the errands stopped completely.

ASSESSMENT

Susan's major reason for entering therapy was that she felt depressed, anxious, and totally hopeless about her future. The major theme of the first therapy interview was that she was very unhappy about not having a relationship with a man, had never had one, and there was no reason for her to believe that things would ever change. At the age of 26, never having had a date, she saw no reason why things would ever be different. She was tearful throughout most of the first session.

In order to understand what problems were contributing to Susan's unhappiness so that treatment interventions could be planned, a thorough evaluation was required. This could best be accomplished by using a BASIC I.D. assessment to identify the problems in all seven personality modalities (Lazarus, 1976, 1981; Brunell & Young, 1982). It would then be possible to determine how the various problems were interrelated and which treatment interventions would be most effective for their remediation. Susan's BASIC I.D. Profile is shown in Table 4-1.

It is just as important to gauge the individual's *strengths* as it is to define the problems requiring therapeutic intervention. Susan's above-average intelligence, excellent verbal skills, her sense of humor, and her good ability to make women friends, were all useful assets for therapy. She also had demonstrated an ability to work hard toward a goal and was very interested in her job, to the extent that she devised means to spend as much time as possible at the office in order to avoid her loneliness at home. She was aware of the significance of this.

BEGINNING CONSIDERATIONS

After the major problems have been identified, it is important to plan an approach to therapy. The first issue that must be addressed is where to start. This is generally decided by determining what must be done to

TABLE 4-1. Susan's BASIC I.D. Profile

Modality	Problem
Behavior	1. Lacks assertiveness skills
	2. Lacks sufficient social and physical activity
	3. Avoids social situations where she fears female competition
	4. Unable to develop a dating relationship with a man
	5. Unable to maintain weight-loss program
Affect	6. Depressed, anxious
	7. Fearful in the presence of male authority figures
Sensation	8. Lacks desired sexual outlet
	9. Lack of enjoyable activities
Imagery	10. Sees self as unattractive to men
	11. Sees self as unattractive compared to other women
Cognition	12. Perceives "nothing will change"; feels that she has no control
	13. Feels men will never be interested in her sexually
	14. Makes deprecatory self-statements
	15. Feels everyone must like her and assertiveness would prevent this
	16. Lacks information about how to find social groups
	17. Lacks information about how to improve appearance
	18. Feels unable to maintain weight-loss program
Interpersonal relationships	19. Lacks social skills in initiating relationships with men
	20. Lacks a social network
	21. Lacks assertiveness in interpersonal relationships
Drugs/biology	22. Overweight
	23. Insufficient physical activity and exercise
	24. Poor muscle tone

permit access to the full range of problems that require remediation. In Susan's case her sense of hopelessness had to be dealt with before any progress could occur. An important diagnostic clue in depression, the feeling that nothing can or will change, is a significant blocking agent in therapy. In forming a therapeutic alliance, it is essential to find some way to convey to the individual that positive changes can occur. It is only after this has been accomplished that the therapy can proceed effectively.

It has been my experience as a therapist that the single most important idea to convey to a depressed client is that he or she can be in control. This helps to alleviate the depressed person's profound sense of impotence. While it is important during the first contacts in therapy to allow the individual to ventilate thoughts and feelings that he or she has stored up for some time, it is just as important to begin immediately to plan a strategy to introduce a sense of control in order to combat the individual's overwhelming feelings of helplessness and hopelessness.

The initial phase of any therapy must focus on establishing a sense of trust so that the therapy relationship can develop. The client requires consistent support when he or she attempts to express unacceptable feelings. Frequently, the client has been troubled by these feelings for a long time and feels that no one else can understand or appreciate how he or she feels. The client may never have had the courage to verbalize these feelings to anyone. The therapist must convey a sense of acceptance and understanding; the client needs to know that the therapist values what he or she is saying, will consider the issues seriously, and will not be judgmental.

An important strategy to demonstrate the therapist's interest in the patient's input and participation, and to help the patient understand that therapy is a mutual effort, is to introduce note taking by the client and other homework assignments (Shelton & Ackerman, 1974). This is usually done by asking the client to record one event (in just one or two words) each day that has stimulated some feeling. The client then labels the feeling the event has caused in a parallel column. The client is instructed to record the notes on a very small piece of paper that can be kept easily out of view; this counteracts privacy concerns and demonstrates that the task will not be a tedious writing exercise. The slip of paper is to be brought to the session, but is to be used only by the client and then discarded. The purpose of the note taking is to train the client to attend to the events that occur in his or her daily life that contribute to his or her unhappiness. It helps him or her to focus on specific therapy issues and identify feelings rather than on vague generalities; it assists the therapist to recognize patterns and problems that the client might not otherwise report.

Many people initiating treatment feel that the therapist could not possibly be interested in the mundane details of their daily lives, that these events and feelings are not dramatic enough to bring to therapy. The therapist needs to emphasize to the client that these daily events are exactly the matters that therapy will deal with and that will enable progress to occur. Frequently, important therapy events and feelings are lost because the client feels them to be insignificant and unworthy to bring to the attention of the therapist. Note taking by the client serves as a kind of "therapy training" and provides a structure that can be used first to find a treatment intervention that will give the client a sense of control and hopefulness and later to develop the other needed treatment interventions and to monitor their progress. Most clients use the note-taking system (if they will follow it at all) long enough to move into a productive therapy routine and then abandon it when no longer needed. It is also important to convey to the client that therapy is a continuous process, that much of the work of therapy has to be accomplished outside of the therapist's office, on his or her own home ground. The notes will help to demonstrate this.

The initial session is perhaps the key to the success of the entire therapy. The therapist must use it to gain an understanding of the problems to be dealt with and how to achieve access, to allow the client to ventilate pent up feelings and concerns, to attain the active participation of the client in the therapy process, and to convey a sense of hopefulness to the individual seeking therapy because he or she has despaired of attempting to deal with his or her problems alone.

TREATMENT SELECTION

The problems that may be defined under the seven BASIC I.D. modalities can be numerous, although sometimes they may be few in number, depending on the situation. It is important that each problem be specifically itemized even though it may be apparent that there is considerable overlap. Frequently, this is due to the "ripple" effect that Lazarus (1976) has described. Each problem in one modality triggers a reaction in another modality; thus a problem in the cognition modality may have a corresponding effect on the individual's affect, behavior, and so forth. Lazarus has referred to this as the "second-order BASIC I.D." (Lazarus, 1981). If it is a significant problem in a particular modality, each problem should be recorded as it affects that modality, regardless of whether it has been previously noted in another modality. This is an important aspect of the assessment that permits a truly comprehensive approach to understanding the problem and selecting effective treatment interventions.

While each problem requires a discrete identification and needs to be worked with in therapy, treatment does not have to be undertaken separately, but can be done through an integrated treatment approach. In order to accomplish successful remediation, a treatment plan is required. This will help the therapist to determine which treatment interventions to use, as well as to establish priorities and to develop an orderly action plan.

The first step in planning treatment is to group the identified problems into categories that include interrelated problems. At first, these may be fairly large groups of problems, and some of the problems may appear in more than one category.

GROUPING IDENTIFIED PROBLEMS

In the foregoing BASIC I.D. assessment, 24 problems were identified under the seven personality modalities. In attempting to categorize these, three major areas of concern emerged: problems related to social–sexual issues (14), to physical matters (10), and to assertiveness (6). They are grouped in Table 4-2 and the modality indicated. In Susan's BASIC I.D. Profile all 24 identified problems could be grouped easily into the three stated categories. There were six repetitions, as shown in Table 4-2, so that a total of 30 items are stated. All six of the repeated items appear in category I, which contains the largest number of problems.

It is apparent that category I, the social–sexual area, will be a major focus in therapy. While it was clear from the client's presenting complaints that this area was the reason for initiating therapy, it was not as clear how many problems existed in this area and precisely how they interacted with each other. The initial treatment interventions selected must provide clients with a sense of hopefulness to demonstrate that changes can be made to alleviate their distress and to encourage their active participation in therapy.

SELECTING SPECIFIC INTERVENTIONS

Since the social–sexual category contained more than half of all of the problems itemized on the BASIC I.D. Profile (14 out of 24), it was important to start with interventions that would have an impact on this area. Susan's image of herself was that she was overweight and therefore unattractive to men: "I'll always be fat and unattractive." This effectively squelched her ability to develop and utilize social skills with men. It was important to assist her with her weight-loss program in order to improve her self-perception and her image. This would help her to feel "in control," an important intervention for her depressed affect. It would also enable work on the development of appropriate social skills with men, a course that was effectively blocked by her negative imagery.

Her reluctance to be assertive (she felt that she could not refuse any request, that everyone must "like" her) caused difficulty in her interpersonal relationships and reinforced her depression. It was important to provide her with assertive skills that would make her feel more in control and more positive about herself. Susan's lack of enjoyable social experiences were both a cause and consequence of her depression, and it was therefore necessary to help her to find some new social outlets. This would help to provide enjoyable social experiences as well as assist her to gain access to new people for future social contacts.

The initial interventions selected to deal with the social–sexual problems in category I were: training in weight-loss strategies and techniques, training in assertiveness, training in social skills with men, and help in developing social outlets. These four interventions would affect all BASIC

TABLE 4-2. Grouping of Susan's Identified Problems

Category	Modality
I: Social–sexual	
2. Lacks sufficient social and physical activity (II)*	B
3. Avoids social situations where she fears female competition	
4. Unable to develop a dating relationship with a man	
6. Depressed, anxious	A
8. Lacks desired sexual outlet	S
9. Lack of enjoyable activities (II)*	
10. Sees self as unattractive to men	I
11. Sees self as unattractive compared to other women (II)*	
13. Feels men will never be interested in her sexually	C
14. Makes deprecatory self-statements (III)*	
16. Lacks information about how to find social groups	
19. Lacks social skills in initiating relationships with men	I.
20. Lacks a social network	
21. Lacks assertiveness an interpersonal relationships (III)*	
Total =14	
II: Physical	
2. Lacks sufficient social and physical activity (I)*	B
5. Unable to maintain weight-loss program	
9. Lack of enjoyable activities (I)*	S
10. Sees self as unattractive to men (I)*	I
11. Sees self as unattractive compared to other women (I)*	
17. Lacks information about how to improve appearance	C
18. Feels unable to maintain weight loss program	
22. Overweight	D.
23. Insufficient physical activity and exercise	
24. Poor muscle tone	
Total = 10	
III: Assertiveness	
1. Lacks assertiveness skills	B
7. Fearful in the presence of male authority figures	A
12. Perceives "nothing will change"; feels that she has no control	C
14. Makes deprecatory self-statements (I)*	
15. Feels everyone must like her and assertiveness would prevent this	
21. Lacks assertiveness in interpersonal relationships (I)*	I.
Total = 6	
30	

*Problem repeated in category indicated.

I.D. modalities, either directly or indirectly. The specific BASIC I.D. Profile problems from category I are grouped with their designated treatment interventions:

- Training in weight-loss strategies and techniques: Problems 3, 6, 10, 11, 13
- Training in assertiveness: Problems 3, 6, 14, 21
- Training in social skills with men: Problems 4, 8, 9, 13, 19, 21
- Help in developing social outlets: Problems 2, 4, 8, 9, 16, 20

The four initial interventions would provide a focus for the beginning of therapy but would not exclude other treatments that would be used to deal with new problems revealed during the process of therapy. It is also apparent that the interventions selected would have an impact on many of the other problems stated in category II (physical) and category III (assertiveness). As therapy continued problems would be reviewed and updated when necessary, and additional treatments implemented as client progress required.

STARTING THERAPY

During the first session Susan talked about herself and her background, repeating several times her unhappiness over the fact that she had never had a male "relationship," just occasional friends. The process of therapy was described to Susan: We would pinpoint specific problems, try to understand their significance and how they interacted with each other, and begin to develop treatment interventions. She was told that she would be given regular feedback about our sessions and that I would request her to provide feedback for me as well so that we might each know how the other was perceiving the progress in therapy. She was asked to take notes (as described above) and advised that she would be given homework assignments that she would be expected to carry out. The importance of her active participation in therapy was emphasized. Her first homework assignment was given: to prepare a list of things she enjoyed doing. She was also told that if she was willing to work in therapy, progress would occur, but that we would both have to work hard at it.

The second session was started by asking Susan how she felt about our initial meeting. She responded that she felt much relieved and more hopeful about her situation. She reported that she felt an immediate sense of relief and lessening depression after the first session. She was then asked whether she had made notes as requested. She produced some rather voluminous notes in shorthand, which she used as a point of reference for her session. (She continued this for about the first 2 weeks of therapy; after that they were no longer needed.)

Susan was asked where she wanted to start. It was pointed out to her that she did not have to proceed in the same order as her notes, nor did we have to cover everything she had written about. If she wished to bring up something we were unable to discuss during this session, she could bring it up again next time. Or, she might decide that she wanted to discuss something entirely different that was not recorded in her notes. The notes were intended to help her use her therapy time productively, but she did not have to feel locked in by them.

Susan immediately launched into the last note she had entered in the waiting room: On the way to therapy, she had "pigged out" on the highway; she had stopped at every fast-food restaurant along the way, purchasing and consuming various high-calorie foods such as "grease burgers and french fries." She was very upset by this since she was sure that she had just "blown" her diet completely and she would now regain all of the weight that she had so painstakingly lost. An old yo-yo pattern would now be repeated. She said of herself that she had "no control" and could never maintain a diet. It was hopeless, she thought. She had felt better all week, but had now demonstrated her self-destructive behavior, which she could not prevent. It was clear that she wanted help with this problem and her feeling of being out of control.

Susan was told, first, that there was no such thing as "blowing" one's diet. That was merely a faulty cognition that ensured defeat in dieting. If one believes that the diet is "blown," that it has been totally ruined by one infraction, this erroneous thinking then leads to the incorrect conclusion that one might as well go on an eating binge since it makes no difference because it is impossible to maintain a weight loss. ("Nothing I do makes any lasting difference. I might just as well enjoy eating.") It was pointed out to her that no weight gain had as yet occurred, and she could, by various strategies, prevent this. She was then asked if she would like to spend the next session on strategies and techniques to help her maintain her weight loss and to help her to continue to lose the rest of her excess poundage. She expressed relief and agreement. She was eager to do this at the next meeting.

Susan then discussed her lack of assertiveness. People asked her to do things that she really did not want to do and she felt unable to refuse. She also felt bored and had nothing to look forward to except work. We discussed the list of things she enjoyed doing, which she had prepared as a homework assignment. Susan commented that she did not like to do things alone and that often there wasn't anyone to do things with. As a homework assignment, she was asked to do one thing each week, even if it was something she did alone. In fact, her list was to include activities that she might be able to do by herself.

CONTINUING TREATMENT

The third session was used to provide weight-loss instruction. The program presented covers all seven BASIC I.D. modalities, six directly and one —affect—indirectly. The main points are outlined below.

WEIGHT-LOSS INSTRUCTION

Techniques

• Use a simple calorie chart. (One is given to the client.) Find a baseline to determine how many calories you usually consume in an average day. Assess quantity of portions as accurately as possible. *Write* the number of calories down each time you eat anything. Put the numbers on a small piece of paper. Add these up at the end of the day.

• Approximately 3500 calories = 1 pound. Therefore, if you want to lose 1 pound in a week, you must eat 3500 calories fewer than the amount you ordinarily consume. This should be divided by seven, or approximately 500 calories fewer each day. It is recommended that weight-loss plans should be targeted for a weight loss of 1½ or 2 pounds per week, *no more*. This is an essential aspect of this program.

• Once you have figured out what your daily calorie consumption can be, plan exactly what you will eat for that day. *Write* down all calories consumed on a small piece of paper. Have a special pad available in the kitchen. It is absolutely essential to record all calories. You need not record the food eaten. If not sure about a particular food, estimate the calories, but *write*.

• Use accepted weight-loss techniques: Eat sitting down in your regular place without distracting material. Cut food into small sections. Chew slowly. Keep physically active (Stuart & Davis, 1972).

• Use *hot* food as much as possible, preferably three times a day. This forces slower eating and creates a feeling of satiation.

• Eat a hot cereal in the morning. Choose by reading labels and select one relatively low in calories. Whole wheat cereals are preferred for nutrition. To prepare, use 1 cup of boiling water and three quarters of the amount of cereal indicated for one portion (thus reducing calories). Into 1/3 cup of hot water, stir a rounded teaspoon of powdered coffee creamer. This will serve as milk and adds only 15 calories. Drink hot coffee or tea. Total: 105 calories for breakfast. *Do not skip breakfast or any other meal.*

• When hungry between meals, *drink hot tea* (not coffee) with an apple, sliced into eight sections and then cored. This is filling and requires slow eating. Add 80 calories to your list. Carrot sticks or low-calorie fresh fruits may be substituted. Be inventive; think of your own low-calorie combinations that are satisfying to you.

• For dinner, a frozen low-calorie (under 300) product is recommended, since it is all prepared and premeasured, and no "seconds" are available. One or two varieties are quite palatable. Choose a product that is packaged in "boil-in" pouches, since they can be prepared in 5 minutes if defrosted in advance. Explore your supermarket. Remove the package from your freezer in the morning and allow it to defrost during the day. Do this as part of your morning routine.

• Avoid beef. Eat mostly chicken (skin removed) and fish. Steam or broil foods with as little shortening as possible. Use "no-stick" spray on cooking pans. Avoid fats and processed sugar. Avoid cheese, other than low-fat cottage cheese. Avoid breads and desserts other than fresh fruit.

• Use a supplementary green vegetable to fill out your dinner (shoestring green beans are best since they are low in calories—about 60 per cup—and blend with the sauce of the packaged low-calorie meal). Add 100 calories for a piece of fresh fruit (cut up), or some canned "packed-in-own-juice" type of fruit. Drink hot tea with your fruit. Plan on approximately 450 calories for your evening meal.

• Total: 105 (breakfast), 450 (dinner), 80 (snack) = 635 calories. Subtract this amount from your planned consumption goal and use the balance left over for lunch, and for other fruit and tea snacks during the day. Use low-calorie foods for lunch such as an omelette prepared with low-calorie cottage cheese, a salad, cottage cheese and fruit, and so forth. *Write down all calories consumed.*

• Count your calories. If you are planning to lose 1½ pounds per week, then your daily calorie consumption will have to be 750 calories under your regular consumption. If you are planning to lose 2 pounds per week, then your calorie consumption will have to be 1000 under your previous consumption that maintained your weight.

Strategies for Successful Weight Loss

• Think of any accomplishment in your past where you had to work hard and persevere for completion (a difficult course, a home project, etc.). If you were able to succeed in the past, you can succeed again.

• The first week on a weight-loss program is generally the most difficult. Stay out of the house and active as much of the time as possible. When you think you might go on an eating binge at home, leave the house. This will not be necessary after the 1st week. Plan to do all of your outside errands during this week.

• Remove all easily consumed high-calorie foods. Do not buy snack foods, except for fruit. If necessary to keep some supplies, store these in the freezer. Preferably, eliminate them entirely. If you need to have them for another member of the family, then buy them in individually packaged portions.

• Know in advance what you are going to eat at each meal, plan your procedure, and *visualize it in your imagery*. Substitute new behaviors for the old ones that kept you fat. Thus, when arriving home for your evening meal, have pots prepared to heat your boil-in pouches. Fill these and your teapot with water, place the pouches in the water to heat, and put your green vegetable on the stove to warm. While your meal is warming, wash up for dinner. By the time you are through, your meal is ready to eat. Repeat this same routine regularly until it is an established behavioral repertoire. This will substitute for previous patterns such as eating quickly consumed high-calorie foods while waiting for food to be prepared.

• Prepare a list of "No-No's." These are items of food that are high in calories, are very tempting to you, and that you have consumed regularly. Include about five or six items on this list. Remember the first letters as a mnemonic device. Rehearse these to yourself frequently. When you are tempted by these foods, repeat the list to yourself. If possible, leave the area of temptation quickly. Notice the visual image of the temptation diminish as you move further away. Notice the good feeling it brings of being in control!

• Keep active. Join an exercise or aerobics class. This will not cause you to lose weight by itself, but will help you to create the kind of figure you want and keep your muscle tone firm. It will also help to keep you aware of your diet. It is enjoyable and will make you feel better and much more energetic. Once this is part of your routine, you will miss it when you cannot participate.

• Do not plan to lose weight too quickly. It is absolutely essential that you remain on this program for a long period of time. You will then become accustomed to the system and be able to maintain it easily and automatically. New eating habits and patterns will have been substituted for the old self-defeating ones. However, this takes time to occur.

• Weigh yourself everyday. Although the scale will not reflect changes daily, and sometimes will not show a weight loss for a few days, it you follow the program, *the weight loss you anticipate will occur within the time limits you had estimated*. Watching your weight daily will help you to be aware of your weight-loss program at all times.

• Plan short-term and long-term weight-loss goals that are realistic. Long-term goals should be geared to special events that you are looking forward to where you want to look especially nice. You will find that the weight will come off exactly as planned if you maintain your system.

• Do not say to yourself, "I blew it." You cannot blow this diet by one infraction. Just continue and you will find that you are losing weight again. You can weigh any realistic amount that you wish. (Health factors should not be neglected in making this decision.)

• When you have lost the desired amount of weight, modify your diet plan, but do not abandon it. Calculate the amount of calories required to maintain your current weight (different from previous amount) and again plan what you will eat to maintain the daily calorie consumption you have targeted. You may decide that you want to eat somewhat more over the weekends and return to your lower calorie foods three or four times a week. At this point you will be able to eat out in restaurants, since you will have learned which foods to order. However, continue to stay away from high-calorie foods, since you are obviously unable to utilize these fully. Should you overdo, you will know how to correct a small weight gain quickly before it is out of hand. After you have learned to control your weight, you may then stop writing, but *do not stop counting*!

• Remember diets do work! Enjoy the heightened level of energy you will experience. Enjoy your new self-image! Enjoy feeling in control!

Multimodal Aspects of Weight-Loss Program

The weight-loss instruction described above covers all seven personality modalities. There are behavioral instructions (B), cognitive approaches (C), and very important imagery suggestions (I). The entire program deals with improving the physical condition of the client (D.). Successful accomplishment then permits access to the interpersonal and social–sexual needs of the individual (I., S). Finally, the improved body image and the feeling of being in control cause changed perceptions about the future. The overall effect is to lessen the depressed affect and to diminish anxiety (A).

One of the most important aspects of this weight-loss program is the utilization of the imagery modality. This was discussed previously when describing the planning and preparation of the evening meal and in utilizing a list of "No-No's." There should be no surprises—the client should know exactly what will be consumed and be prepared to set this up in advance. That prevents the usual high-calorie foraging frequently engaged in by overweight people when seeking out dinner items.

Weight-loss instruction was given to Susan in one session. However, throughout the following sessions we discussed the importance of changing self-defeating cognitions and disrupting old established habit patterns in order to develop new, constructive ones. We discussed all of the techniques and strategies outlined above in order to demonstrate how these could be adapted to her individual needs and integrated into her lifestyle. The effect was to increase her feeling of being in control and to instill a new sense of hopefulness.

IMPORTANT THERAPY ISSUES

During the early sessions Susan frequently expressed her sense of boredom and futility with her unsatisfying personal life. When she was encouraged to find things to do, she said that she could not go anywhere alone. Frequently, when she did think of something to do, she was unable to find anyone who was available to accompany her. This became an important issue in her therapy, as it is in dealing with many depressed women who may not have the regular companionship of a man, or female friends who can be relied upon to follow through with plans.

We talked first about the importance of planning ahead. The idea, "When the weekend comes, I'll think of something to do," is very self-defeating. We discussed the necessity of making a concrete plan in advance and putting it into action. The importance of imagery was emphasized: She was instructed to visualize herself doing the anticipated activity and told that this imagery can be instrumental in triggering the necessary behaviors to carry through with the plan. Susan described a feeling of inertia that usually occurred when the weekend arrived that prevented her from doing what she may have thought of doing. A new cognition was suggested for Susan, "If I don't make specific plans in advance, I will not go anywhere or do anything." She agreed that past experience corroborated this.

Another cognition was explored with Susan that had a great impact on helping her to shape new social behaviors. It was Susan's perception that her single objective in going to any social event was to find a boyfriend. Since she had tried in vain to accomplish this for so long, her motivation to continue with this behavior had been extinguished. When she attended a social event, she was tense and unhappy, moods that were not conducive to encouraging new friendships. It was suggested to Susan that she completely change her cognition about her reason for attending any social event. She was told to choose an activity that was basically enjoyable to her, and then to think of it first as a way of doing something enjoyable, secondly as a way of possibly meeting new *women* friends. With this cognition, she could enjoy the activity and be more relaxed. If she should meet one or two women her age, she would then have some new people available to do things with in the future.

It was pointed out to Susan that her own personal enjoyment was not completely locked into shared experiences. This is an idea that many single women have that causes a great deal of unnecessary unhappiness. Sometimes an enjoyable activity can be fun to do alone. We talked of visiting museums, looking at interesting exhibits, going to concerts, movies, and so forth. Just having the free time to go to an interesting area of the city to look in store windows or at interesting architecture is enjoyable and would be considered a luxury by many people unable to escape their daily responsibilities. Bicycle riding on a nice day is another pleasant solitary activity. Susan agreed that she might like to do these things but felt uncomfortable being by herself. "Other people might think it was weird." We again discussed how self-defeating this perception was.

A homework assignment was given to Susan. She was to do one

enjoyable activity each week, either by herself, or with someone. This was to be planned in advance, arrangements made to do it, and she was to think about it and imagine herself engaged in the activity and having a good time.

As therapy proceeded certain issues came up repeatedly. Susan often saw herself as the "fall guy" between two people. This frequently occurred at work in situations where she found herself trying to please two people with opposing points of view, each insisting that she follow his particular instructions. Her desire to please everyone ("I can't stand to have anyone mad at me.") and to offend no one caused her to be an easy target in these power struggles. Each contender felt that he could find support in her, and she was frequently caught in situations she could not handle. She secretly feared that she would cry when the confrontation became too intense, and she felt her good nature was being abused. This caused her considerable anguish. Assertiveness training helped Susan to develop some new skills in handling herself in these situations. She was asked to read *Assertive Training for Women* (Osborn & Harris, 1975). As she progressed in therapy she felt more comfortable using these skills and the incidence of these confrontations dropped off sharply.

Imagery was again employed to help Susan deal with the feared consequences of assertive behavior (Lazarus, 1978). Instead of trying to please opposing parties in a heated business discussion, she was asked to envision what might happen if she assertively stated her opinion. Her response generally indicated a gross exaggeration of the anticipated consequences. She was asked to try out an assertive behavior to replace her usual "trying to please everyone" response. The new response was rehearsed with her until she felt comfortable with it. She was now asked to imagine herself using this assertive response and to become accustomed to it. She was then asked to utilize her new assertive response in an actual situation at work and report back in therapy. This became easier for her to do as we continued.

Her fear of embarrassment if she were to cry in a business situation when she was under pressure was explored. These were usually situations when she felt abused and unappreciated and were directly linked to her lack of consistent assertive behavior. Susan was actually quite assertive in many situations; however, certain interpersonal situations caused her to retreat into passive, compliant behavior. These were generally times when she was trying to deal with a very authoritarian "top boss," whom she saw as unpredictable, and when she was trying to maintain the goodwill of other people higher on the business hierarchy to whom she reported. After discussion she gradually recognized that the "erratic, unpredictable" top boss was, in fact, quite predictable. Rehearsing planned responses to the anticipated stressful situations with those in authority was helpful, since she no longer saw herself as helpless and unprepared to deal with them. Her fear of crying during these confrontations tapered off.

We also explored what she saw as the "worst possible" situation in which she might, in fact, cry under pressure (or attack as she saw it). When she was able to gain a sense of how she could handle herself, and that it would not mean the end of the world, she relaxed. This was aided by the fact that her new assertiveness training allowed her to feel more in control and less vulnerable in a situation that she dreaded. She was also given a book to read, *Women Making It* (Halcomb, 1981), which describes this very situation.

During the early sessions when her anxiety was out of control, Susan was given relaxation training. This was very helpful to her. At another time when she described herself as unable to stop obsessive thoughts and worries, she was taught the "Stop" technique.

This procedure was modified as follows: She was taught to shout "Stop" to herself, then to breathe deeply, and to say to herself, "I feel calm and relaxed," and then to switch to another matter that required some thinking or planning that was not unpleasant or aversive. This would allow her to use her thought pressures in a constructive way.

At other times we reviewed problem-solving techniques to help Susan to feel that she could choose appropriate options and try them out (Goldfried & Davison, 1976). This helped her to feel that she was not locked into an unsatisfactory and ungratifying life situation. This was applied both to her work and to her private life.

Susan was also given some instruction about where and how to find activity and social groups that she might be interested in and how to make the necessary contacts. We discussed which groups might be suitable for her and which ones to avoid.

SUMMARY

The importance of finding an issue that captured the client's interest was paramount in this case. Susan wanted to lose weight so that she could feel better about herself and, hopefully, interest men. "Being fat" had been a sore point throughout all of her life and she felt completely helpless to alter her body image. The weight-loss program helped her to accomplish this, and made it possible for her to maintain the figure she thought she would never have. When she felt that her weight was being maintained, she changed her clothing style and found much more becoming clothes. She suddenly appeared one day with a new, attractive short hairdo and new makeup. She looked quite attractive, completely different from her first appearance in therapy, and for the first time looked happy.

As Susan felt better about herself, she was able to be more assertive. Her self-deprecatory humor dropped away and was replaced by a more constructive humor. She had a natural talent for being amusing. She seemed more at ease with herself and was more fun to be with. People were beginning to comment on how well she looked, and she became more attractive to men. This was soon apparent to her when a man at the office began to show an interest in her. At that point, her interest in the married man who had obsessed her early in therapy disappeared. She wondered how she had been so interested in such a "nerd."

Susan saw her new romantic interest infrequently, since there were problems in this relationship. However, she finally experienced a man showing sexual interest in her. Later, she seemed again to be pursuing a losing relationship; the man who was the focus of her interest was very ambiguous and would not make any regular social commitments. He just wanted her to be available whenever he wished, and that was infrequently. We discussed how she was handling herself and spent a great deal of time in therapy helping to fill in the gaps in her social experience. She became more assertive and more skillful in dealing with men; her social skills with men improved dramatically. She began to do more things socially, enjoying activities instead of worrying about whether she would "meet a man."

Finally, Susan was exploring more social events. We talked about how to find appropriate activities that she would find pleasing. She then went to a "singles" camp for a weekend, agreeing to accompany a friend to an event that she would have unconditionally avoided in the past. She enjoyed the activities at camp, "had lots of fun," and was surprised and tremendously gratified to find several attractive men interested in her. She received two phone calls, one which surprised her completely since he hadn't asked for her number at camp, and she started dating.

Susan's new feeling of self-confidence extended to all areas of her life. With encouragement in therapy, she began to explore other job options. When she found an excellent position that she was very happy about, at almost twice her current salary, her old fear of authority figures again emerged. She imagined what it would be like telling the owner of the company ("top boss") that she was leaving. We discussed what his reaction might be and how she would handle it. He behaved pretty much as she had feared, engaging in a lengthy tirade and attacking her emotionally; he was as erratic and unpredictable in his choice of issues as she had learned to expect. He berated her for being "ungrateful" and "disloyal," totally ignoring the fact that he had failed to honor his many promises to give her formal recognition for a job well done by promoting her to a job title that would more clearly reflect her actual job assignments and responsibilities and would pay her commensurately. (At one point, he had said to her, "A young girl like you, what do you need so much money for?") Other colleagues told her that they were glad she had found a job where she would be appreciated. Susan felt that her new assertiveness skills served her well during this unpleasant interview, and she was gratified to find that she had handled this most dreaded confrontation in a poised and confident manner and that she had not felt any concern that she might cry.

The use of a multimodal approach in this case provided the much needed specific assessment this case required. This then allowed selection of treatment interventions that could be used in therapy to deal with all of the identified problems. An important aspect of this case was recognizing the impact of particular problems on other modalities. All of the problems identified on the BASIC I.D. were dealt with, and the strengths identified were all utilized constantly during the course of therapy. The result was an integrated and comprehensive treatment that employed all seven BASIC I.D. modalities.

REFERENCES

Brunell, L. F., & Young, W. T. (1982). *Multimodal handbook for a mental hospital: Designing specific treatments for specific problems.* New York: Springer.

Goldfried, M. R., & Davison, G. C. (1976). *Clinical behavior therapy.* New York: Holt, Rinehart & Winston.

Halcomb, R. (1981). *Women making it.* New York: Ballantine.

Lazarus, A. A. (1976). *Multimodal behavior therapy.* New York: Springer.

Lazarus, A. A. (1978). *In the mind's eye.* New York: Rawson. (Reissued 1984, Guilford.)

Lazarus, A. A. (1981). *The practice of multimodal therapy.* New York: McGraw-Hill.

Osborn, S. M., & Harris, G. G. (1975). *Assertive training for women.* Springfield, IL: C. C. Thomas.

Shelton, J. L., & Ackerman, J. M. (1974). *Homework in counseling and psychotherapy.* Springfield, IL: C. C. Thomas.

Stuart, R. B., & Davis, B. (1972). *Slim chance in a fat world.* Champaign, IL: Research Press.

5

Multimodal Therapy with Children: Ernie the Enuretic

DONALD B. KEAT II

The artistry and technical repertoire of an effective child therapist involve specific skills that are not required by a clinician who is gifted with young or elderly adults. To be able to reach certain children, the therapist must frequently transcend formal assessment and treatment procedures by drawing on a storehouse of appropriate games, songs, stories, and by demonstrating a flair for the dramatic. Donald Keat ably demonstrates his capacity for finding appropriate, and often highly inventive, procedures for a variety of specific problems. Over the years, however, I have objected to the fact that Keat links the sensory modality with school-related pressures and requirements. The fact that "sensation" and "school" both start with the letter "S" is no justification for bracketing them together and thus distorting the integrity of the seven modes of personality functioning. In my writings I have stressed that it is essential to include factors that fall outside the BASIC I.D. such as sociocultural, political, and other macroenvironmental events. But external reality (e.g., the school environment) is not part of "temperament and personality." Despite this disclaimer, Keat's chapter shows how a highly talented child psychologist uses the multimodal framework to excellent effect.

The utility of multimodal therapy has been illustrated with numerous cases (Keat, 1976a, 1976b, 1979, 1980a). In those cases I presented children who were predominantly behaviorally disordered (1976a), phobic (1976a), encopretic (1976b), psychotic (1979), as well as a learning-disabled child (Keat & Hatch, 1979), and a child whose primary presenting difficulty was in the interpersonal zone (1980a). Other authors have treated phobias (Lazarus, 1978), insect phobias (Edwards, 1978), anger (Boswell, 1982), aggression (Arace & Franzblau, 1982), weight control (Seligman, 1981), school problems (Starr & Raykovitz, 1982), self-concept (Durbin, 1982), divorce (Green, 1978, 1981), and a broad range of educational concerns (e.g., see Gerler, 1982).

The current case I will present is an ongoing one. The boy's primary presenting concern is enuresis, but the case will illustrate the broadness and richness of the multimodal approach as it is used as a compass to guide the therapist through the assessment–therapeutic maze. The multimodal profile helps provide direction as the therapist searches for effective techniques to aid his or her client.

CASE BACKGROUND

The client, Ernie (aged 10 years), was referred to me by the Mental Health/Mental Retardation (MH/MR) Base Service Unit. Their psychological evaluation indicated that the primary concerns were day and nighttime enuresis, encopresis, fighting with other children, and disruptive behavior in the classroom. Further referral information reflected that he was also sad (suicidal overtures), and there was much fighting in the family both between siblings and parents.

The family composition was the identified client Ernie (aged 10 years), sister Suzie (aged 8 years), his mother, who is primarily a housewife but also a part-time maid, and his father, who is a sometime (in-and-out-of-work) truckdriver. At the time of referral the family was on welfare and living in a trailer. Ernie was born when his mother was 14 years of age. Mother's education went as far as seventh grade and father's eighth grade.

Table 5-1 presents a multimodal listing of the problems and related treatments. On the left side of the table, the zones are rank ordered according to importance. This approach enables the therapist to exercise "clinical judgment" as to where the first zone of intervention should be. The modality to be dealt with first is usually the area where the greatest level of concern is (as presented by parents, agency, and so forth). It is important to try to do something about the primary presenting concern before going on to other zones. The problem and treatment approaches will be discussed in their rank order of concern. The rest of the table includes the seven BASIC I.D. modalities, problems, and related treatments within each modality.

PROBLEM AND TREATMENT INTERVENTIONS

DRUGS/HEALTH

The primary presenting problem of concern was daytime enuresis–encopresis and nighttime enuresis. This type of difficulty requires a broad spectrum of procedures and could indeed benefit from a second-order multimodal analysis (see Lazarus, 1981). The primary procedure tied directly into this concern was the use of audiotherapy. I developed an

TABLE 5-1. Multimodal Profile: Ernie

Rank	Modality	Number	Problem	Treatment
5	Behavior	B1	Chores, responsibility	Behavior contracting
		B2	Behavior at home	Discipline education
		B3	Coping behavior	Modeling
2	Affect/	A1	Deprivation	Relationship enhancement
	emotions/	A2	Fighting	Madness management
	feelings	A3	Tense, nervous	Relaxation training
		A4	Sadness	Fun training
4	Sensation–	S1	Conflict with teacher	School collaboration
	school	S2	Getting work done	Homework contract
		S3	School work	Study skills
		S4	Responsibility	Games
6	Imagery	I1	Low self-image	IALAC
		I2	Performing adequately	Hero imagery
		I3	Imagery	Puppet play
7	Cognition	C1	Self put-downs	Cognitive restructuring
		C2	Decision-making skills	Personal problem solving
		C3	Information	Bibliotherapy
3	Interpersonal	I.1	Poor peer relations	Friendship training
	relationships	I.2	Sibling conflict	Instant Replay
		I.3	Adult relations	Winning Ways
1	Drugs/health	D.1	Enuresis and encopresis	Audio therapy
		D.2	Poor nutrition	Diet therapy
		D.3	Lacks exercise	Activity monitoring

audio cassette tape for Mother, which was later released commercially (Keat, 1981). This particular tape goes through the following procedures in which the parents are to go as far down the list as necessary: rituals, retention control training, nightly awakening time, responsibility training, chart keeping, behavior management procedures, the bell and pad, bibliotherapy (Azrin & Besalel, 1979), hypnosis, drugs, or attending a camp specializing in bed-wetting problems.

The area of nutrition was difficult to implement in this family. Due to low income and lack of mother's interest, there was little that could be done to influence this concern in a broad sense. Therefore, what I tried to do was share granola bars and bananas during our sessions. I also usually bought him a package of a health-food nut mix, which he took home. I hoped that I could have some positive influence on his thinking and actions regarding what he ate.

I also encouraged Ernie to be involved in physical activities. During sessions we accomplished this by engaging in such things as a jump-rope contest. He performed two types (boxing jog and two-feet jump), and I recorded his efforts for the session. Outside of the therapy hours I gave him one of my left-handed son's gloves (there was initially some confusion whether Ernie was left- or right-handed). He writes left-handed and seemed to have some preference for this. After he had it for a week, however, he brought it back and I got him a right-handed glove from one of my sons. He did play Little League baseball this past summer, and at his most recent session he pleasantly surprised me with a trophy. His team had won the Little League championship!

AFFECT/EMOTIONS/FEELINGS

Ernie lived a rather tumultuous life in which he was not sure whether his parents would be together or not (one or the other periodically walked out). Despite this, he seemed to have a close relationship with his mother but a distant one from his father. Ernie impressed me as having an emotional void. He took as much as he could, emotionally and physically, whenever feasible. Our relationship evolved into a close interpersonal one in which things were liberally exchanged. I supported him in any way possible, such as providing the baseball gloves and foods.

As delineated in the original presenting problems, Ernie had difficulty controlling his angry feelings and easily got into fights. Therefore, I employed my madness management (Keat, 1980b) procedures with him. This procedure involved his working on developing physical outlets (hitting pillows and/or bed), picturing humorous things happening to his antagonizer (putting his sister's head in the toilet), and learning what to say and where to say it so that he did not get into trouble. The level of difficulties and number of fights he got into diminished.

Finally, as the antidote for anxiety, he learned relaxation (Keat, 1977b) procedures. His idiosyncratic scenes were imagining that he was fishing and saying the sentence to himself that "this is relaxing." He gained some control of his tenseness.

Finally, as a way of helping him to learn to cope with feelings of sadness, I introduced the concepts of fun training (Keat, 1982a). The audio cassette tape takes the child on a trip with Freddie Funlover as he figures out *what* he likes to do (e.g., go to the Arts Festival sales), with *whom* to do it (with his sister and me), *where* he likes to do it (in State College), and how to get it happening (we plan an annual trip to the Festival). We also shared jokes (the value of humor in life, funny books, e.g., *Whole Mirth Catalog*) and records (e.g., Bill Cosby). These types of activities added some levity and allowed him to begin to "live and laugh at it all."

INTERPERSONAL RELATIONSHIPS

In order to aid Ernie in learning how to get along with peers, he was trained in how to meet, greet, and keep friends (Keat, 1980c). These procedures also involved an introduction to the ABCs of game playing, which means to learn to use appropriate *A*ctions of getting along with others, use the *B*ehavior of taking turns, and to *C*ommunicate (listen to and talk with) the children you're playing with. He has made great strides in this arena.

There was a lot of inappropriate hassling and hitting going on between Ernie and Suzie. When I saw them together, I attempted to give him corrective feedback about how to relate to her ("You say you love her, but when you hit her that hard, it hurts, and tells her that you don't like her very much"). A useful procedure to help siblings learn how to relate is given in the book *Instant Replay* (Bedford, 1974). By reading this book with the two of them together, they were exposed to the ideas of identifying feelings, what they're telling themselves to upset themselves, what else can they do instead of hitting (as actually occurred in the story), and the consequences of each of their proposed actions. Despite a long-standing history of antagonistic relationships, they soon learned to relate more positively.

I also worked with Ernie in the area of adult relationships. He was being instructed in *Winning Ways* (Keat, 1981) of getting along with teachers and parents. Essentially, this involved empathy training, developing his good behavior list, trying to develop listener–talker skills, and working out agreements with adults. He learned more effective ways of getting along with the adults in his life (i.e., both parents and teachers).

Sensation–School

The *Winning Ways* (Keat, 1981) skill was especially important during Ernie's fifth-grade year when he encountered a teacher who had a similar wetting problem but was not tolerant of Ernie's difficulty. By "walking in his shoes" and negotiating with the teacher (with some help from the school counselor), his classroom life was made more tolerable. This school collaboration took place with a meeting of teachers, principal, guidance counselor, caseworker, and me. The parents were encouraged to come to the conference. Indeed, the caseworker stopped by the trailer to pick them up as prearranged, but they were gone. Therefore, it was up to us to effect possible changes in the school. The school situation provided me with an ongoing struggle to achieve adjustments on both sides (i.e., teachers plus Ernie).

In order to coordinate some of these changes, and to help Ernie get his schoolwork done, one part of the contract was payment for the completion of schoolwork. During the fifth-grade school year this was coordinated with the elementary school counselor and her intern who checked in on his accomplishment of this task with the teacher. The following year (sixth grade) the counselor had been on maternity leave, and I switched the responsibility to the mother. Ernie's payoff accelerated (with inflation) from $.03 to $.05 per attainment of each daily goal. His contract usually had four other components (to be discussed under the next mode of behavior). He usually earned from $5 to $7 a month from this contract.

The third skill in this zone was that of helping Ernie acquire the skills in order to more effectively complete his school work. In order to do this, I utilized my study skills audio cassette tape (Keat, 1982b). This approach explains the "STP" formula, which explores the Studying of the subject matter, the best Time of day to accomplish the work, and working out a suitable Place to get the work done. In addition, I reviewed with Ernie the ABCs of studying. These procedures involved such Actions as working in small (15- to 30-minute) concentrated time periods, the Behavior of setting an alarm clock for this time in order to signal break time, and the Consequences of getting some reward (e.g., points or money) when he accomplished what he needed to. On his final contract for this past school year, he got his homework done every day except one and therefore he earned $1.65 for that component of his monthly contract.

The final consideration under this modality was the learning of responsibility. One of the child's main ways of interacting is via games. A component of friendship training (Keat, 1980c) is the ABCs of game playing. During this the child could learn that he or she should show such actions as paying attention, behaving in a cooperative way so that winning is not so important, communicating (talking) during the game, and being fun to play with. One of Ernie's primary difficulties was cheating to win games. I would confront him with this behavior and point out that I knew what he was doing and if he acted that way with his friends, they would not want to play with him. He gradually incorporated this responsibility into his adaptive behavior.

BEHAVIOR

As just discussed in the previous section, I used a behavior contract with Ernie for getting homework done. Although the components of this agreement varied from time to time, the most recent edition has, in addition, four home-related responsibilities. They are putting the garbage out, cleaning up his bedroom, being neat in and out of school, and having a dry bed. His most recent agreement (now on about a monthly basis) showed that he took the garbage out daily, he cleaned up his bedroom 26 of 34 days, did his homework 33 of 34 days, had a dry bed 30 of 34 days, and was neat in and out of school every day (thus earning $7.85 for the month). He was saving his money for a school trip to Hershey Park in June.

In order to integrate the series of rewards and his desired behavior at home, the information from the *Reward Survey for Children* (Keat, 1979) was shared with Mother as a basis for motivating him to respond more favorably to discipline at home. Due to the fact that the mother was essentially a nonreader (for most reading parents I use Keat & Guerney, 1980, for parent bibliotherapy) but a good listener (she also speaks well and spends a lot of time on the phone), with an audiotape set-up in the trailer, I shared *How to Discipline Children* (Keat, 1977a) with her. This audio cassette tape helped her to learn about setting limits, applying consequences (natural, logical, and unrelated), and a variety of procedures to help Ernie to clean his room ("open door/closed door" and putting away clothes—"Saturday Box"). As can be noted from his just cited results, he was cleaning his room more frequently, but not entirely to his mother's satisfaction.

Finally, in order to help Ernie learn more appropriate coping behavior, I served as a model during the sessions. Some examples are: When trying to organize things to remember, I took out a 3 × 5 card and wrote down items; when confronted with decisions, I developed and weighed the alternatives and thought out loud before making a decision; and I demonstrated constantly (by my personal demeanor) how a calm, relaxed person functions. In these ways (and others) I provided a more appropriate role model than he was exposed to at home. In addition, his male caseworker also exposed him to another strong but quiet man who coped with life's concerns very well.

IMAGERY

Ernie would generally make demeaning statements about himself such as, "I'm dumb, no good," and so forth. We read a story, *I Am Loveable and Capable (IALAC)* (Simon, 1973), and talked about how we develop self-confidence. One of my goals was to insert, wherever appropriate, positive statements regarding his capabilities. When he would handle something well, I would comment on this activity. Occasionally I could make statements like "Ernie the Great." Recently, when he brought in a story for me on the "Mission of Halloween," he said, "I like creating something I can be proud of. As long as I'm creating, I'm happy." We are currently working on developing his story and drawings into a book for children.

In a related way to help him perform in music adequately, we used one of his heroes from the muppets, "Zoot." I had let Ernie borrow one of my alto saxophones because the family was too poor to afford buying or renting one. Periodically he would become discouraged because his father, when home and out of work, would not allow him to practice. At these times we would call upon "Zoot" to hang in there and stick with the music program.

Ernie does have a vivid imagination and can develop interesting acting scenes. Therefore, puppet play was a worthwhile avenue for him to work on a variety of conflicts. Two, which recurred during puppet play, were the handling of disagreements with his sister and fighting with peers. By interacting with me during the puppet play, I showed him alternative ways to express affection for his sister (hug instead of hit) and how to avoid fights with other children (e.g., walk away, go to an adult, etc.).

COGNITION

As previously discussed under the imagery modality and illustrating the interactive functions of modes where the "ripple" (Lazarus, 1976, p. 6) or "domino" effect takes place (when action in one area spills over into another sphere), I tried to create competent images of himself (these are the "videotapes" in one's head). The audiotape, concurrently, should be playing the positive sentences such as, "Ernie the great," and so forth. Some of these self-sentences were programmed during the sessions, but he was also encouraged to bring in evidence of positive accomplishments from outside. For example, for his most recent appointment, he brought in a trophy that he had received for being a member of the Little League championship team.

Almost everyone can benefit from improved decision-making skills. To help develop these abilities, we played *Problem Solving for Children* (Keat, 1982c). From this audio cassette tape he learned about developing alternatives for choices, then to figure out the best choice, and finally to try out the choice to see how it goes. We would go through the day (from morning to night) and examine the variety of choices he would be confronted with. It is important for children to have some "voice in the choice" of what happens in their lives. By experiencing some control, they are more likely to become positively involved in their activities.

Finally, in order to share relevant information, a variety of books were read with Ernie. Lazarus (1981, p. 231) has stated, "A well-chosen book can be worth more than a dozen sessions." With Ernie, having such sources to read in between contacts allowed the learning process to continue during the interim. Some which were particularly useful with him were on friendship (Wilt, 1978a), sibling fighting, (Wilt, 1978b), self-image (Palmer, 1977), and values (Johnson, 1978). Another helpful book that covers a lot of areas is *What Every Kid Should Know* (Kalb & Viscott, 1976). This book was later released in audio cassette tape (Kalb & Viscott, 1980) and presents interesting questions for discussion such as

To: Caseworker
Re: Client: Ernie
     Case No. 105-25376

Dear Ms. Caseworker:

Ernie has been transported to sessions by his caseworker. Therefore, he has been able to appear for his appointments as scheduled.

Ernie is in need of continued psychotherapy. The multimodal reasons for this are as follows:

Behavior. We've worked on the *Reward Survey for Children* as a basis for contracts. I also provide lunches, foods (seed packs), and clothes. He is an extremely deprived boy. I'm also supporting his music activities by lending him a saxophone and reeds plus paying for his books.

Affect/emotions/feelings. Ernie has completed the *Madness Management* program to help him with anger control and the relaxation training. Some of these lessons are carrying over into other parts of his home and school life. He benefits from the positive adult male relationship with both his therapist and caseworker.

Sensation-school. I'm in periodic contact with the school counselor and her intern. His classroom placement has been of constant concern this year because of his teacher. We have considered changing his teacher, but I'm currently helping him learn to cope with his present placement.

Imagery. Ernie needs positive feedback to help undo the negatives he's been getting. I do this during sessions and talk to Mother about this. This one-to-one during therapy with Ernie is relatively easy because he is a likable child. He also uses puppet play and fantasy well. To enhance his self-image, we also read books such as *The Value of Believing in Yourself, Learning, Humor,* and so forth.

Cognition. In this mode we've primarily used bibliotherapy. For example, reading relevant parts of *28 Ways to Vent Your Anger* and *What Every Child Should Know.* Now I'm also working on developing his personal problem solving skills.

Interpersonal relationships. Ernie has completed the tape on *Friendship Training for Children.* We also periodically meet jointly with his sister, Suzie, to help them learn to get along better. Mother is currently working, but I hope to see her again in November. I'm working with Ernie on *Winning Ways* to get along better with adults.

Drugs/health. The primary referral reason was enuresis and encopresis. The approach for this has been primarily behavioral (a reward system) and the use of audiotherapy. He seems much improved in this area and uses the bathroom as needed during the day. During our contacts I provide him with healthy foods.

In summary, this is a family in need of continued support and contact. Therefore, psychotherapy for Ernie (primary) and his mother (secondary) should be continued. Therapy is especially needed as he continues to try to cope with his unstable life situation. These contacts could be on a biweekly basis.

If you have any further questions, please call (863-2415), or write 103 CEDAR Building, Penn State, University Park PA 16802.

Sincerely yours,

Donald B. Keat II
Multimodal Child Psychologist

DBK:mh

FIGURE 5-1. MH/MR quarterly letter.

your happiest memories list, three wishes, five people you really admire, unpleasant memories, and five compliments people have paid you. After reading the Kalb and Viscott (1976) book during the session, the tape (1980) provided some carry-over during the interim and thus generalization of learning was enhanced.

SUMMARY

The case of Ernie represents the application of the BASIC I.D. multimodal approach to a wide variety of presenting problems. These concerns were presented in the determined order of importance. This rank ordering of problems allows the clinician to intervene in the primary area of initial concern (e.g., enuresis) and then to proceed to other areas of difficulty. The interactive "ripple" or domino effect was also illustrated wherein treatment in one zone influenced other areas. For example, contracting, which is predominately in the behavioral zone (chores, neatness), effects the sensation–school (homework) and drugs/health (dry bed) areas. In all, 23 treatment interventions were applied in this "technically eclectic" (Lazarus, 1967, 1971) approach. I also used the Multimodal Profile as a means of presenting my quarterly reports to the MH/MR caseworker. In these reports I wrote one paragraph on each mode (see Figure 5-1).

As can be seen from this report, gains have been made, but continued treatment is indicated. Outcomes thus far indicate that Ernie has shown positive growth in most areas of concern. Treatment on a once-a-month basis continues, nevertheless, in order to maintain this close interpersonal relationship, consolidate gains, and to continue helping him to learn to cope with the multimodal concerns of life.

REFERENCES

Arace, R. H., & Franzblau, R. S. (1982). Individual behavioral programs and treatment instructions. In L. F. Brunell & W. T. Young (Eds.), *Multimodal handbook for a mental hospital*. New York: Springer.

Azrin, N. H., & Besalel, V. A. (1979). *A parents guide to bedwetting control*. New York: Simon & Schuster.

Bedford, S. (1974). *Instant replay*. New York: Institute for Rational Living.

Boswell, J. (1982). HELPING children with their anger. *Elementary School Guidance and Counseling, 16*(4), 278–287.

Durbin, D. (1982). Multimodal group sessions to enhance self concept. *Elementary School Guidance and Counseling, 16*(4), 288–295.

Edwards, S. S. (1978). Multimodal therapy with children: A case analysis of insect phobia. *Elementary School Guidance and Counseling, 13*(1), 23–29.

Gerler, E. R. (1982). *Counseling the young learner*. Englewood Cliffs, N.J: Prentice-Hall.

Green, B. J. (1978). HELPING children of divorce: A multimodal approach. *Elementary School Guidance and Counseling, 13*(1), 31–45.

Green, B. J. (1981). HELPING single-parent families. *Elementary School Guidance and Counseling, 15*(3), 249–262.

Johnson, S. (1978). *The value of saving.* La Jolla, CA: Value Tales.

Kalb, J., & Viscott, D. (1976). *What every kid should know.* Boston: Houghton Mifflin.

Kalb, J., & Viscott, D. (1980). *What every kid should know* (Audio Cassette). Waco, TX: Success Motivation.

Keat, D. B. (1976a). Multimodal therapy with children: Two case histories. In A. A. Lazarus (Ed.), *Multimodal behavior therapy.* New York: Springer.

Keat, D. B. (1976b). Multimodal counseling with children: Treating the BASIC ID. *Pennsylvania Personnel and Guidance Association Journal, 4*, 21–25.

Keat, D. B. (1977a). *How to discipline children* (Audio Cassette). Harrisburg, PA: Professional Associates.

Keat, D. B. (1977b). *Self-relaxation for children* (Audio Cassette). Harrisburg, PA: Professional Associates.

Keat, D. B. (1979). *Multimodal therapy with children.* New York: Pergamon.

Keat, D. B. (1980a). Multimodal therapy with children and adolescents. *Journal of Counseling and Psychotherapy, III*, 35–44.

Keat, D. B. (1980b). *Madness management programs for children* (Audio Cassette). Harrisburg, PA: Professional Associates.

Keat, D. B. (1980c). *Friendship training for children* (Audio Cassette). Harrisburg, PA: Professional Associates.

Keat, D. B. (1981). *Winning ways for children* (Audio Cassette). Harrisburg, PA: Professional Associates.

Keat, D. B. (1982a). *Fun training for children* (Audio Cassette). Harrisburg, PA: Professional Associates.

Keat, D. B. (1982b). *Study skills for children* (Audio Cassette). Harrisburg, PA: Professional Associates.

Keat, D. B. (1982c). *Problem solving for children* (Audio Cassette). Harrisburg, PA: Professional Associates.

Keat, D. B., & Guerney, L. (1980). *HELPING your child.* Alexandria, VA: AACD Press.

Keat, D. B., & Hatch, E. J. (1979). Effective helping with learning disabled children. In S. Eisenberg & L. E. Patterson (Eds.), *Helping clients with special concerns.* Chicago: Rand McNally.

Lazarus, A. A. (1967). In support of technical eclecticism. *Psychological Reports, 21*, 415–416.

Lazarus, A. A. (1971). *Behavior therapy and beyond.* New York: McGraw-Hill.

Lazarus, A. A. (Ed.). (1976). *Multimodal behavior therapy.* New York: Springer.

Lazarus, A. A. (1978). What is multimodal therapy? A brief overview. *Elementary School Guidance and Counseling, 13*(1), 6–11.

Lazarus, A. A. (1981). *The practice of multimodal therapy.* New York: McGraw-Hill.

Palmer, P. (1977). *Liking myself.* San Luis Obispo, CA: Impact.

Seligman, L. (1981). Multimodal behavior therapy: Case study of a high school student. *School Counselor, 28*, 249–256.

Simon, S. (1973). *I am loveable and capable.* Niles, IL: Argus.

Starr. .J., & Raykovitz, J. (1982). A multimodal approach to interviewing children. *Elementary School Guidance and Counseling, 16*(4), 267–277.

Wilt, J. (1978a). *A kid's guide to making friends.* Waco, TX: Word.

Wilt, J. (1978b). *Surviving fights with your brothers and sisters.* Waco, TX: Word.

6

Three Multimodal Case Studies: Two Recalcitrant "Ghetto Clients" and a Case of Posttraumatic Stress

JULIAN W. SLOWINSKI

The first two clients described by Julian Slowinski would be classified as "intractable" by many clinicians who might balk at the prospect of undertaking their treatment. Slowinski is not one to shy away from "difficult cases." Armed with the multimodal assessment–therapy framework, he clearly demonstrates how, combined with his own sensitivity, fortitude, and creativity, the BASIC I.D. schema served as a compass, a lodestar, that permitted him to analyze global, diffuse, and seemingly disparate "pathologies" into specific and treatable problems. His third case, that of a woman suffering from a posttraumatic stress disorder, demonstrates operationally what is meant by "systematic and comprehensive assessment and therapy." Again, here is an instance where unimodal, bimodal, or trimodal methods would have been most unlikely to provide the client with a sufficiently diverse range of coping mechanisms to sustain immediate gains. A basic assumption is that the more clients learn in therapy, the less likely they are to relapse afterward.

MULTIMODAL THERAPY FOR TWO "GHETTO CLIENTS"

The two case studies that follow represent an application of multimodal therapy principles developed by Arnold Lazarus. The patients are from a poor urban neighborhood and had received traditional treatment at the community mental health center before beginning treatment with me. I undertook the treatment of Doris F and Alice B in the hope of demonstrating that the methods of multimodal assessment and treatment are applicable to a poor black client population.

The flexibility of the multimodal approach, and the variety of treatment techniques available, gave me a wide range within which to approach the patient and also provided the patients with a degree of coping mechanisms to deal with the problems of daily living in the ghetto community. The history of both patients, particularly Doris F, suggest serious diagnostic and prognostic implications. Multimodal treatment attempted to target a number of areas of therapeutic intervention.

These patients were selected because: they were known to the therapist; they each had a history of traditional treatment, ranging from 3 to 14 years, that had accomplished little in terms of amelioration and maladaptive functioning; they were judged by me to be sufficiently motivated to engage in a multimodal approach, and, in fact, had asked to do so when the method was explained to them. During the course of therapy, in addition to attending the ongoing group therapy with me, each patient also entered into multimodal individual and/or family therapy.

To aid in assessment and in judging the effectiveness of treatment, the Life History Questionnaire (Lazarus, 1981) and the Assertiveness Inventory (Alberti & Emmons, 1982) were administered to both patients at the beginning of multimodal treatment and again following approximately 1 year of therapy. One patient also completed the Fear Inventory (Wolpe, 1973).

CASE HISTORY 1: ALICE B

Alice B was a 49-year-old attractive and well-groomed black female of light complexion. She was first referred to the mental health center by her physician, who was concerned about the possibility of psychosis. At that time she was described as being chronically anxious, suffering from low-grade hypertension, fearful of knives, and fearing she might hurt someone. There was also the question of the presence of auditory hallucinations.

The precipitating event centered around the anxiety aroused when she witnessed a man on the street threaten and stab another man with a knife. Alice reported having been anxious "all her life," and particularly so since the summer before her admission, when she underwent a breast biopsy that proved negative. She was also anxious about the health of her 11-year-old son, who was suffering from central abdominal pain of an unknown etiology. At the time of admission to the center, Alice was given the diagnosis of phobic neurosis and was placed on a low dose of Thorazine (10 mg three times a day). This medication was continued by her physician for 3 years until I requested its discontinuance when I took over her treatment. When Alice began multimodal treatment, she was prescribed Valium (10 mg as needed), which she took only on two occasions. She also received Thiazide (25 mg per day) for hypertension as prescribed by her internist.

Upon her original admission to the clinic, Alice received weekly individual therapy with a traditional psychiatrist for 5 months before being referred to a women's group, where I met her 4 months after she joined the group. While in the group Alice was observed to be overly compliant, generally fearful, anxious, unassertive, and in need of constant reassurance and nurturance.

Alice was the second of six children in a family home she described as having been "full of love." She claimed that both her parents loved her very much. Alice's mother died of cancer at the age of 38 years. Alice had become quite dependent on her father, who at the age of 78 years, was living with his divorced son, whom she described as possibly being "schizophrenic."

Alice got along well with her siblings, and despite being one of the eldest children, she reported being the "baby" in the family and had always been protected and reassured by them about her fears and concerns. The overprotective pattern continued throughout her 25-year marriage to a "loving and understanding" man, who died of a heart attack 1 year previous to her beginning multimodal therapy.

The client lived with her three children, all males, aged 24, 13, and 8 years, her daughter-in-law, and a 1-year-old grandchild. She was quite proud of the fact that her eldest son was a college graduate and that her younger boys were doing well in school.

On the Multimodal Life History Questionnaire (Lazarus, 1981), Alice listed her five main fears as (1) being alone, (2) having pains in the heart and chest areas, (3) knives (someone might pull one on her), (4) afraid she might die and leave her children alone, (5) going places by herself. While Alice recalled being always fearful of being alone, her marked anxiety about having chest pains began 2 years before starting multimodal therapy, when she experienced pain and feared death after admitting her eldest son to the hospital with a diagnosis of high blood pressure. Since then Alice B had not been able to travel alone to the downtown area for fear of having chest pains and dying. While she experienced a generalized fear in traveling alone elsewhere, she was able to come to the clinic by herself.

Alice's responses to the Fear Inventory (Wolpe, 1973) revealed a generally fearful woman who placed 25 of the 87 items in the "much fear" to "very much fear" categories. Only 16 of the 87 items were reported to elicit no fear at all.

In response to items on the Life History Questionnaire that applied to her, Alice listed: headaches, unable to relax, memory problems, lonely, anxiety, horrible thoughts (going to die, anticipating being alone, children might get run over), bored, sympathetic, considerate.

On sentence completion items Alice described herself as liking people, loving to be loved, fearing things all her life, experiencing guilt over hurting someone's feelings, being hurt if people talked about her, denying anger about anything, unable to stand on her own two feet, a good mother, wishing that her own mother had kissed her more, and wanting marriage but not wanting to leave her mother and father.

On the Assertiveness Inventory (Alberti & Emmons, 1982) Alice presented a profile of a generally unassertive woman, who was dependent on others and capable of showing love and affection.

Alice had completed 11th grade and early in her adult life had been employed doing clerical work in a bank. Neither she nor her husband succeeded as well financially as her siblings, a point that caused her some concern and embarassment. Her social activities were centered about her family. She was easily manipulated by the demands of her younger sons in areas such as allowances and buying them expensive clothes. She enjoyed watching television, attending church, movies, and going out to dinner with her family and friends.

Alice was relatively sheltered regarding sexual matters, and when she had become frightened about sex on her honeymoon, she had called her father who had ordered her home; a command her husband had not allowed. While she reported no guilt about sexual relations with her husband, Alice was unable to accept the transition toward the single life after she was widowed, despite being encouraged by her friends to enjoy the company of men.

A Multimodal Profile was established for Alice B (Table 6-1).

Alice B remained in multimodal treatment for 11 months. During that time she was seen 72 times: individual sessions, 32; group attendance, 35; family sessions, 5. She was most reliable in keeping her appointments, cancelling only 4 of her individual sessions during the course of treatment.

While the Multimodal Profile of Alice was extensive, there was much overlap between modalities in the course of treatment. Initial individual sessions focused on relaxation training and coping with stress and generalized anxiety. Cognitive–behavioral and rational–emotive techniques were utilized in dealing with Alice's many self-defeating behavioral and cognitive patterns. She responded very favorably to *in vivo* graded exercises to successfully overcome her agoraphobia. Her assertiveness and socialization skills continued throughout treatment. As mentioned, Alice was taken off Thorazine at the beginning of multimodal treatment and took Valium on only two occasions during the course of therapy.

At the time of collecting the posttest data, Alice's responses on the Life History Questionnaire revealed a considerable improvement in functioning (Table 6-2). Her own perception of the severity of her overall condition changed from moderately severe to mildly upsetting.

At that time Alice also showed a strong shift in her self-description. While she reported some complaints similar to those mentioned in her pretest, she explained that the problems were now experienced to a much lesser degree. Alice was now able to travel alone, was less fearful of being alone under a variety of circumstances, reported fewer somatic complaints, had shown a great reduction in depression, was more independent, had

TABLE 6-1. Alice B's Multimodal Profile

Modality	Problem	Proposed treatment
Behavior	Lacks assertion	Assertive training Behavior rehearsal in group
	Avoids being alone	Graded *in vivo* assignments Positive verbal coping cues Relaxation training Coping imagery Explain secondary gain to client and family Rational disputation of self-defeating statements
	Self-effacing and ingratiating	Assertive training Behavior rehearsal Rational disputation of need to be liked Bibliotherapy
	Behavior directed by what others might think or say	Rational disputation Bibliotherapy Assertive training Modeling by therapist
	Generally fearful in actions	Anxiety management training
Affect	Multiple fears	Relaxation training Eliminate secondary gains Positive coping statements Graded *in vivo* assignments Reassurance Positive imagery
	Chronic anxiety	Relaxation training and reassurance Anxiety management training Evaluate need for medication
	Agoraphobia	Relaxation training Explain secondary gain Graded *in vivo* exercises Positive imagery and self-help verbal cues
	Fears having chest pains, dying, and leaving her children orphaned	Rational disputation Reassurance Thought stopping Relaxation training
	Fears knives	Desensitization
	Lonely	Relationship building Group therapy
	Denies anger—finds it unacceptable	Assertive training Gestalt awareness exercises Modeling Directed muscular activity
	Guilt over the possibility of offending anyone	Rational disputation Bibliotherapy Assertive training

(*continued*)

TABLE 6-1. (*Continued*)

Modality	Problem	Proposed treatment
	Easily hurt by what others say	Rational disputation Group therapy—modeling Bibliotherapy Assertive training
	Fears being a "mental patient"	Rational disputation
	Mild depression	Schedule reinforcing activities Evaluate for medication
Sensation	Chest and heart pains	Relaxation training Examination by physician Reassurance Positive self-statements (coping)
	Urinary urgency and frequency	Physical examination Relaxation training Progressive training in control
	Headaches	Differential relaxation
	Unable to relax	Relaxation training
	Dissatisfied with sex life	Sex education Bibliotherapy Rational discussion of concerns with being widowed
	Mild tachycardia	Examination by physician and need for medication Relaxation training Reassurance
Imagery	Fears death and her children left alone	Rational disputation Thought stopping Positive coping statements
	Mourning dead husband	Empty-chair technique
	Pictures father's disapproval of her behavior, dress, use of make-up, etc.	Desensitization Rational disputation Empty-chair technique
Cognition	Obsessive thoughts; she or her children might die	Thought stopping Reassurance Rational disputation Positive coping statements
	Sexual misinformation	Sex education
	Memory problems	Relaxation training
	Self-defeating statements: "It is wrong to be angry"; "I must do the right thing"; "Others need to come first"; "I might hurt someone's feel- ings"; "I am a baby"; "What will others think of me?"	Rational disputation and correc- tive self-talk Bibliotherapy
	Concerns about being "single" again	Encourage social interactions Rational discussion
Interpersonal relationships	Generally unassertive	Assertive training Graded *in vivo* exercises Behavior rehearsal in group Bibliotherapy Modeling by therapist

TABLE 6-1. (*Continued*)

Modality	Problem	Proposed treatment
	Avoids doing anything to be rejected	Assertive training Rational disputation Bibliotherapy Group therapy
	Dependent on father and feels obligated to accept his opinions	Rational disputation Assertive training Self-sufficiency assignments
	Secondary gain from family regarding her fears	Family therapy—stress nonreinforcement and explain secondary gain
	Smothers and overprotects her children	Rational discussion Assertive training Self-sufficiency assignments Family therapy
	Dependent on others for direction	Self-sufficiency assignments
Drugs/biology	Mild hypertension	Thiazide (25 mg per day) prescribed by physician
	Chronic anxiety	Thorazine discontinued Valium (10 mg as needed)
	Overweight	Diet and exercise
	Sociocultural problems of ghetto environment	Support, stressing reality principles

corrected self-defeating and negative self-statements, and had successfully mourned the death of her husband to the point where she had started dating men.

Alice's responses to the Fear Inventory (Table 6-3) reflected a shift away from the highly fearful woman seen in the pretest (where she reported that 26 of 86 stimulus items evoked much to very much fear). Posttest data showed no items in the "very much feared" category (as compared with 14 items in the pretest), but there were still 14 items in the "much feared" column.

Alice B's responses on the Assertiveness Inventory showed a general increase in assertion (Table 6-4).

CASE HISTORY 2: DORIS F

Doris F was an overweight, 45-year-old, black female, who began treatment 14 years earlier, when she was hospitalized for the first time with a DSM-II diagnosis of schizophrenia, paranoid type. She was the seventh of eight children and described all her siblings as being alcoholics with the exception of her younger sister. After 26 years of heavy drinking

TABLE 6-2. Alice B's Life History Questionnaire: Pretest and Posttest Data

	Pretest	Posttest
Estimated severity of problem	Moderately severe	Mildly upsetting
Main fears	1. Being alone 2. Having pains (heart and chest area) 3. Knives ("someone might pull one on me") 4. "Afraid I might die and leave my children alone, since they have no father now." 5. "Going places by myself"	1. Being alone: "I don't mind being alone now." 2. Going on trips alone: "It doesn't bother me too much now." 3. Knives: "just a little"
Items underlined in Questionnaire that apply to client	Headaches; feel tense; depressed; unable to relax; memory problems; lonely	Headaches ("sometimes"); nightmares ("a little"); feel tense; stomach trouble ("a little"); lonely
Additional words that apply to client	Horrible thoughts; "Going to die"; "Anticipate being alone"; "Children might get run over"; lonely; bored; sympathetic; considerate	Guilty; horrible thoughts ("sometimes"); ("Father or kids might die"; "Oldest son might move out"); lonely; bored; worthwhile; sympathetic; considerate

(beer), Doris joined Alcoholics Anonymous (AA) 1 year previous to multimodal treatment and had abstained from drinking since then.

In her replies to the Life History Questionnaire (Lazarus, 1981), Doris described her family life as a child as chaotic and characterized by much fighting and drinking. Her father, who separated from Doris's mother shortly after the client's birth, was described only as "pleasant." He died of tertiary syphilis when Doris was 16 years old. Her mother died of cancer 20 years ago and reportedly was stern and frequently beat her daughter. Doris grew up feeling unloved and not at all respected by her parents.

Doris had her first sexual encounter at age 16, when she was seduced by a male relative, an event over which she still feels guilty. Her guilt is reinforced by his occasional taunts that he will disclose the incident.

The patient dropped out of school in 11th grade, when she became pregnant with her first of five children. She did not marry her son's father, as her parents were against the union. This son was the focus of much pain for the patient: He served a prison term for rape, later became a drug user, and died of an overdose. Doris was subject to anniversary depressions over this son's death and blamed her drinking problem on his drug addiction and death.

Two years after the birth of her son, Doris met and married another man and bore him a daughter. The marriage lasted 2 years. Doris claimed

TABLE 6-3. Alice B's Fear Inventory: Pretest and Posttest Data

The items in this questionnaire refer to things and experiences that may cause fear or other unpleasant feelings. For each item, put a check in the column that describes how much you are disturbed by it nowadays. [Pretest = A; posttest = B.]

	Not at all	A little	A fair amount	Much	Very much
1. Noise of vacuum cleaners	A, B				
2. Open wounds				A, B	
3. Being alone		B			A
4. Being in a strange place		B	A		
5. Loud voices		B	A		
6. Dead people			B		A
7. Speaking in public			B		A
8. Crossing streets	A, B				
9. People who seem insane			B	A	
10. Falling	B	A			
11. Automobiles		A, B			
12. Being teased		A, B			
13. Dentists		A, B			
14. Thunder		A, B			
15. Sirens	B	A			
16. Failure		A, B			
17. Entering a room where other people are already seated		A, B			
18. High places on land		A, B			
19. Looking down from high buildings		A, B			
20. Worms	A, B				
21. Imaginary creatures		A, B			
22. Strangers	A, B				
23. Bats		B	A		
24. Journeys by train (alone)		B			A
25. Journeys by bus (alone)		B			A
26. Journeys by car (with someone)	A, B				
27. Feeling angry		B	A		
28. People in authority	A	B			
29. Flying insects		A, B			
30. Seeing other people injected		B	A		
31. Sudden noises		B	A		
32. Dull weather		B	A		
33. Crowds	A, B				
34. Large open spaces	B	A			
35. Cats	A, B				
36. One person bullying another		A, B			
37. Tough-looking people		A, B			
38. Birds	A, B				
39. Sight of deep water		A, B			
40. Being watched working		A, B			

(continued)

TABLE 6-3. (*Continued*)

	Not at all	A little	A fair amount	Much	Very much
41. Dead animals		B	A		
42. Weapons				B	A
43. Dirt			A, B		
44. Crawling insects	B	A			
45. Sight of fighting				A, B	
46. Ugly people	A, B				
47. Fire			A	B	
48. Sick people			A	B	
49. Dogs				A, B	
50. Being criticized			A, B		
51. Strange shapes	B	A			
52. Being in an elavator		B			A
53. Witnessing surgical operations				B	A
54. Angry people			A, B		
55. Mice				B	A
56. Blood					
a. Human				B	A
b. Animal				B	A
57. Parting from friends		B	A		
58. Enclosed places (alone)			B	A	
59. Prospect of a surgical operation			A	B	
60. Feeling rejected by others			B	A	
61. Airplanes				B	A
62. Medical odors		B		A	
63. Feeling disapproved of		B		A	
64. Harmless snakes				A, B	
65. Cemetaries		B		A	
66. Being ignored		B	A		
67. Darkness			B	A	
68. Premature heart beats (missing a beat)				B	A
69. a. Nude men	A, B				
b. Nude women	A, B				
70. Lightning		B	A		
71. Doctors	A	B			
72. People with deformities		A, B			
73. Making mistakes		A, B			
74. Looking foolish		A, B			
75. Losing control		B		A	
76. Fainting		A, B			
77. Becoming nauseous		B	A		
78. Spiders		A, B			
79. Being in charge or responsible for decisions	A, B				
80. Sight of knives or sharp objects			B		A

TABLE 6-3. (*Continued*)

	Not at all	A little	A fair amount	Much	Very much
81. Becoming mentally ill			A, B		
82. Being with a member of the opposite sex	A	B			
83. Taking written tests			A, B		
84. Being touched by others	A, B				
85. Feeling different from others		A, B			
86. A lull in conversation	A, B				

that she did not love him at the time of the marriage, but gave in to the urging of her sister-in-law.

Doris used the last name of the man who fathered her final three children, and although they were never married, she referred to him as her husband. He was impotent during the final 2 years of their relationship. She reported that he blamed her for his impotency, which occurred shortly after an unplanned pregnancy and birth of her youngest daughter.

Each of the three youngest children had been a problem for Doris. Her son had served a prison term for murder at the age of 16 years. The 19-year-old daughter was the mother of a 3-year-old illegitimate child and, in the past, was in treatment for sexual acting-out and truancy from school. The youngest daughter came to the mental health clinic at Doris's insistence because of repeated charges by family and neighbors of petty thefts.

Doris's history of treatment and hospitalization was as follows. Her first hospital admission was with a chief complaint of auditory hallucinations. During her 3-month stay at a state psychiatric hospital, she was diagnosed as paranoid schizophrenic and placed on Thorazine. She continued to be medicated with Thorazine for the next 14 years, when Tofranil was substituted to deal with her depression. At the time of her treatment in multimodal therapy, she was medicated with lithium carbonate.

Following discharge, Doris received individual dynamically oriented psychotherapy with a psychiatrist at a local public hospital outpatient clinic. This weekly treatment plus several months of group experience continued for 18 months and, in the client's view, resulted in greater regression and depression, and led to another 3 month's hospitalization in the state hospital.

From that point Doris was seen weekly and medicated by a local nonpsychiatric physician for a 3-year period. Following separation from her husband, the auditory hallucinations returned and the patient was admitted again for a 3-month stay at the state hospital. As with her

TABLE 6-4. Alice B's Assertiveness Inventory: Pretest and Posttest Data

The following questions will be helpful in assessing your assertiveness. Be honest in your response. All you have to do is draw a circle around the number that describes you best. For some questions the assertive end of the scale is at 0, for others at 4. Key: 0 means no or never, 1 means somewhat or sometimes; 2 means average; 3 means usually or a good deal; and 4 means practically always or entirely. [Pretest = boldface; posttest = underlined.]

1. When a person is highly unfair, do you call it to his or her attention?
   0 **1** 2 3 4

2. Do you find it difficult to make decisions?
   0 1 2 3 4

3. Are you openly critical of others' ideas, opinions, behavior?
   0 1 **2** 3 4

4. Do you speak out in protest when someone takes your place in line?
   0 1 2 3 4

5. Do you often avoid people or situations for fear of embarrassment?
   0 1 2 3 4

6. Do you usually have confidence in your own judgment?
   0 1 **2** 3 4

7. Do you insist that your spouse or roommate take on a fair share of the household chores?
   0 **1** 2 3 4

8. Are you prone to "fly off the handle"?
   0 1 **2** 3 4

9. When a salesman makes an effort, do you find it hard to say "No," even though the merchandise is not really what you want?
   0 **1** 2 3 4

10. When a latecomer is waited on before you are, do you call attention to the situation?
   0 **1** 2 3 4

11. Are you reluctant to speak up in a discussion or debate?
   0 **1** 2 3 4

12. If a person has borrowed money (or a book, garment, thing of value) and is overdue in returning it, do you mention it?
   0 **1** 2 3 4

13. Do you continue to pursue an argument after the other person has had enough?
   0 **1** 2 3 4

14. Do you generally express what you feel?
   0 **1** 2 3 4

15. Are you disturbed if someone watches you at work?
   0 1 2 3 4

16. If someone keeps kicking or bumping your chair in a movie or a lecture, do you ask the person to stop?
   0 1 2 3 4

TABLE 6-4. (*Continued*)

---

17. Do you find it difficult to keep eye contact when talking to another person?

    0 **1** <u>2</u> 3 4

18. In a good restaurant, when your meal is improperly prepared or served, do you ask the waiter/waitress to correct the situation?

    0 **1** <u>2</u> 3 4

19. When you discover merchandise is faulty, do you return it for an adjustment?

    <u>0</u> **1** 2 3 4

20. Do you show your anger by name calling or obscenities?

    <u>0</u> 1 **2** 3 4

21. Do you try to be a wallflower or a piece of the furniture in social situations?

    0 1 **<u>2</u>** 3 4

22. Do you insist that your landlord (mechanic, repairman, etc.) make repairs, adjustments, or replacements that are his or her responsibility?

    0 1 **<u>2</u>** 3 4

23. Are you able to openly express love and affection?

    0 1 2 3 **<u>4</u>**

24. Do you often step in and decide for others?

    0 **1** 2 <u>3</u> 4

25. Are you able to ask your friends for small favors or help?

    0 1 2 <u>3</u> **4**

26. Do you think you always have the right answer?

    0 1 **2** 3 4

27. When you differ with a person you respect, are you able to speak up for your own viewpoints?

    0 1 **<u>2</u>** 3 4

28. Are you able to refuse unreasonable requests made by friends?

    0 1 **<u>2</u>** 3 4

29. Do you have difficulty complimenting or praising others?

    <u>0</u> 1 2 3 4

30. If you are disturbed by someone smoking near you, can you say so?

    0 1 <u>2</u> 3 4

31. Do you shout or use bullying tactics to get others to do as you wish?

    <u>0</u> 1 2 3 4

32. Do you finish other people's sentences for them?

    0 1 **<u>2</u>** 3 4

33. Do you get into physical fights with others, especially with strangers?

    <u>0</u> 1 2 3 4

34. At family meals, do you control the conversation?

    0 1 **<u>2</u>** 3 4

35. When you meet a stranger, are you the first to introduce yourself and begin a conversation?

    0 1 <u>2</u> 3 **4**

---

previous hospitalizations, Doris claimed to have received medication, but little or no therapy while an inpatient. Upon discharge Doris was seen for medication and weekly group therapy by a psychiatrist at a local community mental health center for approximately 1 year.

Two years later, the client became assaultive and was admitted to the psychiatric inpatient unit at the public hospital for a 1-month period, with a diagnosis of chronic, undifferentiated schizophrenia. She spent the next 3 months, following discharge, in daily attendance at a day hospital program. She was then re-admitted to the in-patient unit for 1 month, with suicidal ideation and depression over her 16-year-old son's conviction for murder and her guilt over her refusal to help him seek legal assistance. Her diagnosis at that time was psychotic depressive reaction.

Following discharge, Doris was seen weekly for the next year at a mental health center by a psychiatric social worker in a traditional therapeutic approach. She was hospitalized for several months 2 years later, following a depressive reaction centering around the problems with her eldest son.

Doris then returned to the clinic for medication, group therapy, and weekly individual sessions with the same social worker, whom she had seen previously. Several brief attempts at family therapy were unfruitful.

Four years later, Doris was hospitalized for 4 weeks because of a manic episode, centering around an anniversary reaction to the death of her son. At the time of her admission, on New Year's Eve, Doris remarked to me that it was her "lucky day." When questioned about the irony of her statement, Doris replied "because someone [i.e., the therapist] cares."

Three suicide attempts were reported: In 1966 Doris unsuccessfully tried to kill herself by turning on the gas stove. She ingested rat poison in 1971 and roach poison in 1973, but received medical attention each time. She reported no suicidal ideation since then.

Doris's work history covered mainly factory work. She was fired from her last factory job for being "too nervous." She received disability compensation since then. At the time of filing for compensation, the physician's report listed psychotic depression and chronic schizophrenia, paranoid type, as the disabling cause.

What Doris described as a "good" relationship with a man recently ended with his death in an auto accident. She since has been involved with a man who drank heavily. The relationship was characterized by her dependence on him and catering to his needs regarding household duties of cooking and cleaning. She reported that her own needs were not met and she felt "used." However, she had been unsuccessful in attempts to assert herself with him. He had a potency problem, and while Doris was dissatisfied both with the infrequency and quality of their sexual relationship, she was unable to assert herself in this area as well.

The pattern of catering to the needs of the men in her life was replicated with the man whom Doris referred to as her husband. They remained in contact despite their 10 years of separation. Whenever her husband was ill or perhaps ailing from a chronic medical problem, Doris pampered his needs either by going to his apartment to cook meals, and so on, or by allowing him to stay with her and the children. Once again, her behavior was at the expense of her own needs not being met.

On the Life History Questionnaire, Doris listed the following as applying to her: palpitations, bowel disturbances, feeling tense, depressed, unable to relax, excessive sweating, fatigue, suicidal ideations, inferiority feelings, lonely, anxiety, insomnia, alcoholism, home conditions bad, concentration difficulties, worthless, useless, a "nobody," "life is empty," inadequate, incompetent, "can't do anything right," guilty, morally wrong, horrible thoughts, hostile, full of hate, anxious, panicky, aggressive, unattractive, repulsive, depressed, lonely, unloved, misunderstood, bored, restless, confused, unconfident, in conflict, full of regrets, considerate.

Self-descriptive sentence completion responses reflected a woman with an unhappy childhood who had been unable to find love, suffered guilt both over the way she had her children and with the way they turned out, and never found strength in a man. As for meaningful activities, Doris listed reading and taking walks.

Responses on the Assertiveness Inventory (Alberti & Emmons, 1982) presented a profile of a relatively unassertive woman, who tended to inappropriately overreact aggressively to the point of physical confrontation with others.

While Doris claimed to love her children, family interactions observed by the author reflected an indifference and hostility with a general lack of communication of wants, needs, and concerns. She was engaged in a power struggle with her son, who was trying to take over the household and repeatedly reminded her of the sins of her past. The teenaged daughter had been engaged in a cycle of moving in and moving out of the home. When the daughter was at home, there were often violent confrontations with boyfriends who tried to break into the home. The youngest daughter was withdrawn and regressed. The amount of time Doris spent away from home with her boyfriend was a point of contention between Doris and her oldest children.

Doris F was in group therapy with me for 1 year before starting in multimodal treatment. She was gregarious and possessed a fine sense of humor. Doris expressed an interest in engaging in multimodal therapy, and following an evaluation, she began 17 months of multimodal treatment. Her Multimodal Profile is outlined in Table 6-5.

Doris F was seen a total of 109 times over a 17-month period: individual sessions, 74; group attendance, 27; family sessions, 8. During the course of therapy she experienced two episodes that required hospi-

TABLE 6-5. Doris F's Multimodal Profile

Modality	Problem	Proposed treatment
Behavior	Inappropriate aggressive responses	Assertive training Graded *in vivo* assignments Group therapy Behavior rehearsal
	Poor eating habits	Diet regulation
	History of alcoholism	Continuance in AA Reassurance and reinforcement for continued abstention
	Avoids funerals and cemeteries	Rational discussion Graded *in vivo* desensitization Positive coping self-statements
	Avoids speaking in public	Desensitization Positive imagery Group therapy Corrective self-talk Behavior rehearsal and modeling
	Frequently shy	Assertive training Group therapy
	Negative self-statements	Corrective, positive self-talk Bibliotherapy Rational disputation
Affect	Subject to attacks of mania	Medication (lithium carbonate)
	Chronic depression	Medication Assignments in reinforcing behavior Positive self-statements "As-if" exercises
	Anxiety and tension	Relaxation training
	Guilt over way she had her children and anger over the way they turned out	Empty-chair technique Family therapy Rational disputation and corrective self-statements Assertive training
	Feels bored, restless, unloved, inferior	Relationship building Bibliotherapy Rational discussion Assignments in reinforcing activities Positive self-statements
	Fears death by cancer	Rational discussion
	Hostile and full of hate	Empty-chair technique Assertive training Directed muscular activity Bibliotherapy Rational disputation
Sensation	Complains of deficit of sexual pleasure	Sex education Sensate focus Assertive training in dealing with male partner
	Unable to relax	Relaxation training

TABLE 6-5. (*Continued*)

Modality	Problem	Proposed treatment
	Perspires heavily	Relaxation training
Imagery	Distressing scene of son and his death by drugs	Desensitization Rational discussion
	Images of past mistakes while drinking	Desensitization Rational discussion Bibliotherapy
	Loss of virginity to relative	Desensitization Rational discussion
	Images of broken family and unhappy childhood	Desensitization Rational discussion Empty-chair technique
Cognition	Irrational self-talk: "I am useless"; "I am a nobody"; "Life is empty"; "I can't do anything right"; "I am morally wrong"; "I am repulsive."	Rational disputation and corrective self-talk Bibliotherapy "As-if" *in vivo* assignments
	Preoccupied with thoughts of death	Thought stopping Rational discussion, accepting reality but parsing out irrational aspects
	Concentration difficulties	Relaxation training
	Full of regrets about "mistakes" of past life	Cognitive restructuring Bibliotherapy Desensitization Positive self-statements
	Worried about the well-being of her children	Family therapy Rational discussion
	Lacks confidence in her own judgments	Self-sufficiency assignments Group therapy experience
	Doesn't act for fear of hurting the feelings of others	Assertive training
	Sexual misinformation	Sex education
Interpersonal relationships	Poor family interaction and generalized insensitivity	Family therapy Behavior rehearsal Gestalt awareness exercises
	Easily manipulated by and dependent on men	Assertive training Behavior rehearsal and modeling Relationship building Self-sufficiency assignments
	Aggression and loss of control of temper	Assertive training
Drugs/biology	Control of manic episodes and depression	Medication (lithium carbonate; Tofranil, 50 mg, every 3 hours)
	Overweight	Diet and exercise
	Insomnia	Relaxation training Medication (Mrs. F responds to Tofranil)
	Sociocultural problems of ghetto environment	Support stressing reality principles

talization. Therapy visits conducted while Doris was an inpatient were not included in her treatment statistics. Doris canceled or broke 16 individual session appointments during the course of treatment.

The serious nature of Doris's illness and her long psychiatric history present a challenge to any treatment orientation. The lack of adequate support systems in her environment served to complicate her treatment. Medication continued to be a necessary part of her overall treatment. She was placed on lithium carbonate throughout her therapy. On occasion, Tofranil was introduced to deal with depression as a careful balance of medication was sought by the treatment team psychiatrist. Previous to Doris's two hospital admissions, short-term use of Thorazine was prescribed to cope with episodes of mania and psychosis.

Despite her many limitations, Doris proved highly motivated to change the areas of her life over which she had some control. She was energetic in dealing with her struggle with alcohol and responded to behavioral and rational–emotive interventions across many of the modalities targeted for intervention. Her Modality Profile reflects the areas dealt with in therapy.

Considering her lengthy treatment history and numerous hospitalizations, Doris made considerable progress. Her posttest responses on the Life History Questionnaire (Table 6-6) reflected a dramatic change from

TABLE 6-6. Doris F's Life History Questionnaire: Pretest and Posttest Data

	Pretest	Posttest
Estimated severity of problem	Extremely severe	Moderately severe
Main fears	1. Death 2. Cancer	1. Does not want her children to die first 2. Cancer
Items underlined in Questionnaire that apply to client	Palpitations; bowel disturbances; feel tense; depressed; unable to relax; excessive sweating; fatigue; suicidal ideas; inferiority feelings; lonely; anxiety; insomnia; alcoholism; home conditions bad; concentration difficulties	Bowel disturbances; feel tense; depressed; fatigue
Additional words that apply to client	Worthless; useless; a "nobody"; "life is empty"; inadequate; incompetent; "can't do anything right"; guilty; morally wrong; horrible thoughts; hostile; full of hate; anxious; panicky; aggressive; unattractive; depressed; lonely; unloved; misunderstood; bored; restless; confused; unconfident; in conflict; full of regrets; considerate	Considerate; worthwhile; sympathetic; intelligent; attractive; confident

multiple complaints and negative self-esteem, to a woman who, for the first time in many years, had attained a more positive self-image, had overcome negative self-statements, and felt adequate in coping with the demands of life. Doris was able to engage in a number of activities that she previously could not; chief among them was the fact that through *in vivo* desensitization she overcame her fear of funerals, a difficulty that had prevented her from attending the funerals of two of her siblings, a fact that caused much friction between Doris and her family.

Doris's posttreatment data are presented in Tables 6-6 and 6-7. While the data suggested generalized improvement, she continued to be at risk for continued future emotional difficulty. Her two hospitalizations during the course of treatment reflected the seriousness of her problems despite the intensive efforts of therapist and patient during the treatment process. I anticipate that she will require continued treatment and monitoring in the future.

MULTIMODAL THERAPY IN A CASE OF POSTTRAUMATIC STRESS DISORDER

The DSM-III includes a new diagnostic category, Posttraumatic stress disorder, whose essential feature is the development of a set of characteristic symptoms following a psychologically traumatic event that is beyond the usual life experience of most people. The response to the trauma may be either acute or chronic (delayed), and the development of symptoms usually involves reexperiencing the traumatic event via recurrent and intrusive recollection or dreams and/or sudden acting or feeling that the events are recurring. This is often in response to ideational or environmental stimuli or associations. Allied features of the syndrome include diminished interest in significant activities and reduced involvement with the external world. A number of symptoms not present before the trauma are also seen, such as sleep disturbance, hyperalertness, and avoidance of activities that arouse recollection of the traumatic event. Anxiety, depression, and emotional lability are also common in persons who present with posttraumatic stress disorder.

Recent literature has given much emphasis to the syndrome as seen in Vietnam veterans. More commonly the syndrome can result from trauma suffered alone as in being the victim of assault or rape. The case study that follows is an example of the application of multimodal therapy in treating a victim of assault who presented with the DSM-III diagnosis of posttraumatic stress disorder, chronic, with anxiety and depression as associated symptoms.

TABLE 6-7. Doris F's Assertiveness Inventory: Pretest and Posttest Data

The following questions will be helpful in assessing your assertiveness. Be honest in your response. All you have to do is draw a circle around the number that describes you best. For some questions the assertive end of the scale is at 0, for others at 4. Key: 0 means no or never, 1 means somewhat or sometimes; 2 means average; 3 means usually or a good deal; and 4 means practically always or entirely. [Pretest = boldface; posttest = underlined.]

1. When a person is highly unfair, do you call it to his or her attention?
0 1 2 3 <u>**4**</u>

2. Do you find it difficult to make decisions?
0 <u>**1**</u> 2 3 4

3. Are you openly critical of others' ideas, opinions, behavior?
0 <u>**1**</u> 2 3 4

4. Do you speak out in protest when someone takes your place in line?
0 1 <u>**2**</u> 3 4

5. Do you often avoid people or situations for fear of embarrassment?
0 1 <u>**2**</u> 3 4

6. Do you usually have confidence in your own judgment?
0 1 2 <u>**3**</u> 4

7. Do you insist that your spouse or roommate take on a fair share of the household chores?
0 <u>**1**</u> 2 3 4

8. Are you prone to "fly off the handle"?
0 <u>1</u> 2 **3** 4

9. When a salesman makes an effort, do you find it hard to say "No," even though the merchandise is not really what you want?
0 **1** 2 <u>3</u> 4

10. When a latecomer is waited on before you are, do you call attention to the situation?
0 1 <u>2</u> 3 4

11. Are you reluctant to speak up in a discussion or debate?
<u>**0**</u> 1 2 3 4

12. If a person has borrowed money (or a book, garment, thing of value) and is overdue in returning it, do you mention it?
0 1 2 3 <u>**4**</u>

13. Do you continue to pursue an argument after the other person has had enough?
<u>**0**</u> 1 2 3 4

14. Do you generally express what you feel?
0 1 <u>2</u> **3** 4

15. Are you disturbed if someone watches you at work?
0 1 2 **3** <u>4</u>

16. If someone keeps kicking or bumping your chair in a movie or a lecture, do you ask the person to stop?
0 1 <u>2</u> **3** 4

17. Do you find it difficult to keep eye contact when talking to another person?
<u>**0**</u> 1 2 3 4

18. In a good restaurant, when your meal is improperly prepared or served, do you ask the waiter/waitress to correct the situation?
0 <u>1</u> 2 3 **4**

19. When you discover merchandise is faulty, do you return it for an adjustment?
0 1 2 3 <u>**4**</u>

TABLE 6-7. (*Continued*)

20. Do you show your anger by name calling or obscenities?
    0 <u>1</u> 2 3 4

21. Do you try to be a wallflower or a piece of the furniture in social situations?
    <u>0</u> 1 2 3 4

22. Do you insist that your landlord (mechanic, repairman, etc.) make repairs, adjustments, or replacements that are his or her responsibility?
    0 1 2 3 <u>4</u>

23. Are you able to openly express love and affection?
    0 1 2 <u>3</u> 4

24. Do you often step in and decide for others?
    0 <u>1</u> 2 3 4

25. Are you able to ask your friends for small favors or help?
    0 1 2 3 <u>4</u>

26. Do you think you always have the right answer?
    <u>0</u> 1 2 3 4

27. When you differ with a person you respect, are you able to speak up for your own viewpoints?
    0 1 2 3 <u>4</u>

28. Are you able to refuse unreasonable requests made by friends?
    0 1 2 <u>3</u> 4

29. Do you have difficulty complimenting or praising others?
    <u>0</u> 1 2 3 4

30. If you are disturbed by someone smoking near you, can you say so?
    0 1 2 3 4

31. Do you shout or use bullying tactics to get others to do as you wish?
    0 <u>1</u> 2 3 4

32. Do you finish other people's sentences for them?
    <u>0</u> 1 2 3 4

33. Do you get into physical fights with others, especially with strangers?
    <u>0</u> 1 2 3 4

34. At family meals, do you control the conversation?
    <u>0</u> 1 2 3 4

35. When you meet a stranger, are you the first to introduce yourself and begin a conversation?
    0 <u>1</u> 2 3 4

CASE HISTORY 3: SALLY D

Sally D was a 30-year-old unmarried woman executive who was the victim of an unprovoked attack while walking along a city street. Her assailant repeatedly punched her and stabbed Sally in the face, the weapon piercing her cheek and tongue. The man fled the scene but was later apprehended by the police. Sally received emergency hospital treatment and eventually required plastic surgery and follow-up treatment with a neurologist as a facial nerve was severed in the incident.

The procedure surrounding the trial of the assailant took over a year and was quite stressful. Sally was required to testify a number of times and had to confront her assailant at the court appearances. She also was harassed by people who were suspected to be friends of the assailant.

Sally was referred for therapy more than 2 years following the stabbing incident chiefly because of labile affect that alarmed friends and colleagues. She had never seen a therapist before. Sally presented as an anxious, sad, and tired-looking woman. Sally wore no make-up, dressed plainly, and wore her hair in a short style that contributed to her overall timid appearance.

Sally complained of difficulty sleeping and of recurrent nightmares about her past attack. During the 2 years since the incident, she had developed avoidance behaviors that severely limited her freedom. She was frightened of being alone and as a result was escorted by friends or family whenever she was in public. She was taken to and picked up from her job. Sally would not leave her office alone and would not take her lunch hour if she could not be in the company of a colleague. Well-intentioned family, friends, and colleagues were maintaining the avoidant behavior by their solicitude. Sally reported that no one ever told her *not* to be afraid. She avoided crowds and had cut herself off from previously enjoyed activities. Sally described a 50-pound weight loss since the incident. Her interpersonal relationships were characterized by tension, anxiety, and passive behavior that was followed by outbursts of temper. She had become extremely dependent upon her boyfriend who was supportive, as were solicitous family members and friends. Sally reported that her personality and behavior before the incident were directly at variance with her current state. Sally completed a Life History Questionnaire and Assertiveness Inventory. Her Multimodal Profile (Table 6-8) revealed her

TABLE 6-8. Sally D's Multimodal Profile

Modality	Problem	Proposed treatment
Behavior	Fear of being alone	
	Avoidance of crowds and strangers	Desensitization via imagery and *in vivo* experience
	Generally unassertive	Assertive training
	Angry outbursts	Assertive training, bibliotherapy
Affect	Fear, panic, anxiety	Reassurance, anxiety management training
	Depression	Discuss with Ms. D possible use of medication
		Proper use of reinforcers
	Fears rejection	Corrective self-talk
	Negative feelings about self and others	Rational disputation

TABLE 6-8. (*Continued*)

Modality	Problem	Proposed treatment
	Anger	Role playing
	Guilt about "everything"	Rational disputation, bibliotherapy
	Lonely	Relationship building
	Unresolved mourning over death of father	Empty-chair technique
Sensation	Somatic complaints: stomach up-set, bowel disturbance, headache	Relaxation training Abdominal breathing exercise Consultation with Sally's physician
	Decreased interest in sex	
	Tension	
	Fatigue	Relaxation and prescribed exercise
Imagery	Nightmares of attack (frequent)	
	Images of being attacked	Desensitization
	Negative self-image as unattractive	Corrective self-talk
	Hypersensitive about facial scar	Positive imagery
	Disturbing image of father's death	Desensitization Empty-chair technique
Cognition	Negative statements about self-worth	Cognitive restructuring
	Needs approval of others	Coping imagery
	Sees self in stereotyped role of passive and compliant daughter and female ("doormat")	Assertive training
	Unfulfilled wishes for further professional advancement and education	Vocational counseling
	Fears not finding a spouse	Relationship building
	Perfectionistic beliefs about performance	Rational–emotive therapy
	Thoughts of people harming her	Desensitization Rational–emotive therapy
Interpersonal relationships	Passive and compliant at expense of self-esteem	Assertive training
	Avoidance of men and strangers	Desensitization Positive imagery rehearsal
	Frequent volatile encounters with colleagues	Role playing, assertive training
	Unassertive with family members	Assertive training
	Secondary gain from concerned persons	Explain reinforcement principles and elicit cooperation
Drugs/biology	Sleep disturbance	Referral to physician for check-up
	weight loss/poor appetite	
	Cigarette smoking (2 packs per day now one-half pack)	Smoke-stopping program
	Frequently catching cold	
	Lack of exercise	Exercise program

chief complaint as well as additional concerns that also were to become the target of therapeutic intervention.

Sally's Modality Profile revealed much more than the diagnosis of posttraumatic stress disorder would imply. While her symptoms reflected the classic aspects of the delayed stress syndrome, Sally's assessment also disclosed a basically shy, unassertive woman with negative feelings about herself. She carried with her a host of cognitive imperatives that were the result and residue of a strict, traditional ethnic upbringing that severely hampered her behavior and interpersonal relations. Her family history revealed that as a child at home her role was to nurse a sickly father and be protected by siblings. Her father's death a decade before treatment had left her with unresolved feelings that brought immediate resistance and tears when it was discussed in therapy. In addition, Sally was locked in a long-term relationship that was not meeting her needs or goals for the future. While she was respected and successful in her career, Sally felt frustrated by not being able to advance further without more formal education.

Treatment

While Sally recognized both the chronicity and seriousness of the symptoms of the delayed stress syndrome, she requested that initial therapeutic intervention was best directed at her interpersonal difficulties on the job. Sally's labile affect irritated her colleagues to the point that she received several severe admonitions from her boss.

From the viewpoint of the therapist, the initial intervention was one that served several purposes: Rapid rapport was established, results were easily measurable, and the techniques employed could and would be used to deal with many of the same symptoms seen in the delayed stress syndrome.

In fact, treatment was directed in several areas simultaneously. Relaxation training was begun with immediate positive results reported by Sally. Evaluation showed that she was adept at visual imagery, and appropriate behavior rehearsal was begun in this modality using day-to-day scenes of coping appropriately on the job. This laid the foundation for the transition to using images to cope with the avoidance behavior and fears Sally had developed. Behavioral rehearsal and rational discussion of dealing with problematic people at the office yielded rapid positive results and built Sally's confidence in tackling her greater fears. Consultation with Sally's physician gave assurance that her condition and physical complaints were being monitored, and no medical intervention was required at the time therapy began.

Detailed second-order BASIC I.D. tracking of Sally's response to fear, and her subsequent avoidance behavior, yielded valuable clinical information. For example, Sally's first awareness of becoming anxious when she was with strangers or in public places was the feeling of tension in her stomach. The sensation triggered thoughts that people were going to harm her. She then would begin to walk rapidly and engage in various avoidance behaviors. Once Sally was safely back at home or in the office, she would become angry with herself for having behaved in such a way. She then engaged in generating negative self-statements and feelings. Eventually Sally became angry at others and believed that she then behaved by displacing her anger on colleagues. Specific treatment was prescribed to assist Sally to cope through each step along her own "firing order." Relaxation, corrective self-talk, and self-monitoring were recommended. Graded desensitization exercises were begun, which exposed Sally to public places and strangers.

As Sally progressed a series of graded *in vivo* exercises were also conducted, accompanied by the therapist in the crowded downtown areas. Sally eventually walked at noon down busy streets that she had avoided for 2 years. Graded tasks involving decreasing dependency on friends and family also met with continued success. Selected "bibliotherapy" readings paralleled treatment and helped deal with cognitive distortions and irrational interpretations of events. As Sally gained more mastery of her fears of people and public places, *in vivo* desensitization sessions with the therapist included visits to the day hospital, psychiatric unit, and retardation services at the hospital where the therapist is on staff.

Imagery was repeatedly employed in sessions to deal effectively with the painful images of the traumatic event. The fact that she was finally able to talk freely about the episode was a breakthrough for Sally. During this time there was a noticeable decrease in the frequency of nightmares. Sally continued to master her fears through daily practice using both *in vivo* exposure and imagery rehearsal. She became increasingly more adept at discriminating both internal and environmental stimuli that had previously been associated with maladaptive responses. As Sally's confidence grew she reported improvement across the BASIC I.D. modalities. Earlier somatic complaints were no longer a concern. Associated vegetative signs and symptoms of depression decreased and eventually were absent. Interpersonal relations improved as Sally's new assertive skills were supported and reinforced by her friends and colleagues. A significant event occurred when Sally witnessed a mugging of a woman on a city street and came to the victim's aid after the attacker fled. Rather than becoming fearful and upset over the incident, Sally used the opportunity in therapy to constructively deal with her anger over her own attack. Also by chance, and well along in therapy, Sally reported seeing her attacker standing on a street corner one day. She reported that she was not upset at seeing him and only "felt sorry for him."

By her own admission, Sally recognized that she had become extremely self-conscious about the residual scar on her cheek and had developed defensive behaviors and negative cognitions that interfered with her interpersonal functioning. Through the use in the sessions of behavior rehearsal, shame-risk exercises, rational disputation, and flooding techniques, Sally's hypersensitivity about her facial scar was dramatically reduced.

Once Sally's chief complaints involving the sequelae of the trauma responded to treatment, attention was turned to additional problems presented in her modality profile.

Sally overcame her initial resistance, and managed to face the conflicts connected to the memory of her father's illness and death. The empty-chair technique and imagery exercises allowed for therapeutic gains in assisting Sally to experience and put to rest a host of negative experiences and affective associations she had previously avoided.

Sally turned her attention to the interpersonal area. After thoughtful consideration she terminated a long-standing relationship that was not meeting her needs and, in her mind, did not predict a future that she wanted. Similarly, Sally dealt assertively and more appropriately with family members with whom her previously unassertive behaviors had locked her into dependent relationships.

As a better sense of self emerged, Sally concentrated on her physical and personal appearance. She began wearing make-up, changed her hair style and bought fashionable clothes. Her appearance was significantly improved, and Sally was determined to enjoy socializing and expanding her network of friends. Plans were also made for career advancement by exploring appropriate on-going education programs.

Discussion

The case of Sally reports her progress in 30 sessions of multimodal therapy spanning over 6 months. Initial sessions were scheduled twice weekly to allow for assessment and initial intervention in Sally's stressful psychological state.

A multimodal analysis of Sally's status allowed the therapist to simultaneously intervene across several modalities. Flexibility was essential, for not only was Sally suffering from the on-going results of the traumatic stress disorder, but also from situational difficulties in her professional and personal life. Sally was a very cooperative patient who readily followed specific suggestions and assignments between sessions. While Sally's cooperation might have reflected her basically compliant personality style, her commitment to treatment worked in her favor as gains were rapidly achieved. It is a shame to think that Sally had not come to treatment for 2 years despite the severity of her problems. It appeared that as long as Sally remained passive and dependent, her supportive network maintained her. However, the system could not cope with her eventual anger and depression, and she was urged to seek treatment.

As mentioned, Sally responded quickly to initial therapeutic interventions, especially relaxation training and anxiety management. The techniques provided her with coping skills as "ammunition" to deal with her daily stress. Imagery techniques were extremely helpful for Sally. They were used as a form of behavior rehearsal in helping her to successfully cope with her fears of being in public places. Imagery was also important in dealing effectively with memories of her trauma flowing from the event itself right through to the discomfort caused by the protracted process of the trial of Sally's assailant. *In vivo* desensitization exercises proved to be a valuable adjunct to imagery and relaxation training in overcoming the variety of avoidance behaviors she had developed. Attention was paid at the same time to the contributing cognitions that maintained Sally's maladaptive behaviors. Much of therapy centered around examinations of her faulty beliefs and the use of cognitive and rational–emotive techniques.

Once Sally began making progress with her chief causes of anxiety, rapid progress was seen across other modalities. The signs and symptoms associated with depression lessened, the frequency of nightmares diminished, and general interpersonal functioning improved. Somatic complaints all but disappeared. Sally's new confidence allowed her to be less resistant in dealing with issues surrounding her father's death. The Gestalt therapy technique (the empty chair) gave Sally an avenue to deal with her affect appropriately and helped to resolve long-standing painful memories.

Sally's therapy is ongoing at the time of this writing. We are emphasizing future planning and continued adjustment to the changes in daily events and relationships that flow from her improved behavior and openness. Attention will also be paid to periodically reviewing events that may recall the initial traumatic incident so that Sally will be prepared to cope with future anxiety-producing situations. This allows for a type of "emotional fire drill" that supports appropriate behavior patterns and emotional responses.

While Sally's case is certainly not unique in terms of presenting with a cluster of symptoms following a trauma, it serves to demonstrate the effectiveness of multimodal therapy for a specific diagnostic category that is receiving increased attention. Multimodal assessment and therapy provided for Sally's treatment a specific and systematic set of interventions that met both her clinical needs and her own expectations.

REFERENCES

Alberti, R. E., & Emmons, M. L. (1982). *Your perfect right* (4th ed.). San Luis Obispo, CA: Impact Publishers.
Lazarus, A. A. (1981). *The practice of multimodal therapy.* New York: McGraw-Hill.
Wolpe, J. *The practice of behavior therapy.* (1973). New York: Pergamon Press.

7

Multimodal Therapy and Cognitive Dissonance in a Behavioral Medicine Context

JAMES T. RICHARD

The multimodal framework is "tailor made" for assessing and thoroughly treating most problems that fall within the purview of "behavioral medicine." Stress reduction methods that systematically attend to the BASIC I.D. provide clients with a broad array of coping responses. This is in contrast to various "biofeedback clinics" where clients are apt to be treated on too narrow a spectrum for enduringly positive outcomes. James Richard shows how the construction of Modality Profiles revealed a range of discrete but interlocking problems that called for therapeutic attention beyond the presenting complaints. The two cases that Richard presents both benefited predominantly from cognitive interventions that resulted in significant behavioral changes. This is by no means prototypal, but it does reveal how rapidly and effortlessly the perusal of the seven vectors tends to pinpoint otherwise illusive nonconscious conflicts.

INTRODUCTION

This chapter is presented with two purposes in mind. First, it is an attempt to illustrate the utility of the concept of cognitive dissonance in treating behavioral medicine problems. Second, two cases will be presented in the context of Lazarus's (1976) multimodal therapy model to illustrate the utility of that approach as a unifying paradigm for the treatment of behavioral medicine problems. By systematically touching base with the seven BASIC I.D. categories, the therapist can operationally achieve the goal of a holistic behavioral medicine protocol (Richard, 1978, 1981).

The following cases are presented not to support the clinical efficacy of the multimodal therapy approach, but to illustrate the fact that if the clinician had narrowly applied the accepted clinical protocol to these two behavioral medicine problems, valuable clinical data would have been overlooked. In addition, the theory of cognitive dissonance (Festinger, 1957) will be employed to illustrate the sources of stress in each of the cases presented and to suggest possible therapeutic interventions.

COGNITIVE DISSONANCE

Cognitive dissonance was first proposed as a psychological construct in 1957 by Leon Festinger. It has been further elaborated on and reformulated by Aronson (1976), who defines it as "a state of tension that occurs whenever an individual simultaneously holds two cognitions (ideas, attitudes, beliefs, opinions) that are psychologically inconsistent."

This state of tension is unpleasant and, therefore, according to Aronson (1976), people are motivated to reduce this tension much as they would the thirst–hunger drives, except that the force is psychological rather than physiological discomfort. The tension reduction can take place if one or both cognitions are changed or modified so as to be more harmonious with each other, or by adding a new cognition that can resolve the inconsistency in the original cognitions.

Aronson (1976) further suggests that the dissonance is greatest when the self-concept is threatened, that is, when the individual believes that "I am an honest person" and behaves dishonestly in a romantic relationship (see the case of Kay later in this chapter).

THE CASE OF SALLY

The case of Sally, who was a 33-year-old married woman with two children, illustrates a patient who was suffering from persistent migraine headaches. She was referred by her physician for biofeedback training because the doctor was worried about her possible dependence on medication.

Because she came with some optimistic expectations regarding this treatment approach and because it was an appropriate treatment, the therapist began thermal biofeedback training. Before and after the biofeedback training periods, the therapist continued to expand on the client's BASIC I.D. Profile (see Table 7-1) in subsequent sessions.

Initially, Sally was started on thermal biofeedback training. It was suggested that she avoid some common food substances (monosodium glutamate, sodium nitrate and nitrites, salt, and tyramine) that have been associated with headaches. In addition, she was instructed to chart any stressful incidences and record the frequency and intensity of her headaches.

After practicing autogenic relaxation training for homework using an audio cassette, Sally reported increased feelings of relaxation and some small reduction in the incidence of migraine headaches.

While therapy was progressing the patient revealed that there were considerable risks involved in her becoming pregnant again, and that she was under increased pressure from her uncle (a physician in another state)

TABLE 7-1. Sally's Multimodal Profile

Modality	Problem	Intervention
Behavior	Frequent visits to physician for migraine headaches	Daily charting of incidence and severity or pain
Affect	Anxiety in crowds and super-markets	Guided imagery of crowd scenes while doing relaxation training
	Guilt over not doing more for sick in-laws	Discuss cognitive dissonance theory
	Fear of pregnancy	
	Fear of rejection by husband	
Sensation	Light-sensitive before headaches	Autogenic training in office and cassette tape for home practice (Richard, 1982)
	Internal sensations of pressure–scream inside	
		Followed by office thermal bio-feedback on index finger of right hand
Imagery	I see myself trying to be "Wonder-Woman"	Discuss perfectionistic standards
	My insides are going wild!	Use calming images
Cognition	I should lose more weight	Weight Watchers class. Examine possible secondary gains to being fat
	I should not practice birth control	Discuss the principle of "Double Effect" (described in text below)
	Husband fearful of losing job	Examine the consequences of husband losing his job
	I want to run from responsibilities for sick parents	Discuss getting other family members to help
		Discuss ABCs of rational–emotive therapy
Interpersonal relationships	Physician–uncle advising her to have to a tubal ligation	Discuss time management and hierarchy of values and her home responsibilities
	Trying to care for agoraphobic neighbor	
	Trying to care for sick neighbor	
Drugs/biology	She enjoys gin, vodka, cheese, chocolate	Discuss eliminating common allergic substances that are linked to migraine headaches
	Medications: Inderol and Furinal with codeine	
	Tubal ligation recommended by gynecologist because of Rh factor	

to consider having a tubal ligation. However, this suggestion was in conflict with her religious training, and she was concerned about the importance of the birth-control issue for her husband.

She expanded on her conflicts in the cognitive realm—to get a tubal ligation and improve her love life with her husband, but not to go against her religious convictions. This was a critical point in the therapeutic process. In a eureka kind of explanation Sally exclaimed, "This is what is really bothering me and causing the headaches." At this juncture the therapist described the following ways of resolving the resulting tension state within the context of cognitive dissonance theory.

In formulating additional interventions, it was necessary to focus on the following areas: uncle's urging of the tubal ligation and her husband's religious and romantic reactions, fear of pregnancy and fear of spiritual–religious consequences, and ways of decreasing her tendency to dwell on headaches.

Sally's cognitive dissonance was generated by two conflicting thoughts: "I must respect my husband's religious wishes and follow my earlier religious teachings" versus "I want to practice birth control because I'm scared of the consequences of another pregnancy." The latter cognition was in conflict with her actions or behavior, that is, not practicing birth control.

Her conflict was further intensified by the fact that she and her husband had a very good marriage in general, and a very satisfying romantic life in particular. She reported that many times in the past she would deliberately put her husband off when she suspected she was ovulating. Suffice it to say, both husband and wife found these times of the month very frustrating.

Festinger (1957), in his cognitive dissonance model, stated that a person is in a state of tension if there is disparity between what a person thinks (and feels) and how he or she behaves. Sally's conflicted thinking was focused on wanting to use some form of birth control and yet not wanting to compromise her religious training.

According to Aronson (1976), dissonance can sometimes be resolved by introducing a third cognition that bridges the gap between the original cognitions.

Again, using Lazarus's (1981) concept of bridging, the therapist initiated some cognitive disputations that were familiar to her, since they originated from her religious–cultural tradition. The first was a suggestion that she discuss her value priorities with her husband, vis-à-vis marital harmony and family integrity versus adherence to a religious prohibition against artificial birth-control techniques.

The second cognition was the principle of "Double Effect," which states that if one is confronted with two alternatives (birth control vs. no birth control) the less good or less desirable (birth control) can be elected if it leads to the achievement of a greater good (family solidarity and marital survival) that could not be reached if the more desirable alternative were chosen. This rather elaborate philosophical-religious principle was readily understood by the patient and her husband, because it came out of the religious training that both had received in their earlier years. This cognitive disputation, adding a new cognition, reconciled the two conflicting cognitions and legitimized the change in behavior—practicing birth control.

A 1-year follow-up revealed that she is still involved with community activities, but they are fewer in number and only include those that she really enjoys. She underwent tubal ligation, and she and her husband feel comfortable with their decision.

THE CASE OF KAY

This patient was referred by her gynecologist for biofeedback training because she was exhibiting symptoms of anxiety and depression and complained of vaginismus. She presented herself at the end of regular office hours without calling for an appointment. Since she was extremely distressed, she was seen immediately.

Kay, 37 years old, was employed as a salesperson in a department store. She was married, for a second time, 10 years ago. Her first marriage occurred when she was 17 years old and lasted about 7 months. She had two children from the marriages, aged 19 and 9 years.

In subsequent sessions the therapy centered on symptomatic relief of painful colitis attacks, which she reported having experienced two to three times a day. This colonic disorder, for which she had been receiving medical treatment for the past 5 years, came to light as the therapist was completing the drugs/biology modality questions. The colitis, rather than the original presenting problem of vaginismus, was monitored because the colitis was far more disruptive and tended to be incapacitating.

Autogenic relaxation training was administered in the office with a subsequent recommendation that it be continued twice daily at home, using a cassette tape which was given to her. A thermal biofeedback instrument was attached to her finger and was used to monitor her stress levels while in the office.

In the process of completing the Multimodal Profile (Table 7-2), the therapist, while exploring the cognitive and affective modalities, asked the patient if she loved her husband. She unhesitatingly responded, "No." When asked how long she was aware of the loss of feelings, she blurted out, "Nine years."

In an attempt to highlight this very apparent conflict, the therapist asked her why she did not leave her husband. She responded that she was

TABLE 7-2. Kay's Multimodal Profile

Modality	Problem	Intervention
Behavior	Frequent trips to bathroom because of spastic colon	Chart number of colonic attacks per day
Affect	Doesn't love husband	Discuss the practicality of trying to act married in a loveless relationship
	Fearful that she cannot survive financially living alone	
	Fears children's reactions if she leaves	Challenge her assumptions on how her children might react
Sensation	Burning pain in the abdomen	Autogenic relaxation training in office
	Muscle tension in neck and shoulders	Thermal biofeedback instrument attached to index finger of right hand
Imagery	I cannot see myself making it alone	Guided imagery of successful scenes of living alone
		Use rubber band to demonstrate dissonance
Cognition	I want to leave marriage	Explain cognitive dissonance
	I cannot leave the marriage	Detail for strong traits—
	I don't make enough to leave	economic, social, vocational
	My kids will never forgive me if I leave	Suggest discussing leaving with children
Interpersonal relationships	Loses arguments to husband	Role play successful confrontations with husband
Drugs/biology	Sought medical attention for chronic vaginismus	
	Under medical care for chronic spastic colon for 5 years	

afraid of his persuasive skills. Basically, she lost every argument because of his superior education, and because she did not think she could survive financially on her own. She was also afraid of adverse reactions from her children.

This negative self-image gave rise to the pessimistic cognition, "I cannot successfully leave this marriage."

To illustrate to the patient the impact of her conflicting thoughts ("I want to leave this marriage" vs. "I cannot leave this marriage"), the therapist hyperextended a rubber band to depict cognitive dissonance, that is, her actions going in one direction and her thoughts and desires going the opposite way, thus creating a state of tension that exacerbated or caused her physical problems.

This visual mode was chosen because during tracking procedures (Lazarus, 1981) she repeatedly responded in the visual/imagery modality

—"I don't *see* how I can leave," "I *see* myself folding again after arguing with my husband." Visualizing rubber bands being stretched to capacity afforded an image that had idiosyncratic value.

As a way of challenging her negative self-image and her pessimistic cognitions, the therapist listed her many friends, her steady job, and the fact that she had recently been offered two jobs. Next in the sequence the therapist challenged her with the question, "How long can you see your body allowing you to maintain this dishonest contradiction, that is, trying to act married and not feeling married?" Inherent in this question, a third cognition was presented that buttressed learning and resolved the dissonance: "I must leave to save my health." Furthermore, she was informed that the foregoing cognition was both legitimate and honest, and Kay pictured herself as an honest person.

In addition to the relaxation training conducted in the office, the therapist next bridged (Lazarus, 1981) into the interpersonal modality, which took the form of role-playing a scene in which Kay told her husband that she wanted to leave the marriage and in which she detailed the support arrangements she wanted for her children.

To her surprise, when she did confront her husband, she was able to stay focused on the topic and got her husband to agree to a divorce. Even more surprising, her children reacted exactly opposite to the way she had anticipated.

A 6-month follow-up of Kay's brief psychotherapy revealed that since she left her husband, her colitis had "miraculously cleared up." In addition, she was quite happy with her relationship with her children.

This case illustrates a person trying to fake being married—a feat that takes an incredible amount of energy and that this clinician thinks is close to impossible!

The focus of this chapter has been on the consideration of cognitive dissonance theory and multimodal assessment in the treatment of behavioral medicine problems. It is the author's opinion that if it were not for his thorough investigation of the BASIC I.D., the therapist would have missed the cognitive stressors and would have relied only on biofeedback/relaxation and assertive behavior training interventions.

The preceding two cases illustrate a basic caveat for psychologists and physicians in treating presenting problems that fall within the purview of behavioral medicine: *Be on guard for discrepancies between how people are thinking and how they are acting.*

ACKNOWLEDGMENT

The author would like to thank Doctors Ronald Goldstein and William Ford of the Bucks County Community College for their helpful comments and suggestions in the preparation of this chapter.

REFERENCES

Aronson, E. (1976). *The social animal* (2nd ed.). San Francisco: W. W. Freeman.

Festinger, L. (1957). *A theory of cognitive dissonance*. Stanford: Stanford University Press.

Lazarus, A. (1976). *Multimodal behavior therapy*. New York: Springer.

Lazarus, A. (1981). *The practice of multimodal therapy*. New York: McGraw-Hill.

Richard, J. (1978). Multimodal therapy: An integrating model for behavioral medicine. *Psychological Reports, 42*, 635–639.

Richard, J. (1981, November/December). Multimodal therapy approach to headaches. *Pennsylvania Psychologist*, 4–5.

Richard, J. (1982). *Learn to relax* (Audio Cassette). Newtown: Newtown Psychological Centre.

8

Multimodal Residential Therapy in Two Cases of Anorexia Nervosa (Adult Body Weight Phobia)

MAURITS G. T. KWEE

In collaboration with
HUGO J. DUIVENVOORDEN

People suffering from anorexia nervosa are anything but "easy cases."
The successful resolution of this life-threatening condition calls for an
intricate treatment repertoire. Here, unimodal, bimodal, or trimodal
therapies are unlikely to meet with success—treatment must indeed be
multimodal. *In this chapter Maurits Kwee and Hugo Duivenvoorden*
provide the details of numerous procedures employed and the rationale
behind them. This work was carried out in The Netherlands, and called
for a team approach in the context of an inpatient psychiatric facility.
This is a first-hand account of the "battlefront conditions" of patient care
and responsibility. When confronted by patients who are capable of
starving themselves to death, the clinician must set aside any pretenses
toward theoretical purity and embrace a comprehensive, systematic, and
essentially eclectic stance. To do otherwise would simply jeopardize the
treatment outcome. While reading this chapter, I was impressed by the
fact that the successful outcomes were predicated on hard work. *There*
was little, if any, glamour involved. If therapists wish to be effective rather
than personally fascinated or enthralled, they must step down from the
role as high priests and serve as caretakers, custodians, warders, and fill
different pedagogic roles. This chapter clearly describes how this can be
achieved.

ANOREXIA NERVOSA DEFINED

Primary anorexia nervosa is a rare and complex condition that occurs in individuals usually under 25 years of age who tend to starve themselves. The average incidence is 0.24–1.6 cases per 100,000 in the general population. It is more prevalent in females than in males, with a consensus ratio of about 15:1. Mortality rates lie between 5% and 22% according to studies following cases of diagnoses over 4 years or longer (Bemis, 1978; Brownell, 1981; Dally & Gomez, 1979; Halmi, 1980).

There are several diagnostic criteria for anorexia nervosa, including those of Russell (1970) and Feighner *et al.* (1972). For the sake of uniformity DSM-III diagnostic criteria (American Psychiatric Association, 1980), subsumed under six headings, are employed:

1. Intense fear of becoming obese, which does not diminish as weight loss progresses.
2. Disturbance of body image with inability to accurately perceive body size.
3. Weight loss of at least 25% of original weight, or, if under 18 years of age, weight loss from original body weight plus projected weight gain expected on growth charts may be combined to compromise the 25%.
4. Refusal to maintain body weight over a minimal normal weight for age and height.
5. No known medical illness that would account for the weight loss (amenorrhea in females).

To encompass anorexia nervosa at a descriptive level, Crisp (1980) coined the term "adult body weight phobia" emphasizing the consistent psychological striving for weight loss in spite of all biological defenses, and stressing: "(i) the primary importance of normal adult body weight (and hence shape and fatness), and (ii) the central role of this as a source of the intense panic which also characterizes the condition" (p. 78). Apart from its diagnostic relevance, this view provides an opportunity to talk the anorectic client's language and to compare the aberrant condition with other phobic avoidance reactions in the construction of a multimodal functional analysis.

FUNCTIONAL ANALYSIS

Surveys of the literature and close observations of a dozen primary anorectic clients form the basis for the following multimodal functional analysis, which ties in with the hypothetical psychological analyses of the condition by Garner and Bemis (1982), Hautzinger (1980), Vandereycken (1980), and Wright, Manwell, and Merrett (1969).

The onset of the functional loss of appetite and food refusal is frequently triggered by a decision of the client to lose weight in order to achieve a certain cultural ideal of slenderness. Many clients remember being teased once or more because of fatness during puberty. Then a "pursuit of thinness" (Bruch, 1973) escalates into an addictive self-starvation that is very probably motivated by a rejection of the adult role, especially sexuality. Anorectics are identified premorbidly as introverted, scrupulous, diligent, obedient, successful in their schoolwork, and as model children who lack social skills and are unable to express their emotions adequately. When anorectic, they become obsessional, stubborn, socially withdrawn, and ruthlessly egocentric-behaving persons who, from a powerless stance, conduct an "alimentary tyranny" (Van de Loo, 1981) in the family situation.

Disturbed family relationships in general, and parental overprotection in particular, plus a self-rejecting, perfectionistic, and absolutistic style of self-talk, are considered to be the major stress-factors antecedent to the dysfunctional condition. The stressful family situation is characterized by a conflictful parental and sibling relationship that can manifest itself in many variants. In most instances, the anorectic child grows up in an emotionally deprived surrounding where high standards of achievement exist, while the expression of aggression and sexuality are repressed. Frequently the father is experienced as a rigid and demanding person, and the mother as a dominant and nonaffectionate parent. Not seldom the mothers of anorectic clients tend to be overweight and seem to be restrictive in the sense that they do not allow their children to solve their own problems. Most of the time there is no respect for the vital needs of the child who learns to distrust his or her experiences, including bodily signals such as hunger (Yager, 1982).

The facilitating stress factors during the transition period of sexual maturity, which hypothetically lead to the anorectic reaction, are summarized in the left corner of Figure 8-1.

Figure 8-1 is a tentative model of the functional analysis of anorexia nervosa in terms of the BASIC I.D. The multimodal schema gives an integrated psychologic construction with five hypothetical vicious cycles, explaining both the onset and maintenance of the aberrant condition. They are centered around the maintaining consequences: cognitive factors (C), anxiety reduction (affect) (A), and (the perception of) reinforcing reactions of the social environment, especially family members (interpersonal relationships) (I.).

The first vicious cycle (1) follows the firing order S-I-C-A and starts from Ellis's (1962) premise that it is not food and eating situations *per se* (S) that lead to feelings of anxiety (A), but the dysfunctional images (I) and faulty thinking style (C). Anxiety and panic (A) are the result of absolutistic demands and rigid norms about having a thin body image in order to be accepted (I) and strivings for perfectionism while reasoning in a dichotomous manner (C) (e.g., "Being fat is bad and being thin is good").

The second vicious cycle (2) is characterized by hunger as *intrinsic pressure of pain* and follows the sequence A-B-S-D. Feelings of anxiety

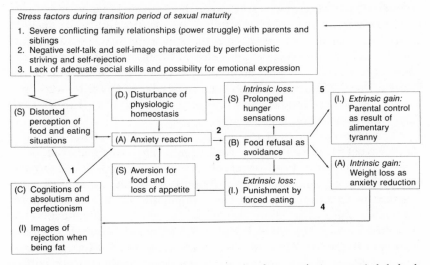

FIGURE 8-1. A multimodal functional analysis of anorexia nervosa (adult body weight phobia) in terms of the BASIC I.D., containing five vicious cycles.

(A) and the act of eating (B) are two reciprocally inhibiting reactions, as demonstrated and supported by neurophysiologic research (Wolpe & Lazarus, 1966). Anxiety blocks gastric motility and raises the blood-sugar level, which may result in a drastic reduction of physiologic hunger, while at the same time the person experiences a chronic empty sensation in the stomach (S). This leads to a sense of (quasi) control of the body, and at the same time to a biological (endocrinologic) imbalance (D.), such as amenorrhea, hypothermia, bradycardia, (arterial) hypotension, and edema. These protection signals against starvation are inherently anxiety-provoking phenomena.

The third vicious cycle (3) is characterized by punishment as *extrinsic pressure of pain* and follows the sequence A-B-I.-S. The A-B part has been explained previously. The avoidance behavior of food refusal elicits care and attention, mostly negative reactions from alarmed parents who employ several measures of punishment and disregard (I.). Usually the desperate parents alternate caring and punishment, aggravating in both instances the aberrant avoidance behavior by what can be called positive and negative reinforcement. They tend to force their child to eat certain amounts, and the already aversive situation becomes even more aversive when the meals become a theater of struggle. Food becomes aversive, and in the long run, the client may experience a loss of appetite (S) (Jacob, Nordlund, & Schwieler 1975).

The fourth vicious cycle (4) follows the firing order B-A-C-A and is characterized by *intrinsic or primary gain*. The phobic avoidance reaction of food refusal (B) results in weight loss that leads to anxiety reduction, a pleasurable result of the self-discipline (A). At first peers are likely to compliment the anorectic, but when the weight drops under socially acceptable norms, fear of rejection is elicited again. The client's answer to repress the fear is persistent slimming (A) (Hallsten, 1965). But an absolutistic, perfectionistic, and rigid self-talk (C) may be the reason why a satisfactory level of weight loss will never be reached so that anxiety and fear (A) become more or less permanent.

The fifth vicious cycle (5) follows the firing order B-I.-S-A and is characterized by *extrinsic or secondary gain*. The avoidance reaction of food refusal (B) is in most instances the beginning of a power struggle between the client and the parents. By refusing to eat, the anorectic discovers a strong means of power. The manipulative hunger strike acquires reinforcing value. The anorectic child secures a powerful position by alimentary tyranny (I.) (Crisp, Harding, & McGuiness 1974). This problem feeds back to the first of the assumed facilitating stress factors, which has led to the anorectic way of perceiving and dealing with food and eating situations (S). As has been explained by Beck (1976), the perception of food can lead to feelings of anxiety (A) without the intermediate cognitions that can have become "automatic" in the long run.

RESIDENTIAL THERAPY

Multimodal residential therapy encompasses a broad spectrum of treatment modules that is embedded in the therapeutic program of the Department of Behavioral Psychotherapy, an autonomous-functioning unit situated in a mental hospital.[1] In this department, with a capacity of 16 beds, only clients with severe neurotic complaints are admitted, especially obsessive–compulsives, severe phobics, and anorectics. The art and science of multimodal psychoeducation (Kwee, 1981) for chronic anorexia nervosa is necessarily applied in a residential setting, where, in a total care situation, the client is simultaneously treated by a psychotherapist (usually a clinical psychologist) and a cotherapist (usually a psychiatric nurse). Following a learning model, the clinical department can best be considered *a boarding school for problems of living*, with a maximum-stay period of 36 weeks, divided into three subsequent phases of 12 weeks each. The multimodal treatment strategy is meant to design an individualized "inpatient" psychotherapy that meets the idiosyncratic requirements of the client by addressing Frank's (1959) admonition: "What kinds of therapist activity produce what kinds of change in what kind of

1. The Algemeen Psychiatrisch Instituut "Het Sint Joris Gasthuis," Delft, The Netherlands, is a 600-bed general mental hospital.

patients?" (p. 10). Based on a technical–eclectical doctrine (Brunell 1982; Lazarus, 1981), the program is structured in (semi)-individual therapeutic activities and group therapeutic activities. These activities altogether constitute the elements of a BASIC I.D. approach that will be specified for the treatment of anorexia nervosa in the following section (see Table 8-1).

INDIVIDUAL SETTING

Individual Assessment (Client, Cotherapist, and Psychotherapist)

During intake and the whole process of therapy, individual assessment is carried out by means of interviewing the client and administering the Multimodal Life History Questionnaire (Lazarus, 1981).

Information is further gathered by: (1) occasional psychiatric consultations for differential diagnosis and biomedical questions (e. g., withdrawal of laxatives or management of vomiting); (2) administering psychometric questionnaires concerning complaints, relational problems, and psychological functioning; and (3) keeping a problem-oriented notebook and self-monitoring of weight and caloric intake. Usually the functional analysis for the individual anorectic client will differ only slightly from the general scheme presented above.

TABLE 8-1. Matrix of (Semi)-Individual and Group Therapeutic Activities and the BASIC I.D.

	Frequency per week	Modality*						
		B	A	S	I	C	I.	D.
(Semi)-individual								
Individual assessment	1	X	X	X	X	X	X	X
Individual training	5	X	X	X	X	X	X	(X)†
Individual therapy	1	X	X	X	X	X	X	
Marital therapy	1	X	X			X	X	
Family therapy	1	X	X			X	X	
Group gatherings								
Evaluation training	2	X		X	X	X	X	
Insight training	1			X	X	X	X	
Rational training	1	X	X	X	X	X		
Assertion training	1		X	X	X		X	
Relaxation training	5	X	X	X	X			

*B = Behavior, A = Affect, S = Sensation, I = Imagery, C = Cognition, I. = Interpersonal relationships, D. = Drugs/biology.

†The withdrawal or administration by a consultant psychiatrist of drugs (if necessary).

Further, a BASIC I.D. scheme is constructed, which might look as follows:

B   Food refusal and hyperactivity
A   Inability to express feelings and depressive mood
S   Poor discrimination of hunger sensations
I   Negative self-concept and poor body image
C   Perfectionistic style of self-talk
I.   Creating an alimentary tyranny in the family
D.   Weight loss

These aspects are all possible starting points in the various parts of the multimodal therapy program.

Individual Training (Client and Cotherapist)

In the individual training the cotherapist performs mainly behavioral procedures and techniques under supervision of the psychotherapist. Operant interventions are usually applied in the context of a behavioral contract and are focused upon weight gain, usually to a level of 85–95% of the average height for weight according to actuarial tables.

When the anorectic complaints become "ego-dystonic" and exist as a *corpus alienum*, operant technology might be helpful (Eckert, Goldberg, Halmi, Casper, & Davis, 1979). Schedules of self-reinforcement can be used to strengthen eating behaviors, while noneating behaviors are ignored. To secure durable results, other modalities must be dealt with in addition (Erwin, 1977).

Systematic desensitization (Schnurer, Rubin, & Roy, 1973), may be helpful in eliminating phobic avoidance responses to eating and weight gain. "Flooding" ("prolonged exposure" to weight-related stimuli and "response prevention" of compulsive exercising) might also be effective in helping the client to gain weight as suggested by Mavissakalian (1982).

Success seems to depend on the extent to which the fear of being obese plays a major role in the functional analysis of the individual client. The shorter the existence of the anorexia nervosa, the more chance that desensitization or flooding procedures may produce a positive outcome.

Individual Therapy (Client, Cotherapist, and Psychotherapist)

Every week an individual therapy session is programmed. In these sessions assessment and therapy are intertwined. A strong working alliance is considered a necessary but insufficient condition for behavioral change (cf. Lazarus & Fay, 1982). The therapy is oriented toward problem solving of the client's intra- and interpersonal problems for which the whole armamentarium of multimodal techniques can be used.

The imagery modality in particular (the self-concept and body-image) can be dealt with in the individual therapy sessions (Lazarus, 1978). It must be emphasized that many authors have stressed that anorectic clients tend to overestimate the size of their bodies, in particular the widths of their faces, breasts, waists, and hips (Ben-Tovim, Hunter, & Crisp, 1977; Casper, Halmi, Goldberg, Eckert, & Davis, 1979; Crisp & Kalucy, 1974; Garner & Garfinkel, 1981; Slade & Russell, 1973). These body-size misperceptions cannot be modified only by self-image confrontation. It is recommended that the client reinterpret the body-image misperceptions by learning to distrust the anorectic way of self-perception and by developing an experimental attitude throughout by relying on empirical evidence.

Marital Therapy (Client, Partner, Cotherapist, and Psychotherapist)

If indicated, the individual therapy sessions are substituted by or added to a setting in which the partner of the client is involved. There seem to be a growing number of anorectic clients between the ages of 20 and 40 years, who have unconsummated marriages. The married anorectic may consolidate his or her aberrant behaviors and be the architect of communication barriers and sexual problems.

In general, the client transfers the pubertal problems and conflicts onto the spouse, who is expected to be altruistic regarding the anorectic's needs. Often, the husbands of anorectic clients deliberately choose an immature partner so that they can take up the protector's role. Usually both partners are unable to develop a mutually meaningful and thus satisfying relationship. At first it might be promising if the husband tries to change his anorectic wife, especially when this strengthens and maintains the marital homeostasis. The therapist must be careful not to impair the husband's self-esteem. In marital therapy the anorectic client and the spouse run the risk of the relationship breaking up as the anorectic symptoms recede.

Family Therapy (Client, at Least One Family Member of Another Generation, Cotherapist, and Psychotherapist)

The individual or marital therapy sessions can be extended or substituted by a family therapy setting. Lazarus (1981) emphasizes that

> it is a serious mistake to shift *all* attention away from disturbed *individuals* to dysfunctional *systems* . . . more rapid, elegant and longer lasting gains

are achieved when the therapist swings the focus of attention back and forth from the individual and his or her parts to the individual in his or her social setting. (p. 41)

Family therapy as practiced by Selvini-Palazzoli (1978) or Minuchin, Rosman, and Baker (1978) may be different on a theoretical level, but there are many similarities with a behavioral or multimodal approach in practice (Liebman, Minuchin, & Baker, 1974).

Pathogenic interaction patterns as observed by Minuchin *et al.* (1978) in families with an anorectic child can be confirmed: (1) triangulation— the child is forced to be sensible in his or her choice for one of the two disagreeing parents; (2) coalition—the child has selected a parent and safeguards this parent against the other parent; and (3) detouring—the parents are united in giving attention to the child, who is blamed and praised and who functions at the same time as a conductor for other existing family tensions.

During so-called "family therapy lunches," the anorectic problem can be brought into clearer focus, so that problems between the child and the other family members, and marital problems of the parents, can be dealt with.

GROUP SETTING

Evaluation Training (Clients, Cotherapist, and Psychotherapist)

All clients participate in a group that takes place twice a week, one on the weekend and the other on a weekday. The aim of these groups is to teach the client responsibility for success or failure through the self-monitoring of diligence (of the past week) and of the application of learned skills (during the weekends) on a 10-point scale. Therapy progress (being "symptom" free) is measured in percentages. For anorectic clients weight may also be used for self-monitoring purposes. The therapist must be careful not to become engaged in a power struggle with the client.

The therapist gives specific instructions and provides feedback and reinforcement of the goals that are reached. Questions asked in the training are: "What have you done this week to solve your problems? What was your specific contribution for success or failure? What is your homework assignment and how do you intend to bring this into practice? What do you say to yourself when you succeed in problem solving?"

Insight Training (Clients, Cotherapist, and Psychotherapist)

Every 12 weeks after admission each client is interviewed by the psycho-therapist in the group in front of all the clients and staff members who provide the client with the necessary feedback. Intellectual and emotional insight on the functional relationships between neurotic (anorectic) complaints and antecedent stress factors on the one hand, and maintaining variables on the other, are sought after.

A functional analysis of the individual's complaints and family or relational problems is concisely brought into the picture. The psychotherapist avoids technical terms and relies on metaphors for rhetorical purposes to implement the functional insights. Often, the client uses "face-saving" complaints as maneuvers to manipulate others, seek attention, be excused, or avoid responsibilities. In confronting the client with these extrinsic or other intrinsic gains (e.g., tension reduction in avoidance or flight reactions), the therapist must be careful in handling the client's resistance in the group, especially when using paradoxical interventions. As Lazarus and Wilson (1976) state, "To prescribe a 10–15 pound weight loss is hardly a cure for anorexia nervosa" (p. 124).

Anorectics might be adversely defensive and sensitive to deception (or the appearance of it), so that a meticulously honest attitude is a prerequisite for the helping alliance (Garner & Bemis, 1982).

Rational Training (Clients, Cotherapist, and Psychotherapist)

The basic idea in rational–emotive training, as developed by Ellis (1962), is Epictetus's (1st century A.D.) adage, "Men are not disturbed by things but the views they take of them." Ellis speaks about the ABCs of emotional disturbance, in which A stands for the *A*ctivating event, B for (ir)rational *B*eliefs, and C for emotional and behavioral *C*onsequences. Beck (1976) starts from this same principle and formulates several dysfunctional cognitions that have been specified by Garner and Bemis (1982, p. 137) for anorectics:

- *Selective abstraction*—"The only way that I can be in control is through eating."
- *Overgeneralization*—"I must avoid carbohydrates so I won't become obese."
- *Magnification*—"Gaining 5 pounds would push me over the brink."
- *Dichotomous reasoning*—"If I gain a pound I'll go on and gain a hundred pounds."
- *Personalization*—"When I see someone who is overweight, I worry that I will be like her."
- *Superstitious thinking*—"If I eat sweets, it will be converted instantly into stomach fat."

Kwee (1982a) discusses the practice of "General Semantics" in psychotherapy and concludes that irrational thought patterns and cognitive distortions are mainly based on incorrect abstractions of reality.

To unmask each irrational self-verbalization, the therapist teaches the client in a "Socratic dialogue" to ask himself or herself the following questions: (1) "Is my thinking factual?" (2) "Does my thinking help me to achieve my short- and long-term goals?" (3) "Does my thinking help me to feel what I want?" (4) "Does my thinking help me to avoid significant conflicts?" (Maultsby, 1978). It is of the utmost importance to uncover the underlying irrational assumptions and to dispute these ideas in combination with reality-testing exercises.

Assertion Training (Clients, Cotherapist, and Psychotherapist)

Frequently, anorectic clients are socially reclusive and inhibited. They feel insufficient, uncertain, and powerless. Emotional freedom can be promoted by showing clients how to express feelings or emotions in a direct, open, and honest way so that the possibility of getting one's needs can be maximally met (Lazarus, 1971).

In each session of the assertion training, the client is motivated to behave assertively. A problem situation is selected, discussed, and practiced by means of behavioral rehearsal. In this procedure the therapist models an effective response, in which a significant effect can be brought about by a minimum of effort. Through feedback of the group members and coaching by the therapist, the client is taught coping skills to practice in a variety of interpersonal problem situations. The client is encouraged to keep an assertiveness notebook where brief reports are recorded of problems that were encountered and of homework that had been carried out.

The use of assertiveness training in the treatment of anorectics appears to be an important intervention (Agras & Werne, 1977).

Relaxation Training (Clients and Cotherapist)

Relaxation training can be induced as a self-regulatory skill to refine the anorectic client's bodily experiences. Progressive relaxation and autogenic training appear to be helpful in learning to separate internal sensations from emotional feelings.

Whereas progressive relaxation is based on the contrast effects of muscle tension and muscle relaxation, autogenic training is based on proprioceptive awareness that is sharpened by concentration and self-suggestions. Differential muscle relaxation can also be applied by deliberately relaxing those muscle groups that are not in use while performing various activities. For instance, when chewing it is possible to relax the shoulders, arms, chest, abdomen, buttocks, and back muscles. (There are several relaxation-training cassettes on the market that clients can use to practice at home.)

Biofeedback relaxation might also be useful in identifying and controlling internal and external bodily experiences, so that recovery of weight becomes a less anxious process.

CASE DESCRIPTIONS

Bergin and Strupp (1972) have concluded: "In view of the current state of knowledge and technology in the area, it is considered more desirable to encourage research developments along lines other than large-scale collaborative studies, such as systematic research on basic mechanisms, naturalistic observations of psychological change, and intensive study of single cases" (p. 427). Outcome research is almost exclusively based on group studies, and the mean change score of a relatively small number of clients. Considering the fact that clinical practice concerns unique individuals, one may dispute the relevance of the group approach. This is connected to what Kiesler (1966) calls the "uniformity assumption myth," implying that client characteristics (or therapeutic changes of the individual) do not differ from each other. In so doing, exceptional cases may be lost sight of, especially those with a negative outcome (Strupp, Hadley, & Gomes-Schwarz, 1977).

Lazarus and Davison (1971) summarize the rationale for the use of experimental case studies. Single-subject research may (1) cast doubt on generally accepted theories; (2) give rise to better-controlled inquiries; (3) be useful for the study of rare phenomena; (4) offer the opportunity to apply new techniques; (5) yield acceptable scientific information to a certain degree; and (6) place meat on a theoretical skeleton. Chassan and Bellack (1966) explain that when the same study is repeated several times with different individuals, these studies may constitute a group study in which it is possible to discover whether the specific treatment was suitable and if so, for which specific individual and under which set of specific circumstances.

A plea is made here to combine nomothetic data from group experimental studies with idiographic data from single-subject research strategies, as each tends to complement the other. Bandura (1976) states:

> One can examine how each individual is affected by experimental procedures during induction or successive phases and also compare statistically whether the individual demonstration of the phenomenon occurs more frequently among subjects who receive the procedures than among those who do not. Adding baseline comparison groups and quantitative evaluation of data in no way detracts from inspection of individual variability. (pp. 150-151)

With this philosophy in mind, two cases of anorexia nervosa are presented in the following section.

THE CASE OF ANNY

The client, Anny, was a just-married woman, aged 21 years, height 1.63 m, weight 40 kg. Before she became anorectic, her weight was 55 kg, so that there was a weight loss of 37.5%. Anny's profession was that of dental assistant; her husband worked as a clerk in a big firm. She had been hospitalized for 3 months in a nearby psychiatric institution.

The anorectic behaviors started at the age of 16 years. Looking in a mirror Anny became discontented with her bodily contours and decided to lose a few kilograms. This slimming escalated into a long-lasting and uncontrollable process. When she was 17 years old, her weight was 52 kg, and in the subsequent 4 years this decreased to 40 kg. However, she was still discontented and pursued losing weight by physical exercises, frequent weighing, and keeping tables. She started each morning with the ritual of mirror gazing, calculating calories, and composing the food allotment for the day. When she ate more than intended, she suffered from guilt feelings and remorse so that she ate by bits and pieces with chopsticks. The end result was that Anny was no longer able to take care of herself, and several physical complaints became manifest: for example, aches over her whole body (especially in the stomach), sensations of passing out when standing up, difficulties in defecating, low blood pressure, and absence of menstruation. Meanwhile, Anny had fantasies about delicacies, such as pastry and cake. By smoking she could suppress her appetite. On weak moments, once or twice a week, she ate on the sly, from the cookie jar, during those times she had compulsive binging attacks. Having read many cookery books, Anny knew the caloric value of most foods and products. Because she was able to camouflage her preoccupation with and avoidance of food, only a few people knew about her condition.

Anny's adult body weight phobia seemed to be connected with a problematic family situation in view of the long-lasting tense atmosphere at her parental home. There were five in the family of which Anny was the eldest child. As long as she could remember, her parents quarreled with each other almost daily, especially during meals. When Anny was a toddler, she and her mother teamed up against the father. In the course of time Anny, her brother, sister, and mother formed one camp against the father, who used to beat the mother. Anny and her father also came to blows. Anny and her father were both introverted, perfectionistic, stubborn, and moody. Furthermore, the father suffered from a severe disease for which he adhered to a strict diet for many years. A year before Anny became anorectic, her parents divorced. While visiting her father, Anny was able to make contact with him for the first time in her life. Several weeks thereafter, he died in a hospital, as he refused to remain on the prescribed diet.

Anny was unable to mourn, although she blamed herself for misjudging her father and for having taken her mother's side uncritically. When the anorectic behaviors, especially the food refusal, were manifest, every meal became a theater of war between Anny and her mother. To escape the tense atmosphere at home, she decided to marry an obliging schoolmate. However, in her marriage she was not able to feel happiness. Problems with her mother-in-law led Anny to consider a divorce, shortly before she was hospitalized.

To complete the case of Anny, the Modality Profile of her complaints and problems that permitted the tailoring of successful interventions is presented in Table 8-2.

The Case of Bill

If the epidemiologic numbers are correct, the phenomenon of a male anorectic occurs in 1 out of 1,000,000 people in the general population. Considering the fact that The Netherlands had about 14 million inhabitants, Bill was one of the 14 anorectic male persons in the country.

The client, Bill, was an introverted man with a lean appearance. He was roughly 30 years old, with a height of 1.83 m and a weight of 55 kg. Before the onset of the anorexia nervosa, he weighed 80 kg, so that there was a body weight decrease of 31%. Bill, who worked as a civil servant, did not function well in his job. After several pharmacologic treatments he was rejected as medically unfit a few years before his admission for residential psychotherapy.

The anorectic behaviors became manifest a few months after his marriage, 10 years ago, when he was confronted with the problem of detachment from his parental home. Bill experienced sadness after visiting his parents and noticed that he lost his appetite when feeling sorrow. He began to become obsessed with the "higher" value of not eating and got absorbed in the various ways of losing weight. Being able to eat as little as possible and losing weight were signs of "willpower," while gaining weight meant being weak. However, Bill was not always as strong as he wished to be, in view of the fact that he suffered from "eating attacks" about four times a week. During such an attack, that could last up to 1 hour, Bill could ingest an enormous amount of carbohydrates. After eating too much, Bill suffered from stomach aches, whereupon his caring wife was ready to put him to bed with a hot-water bottle. However, most of the time Bill was grossly overactive in order to lose weight, especially in his work where he stood for most of the day, and then played sports or went walking.

Bill came from a six-children family, of which he was the third. The atmosphere in the parental home was dominated by father's severe and

TABLE 8-2. Anny's Modality Profile

Modality	Problem
Behavior	Avoidance of eating situations
	Minimal eating
	Prolonged eating
	Counting calories
	Mirror gazing
	Rituals of composing the food allotment of the day
Affect	Feeling bad after eating
	Guilt feelings about father
	Unable to express emotions
	Mourning father's death
	Pictures of having a fight with father
	Feeling anxious in company of others
Sensation	Unaware of own body
	Insensitive to sexuality
	Rejection of bodily sensations
	Unable to discriminate between feelings and sensations
	Feeling tense generally
Imagery	Poor self-image
	Overestimation when imagining body size
	Having images that people are watching and judging her
	Being obsessional about (exotic) foods
Cognition	Eating much is bad
	Losing weight is an exceptional achievement
	One must be slim to get accepted
	Self-downing ("I am a worthless human being")
	It is forbidden to quarrel
Interpersonal relationships	Living in social isolation
	Conflicts with mother and in-laws
	Dissatisfying marital interactions
	Unconsummated marriage
	Introverted attitude
Drugs/biology	Amenorrhea
	Exhausted bodily condition
	Constipation
	Stomachaches
	Low blood pressure
	Hair is beginning to fall out

rigid discipline. Mother obeyed father inexorably, just like the children who grew up in a milieu of overprotection. Nevertheless, Bill experienced emotional problems about having broken away from home. He felt continuously homesick. A year after having left home, Bill's father suddenly lost a lot of weight because of a serious disease that ultimately led to his death. During the same time, Bill became preoccupied, and later obessed with his own weight, so that he could not mourn the important loss. However, he felt a great emptiness, as his father used to arrange and decide many things in Bill's life.

To complete the case of Bill, a Modality Profile of his complaints and problems is drawn up and represented in Table 8-3.

TABLE 8-3. Bill's Modality Profile

Modality	Problem
Behavior	Binge eating about four times a week
	Doing physical exercises or standing for a long time at work after overeating
Affect	Feeling depressed while still mourning father's death
	Anxiety and panic attacks when gaining weight or after eating something substantial
Sensation	Dizziness
	Feeling shaky
	Sensations of passing out
	Ignoring signs of hunger
	Lack of libido
	General tension
Imagery	Wishful imagining that father is still alive to lead and guide
	Negative self-image of being a "nobody"
	Nostalgic images of still being a child in the parental home
Cognition	To eat means to be weak and not having "willpower"
	Thinking about being an insufficient person
	Lacking self-confidence and self-respect
	Strivings of perfectionism and categorical imperatives
Interpersonal relationships	Dependence of mother and wife
	Reclusive in social situations (e.g., in presence of brothers and sisters)
	Unassertive in various situations
	Introversion
Drugs/biology	Stomachaches
	Headaches
	Constipation
	Physical exhaustion
	High blood pressure after eating too much licorice

TREATMENT RESULTS[2]

To evaluate the multimodal residential psychotherapy, five relevant target variables were chosen and measured by means of the following methods:

1. "Neurotic" complaints by a symptom checklist[3]—57 items (Luteyn, Kok, Hamel, & Poiesz, 1979)
2. Introversion (as a trait) by an introversion scale—13 items (Luteyn & Kingma, 1978)
3. Rational ideation by a rationality questionnaire—15 items (Kwee, 1982b)
4. Assertive behavior by an assertiveness schedule—46 items (Rathus, 1973)
5. Psychophysiological arousal by an S-R inventory—154 items Endler, Hunt, & Rosenstein 1962)

These psychometric instruments were administered five times: at intake, at admission, after 12 weeks, at discharge, and at follow-up. For both Anny and Bill the time between intake and admission lasted 15 weeks; between admission and discharge, 30 weeks; and between discharge and follow-up, 30 weeks.

The sum scores of all variables have been transformed to a mean score of 50 and a standard deviation of 10, whereby the second measurement, at admission, was used as a reference point of each variable. The mean is evaluated according to the following arithmetic formula:

$$\bar{X}.j2 = \frac{\bar{X}pj2 + \bar{X}oj2}{2} \times 100$$

where $\bar{X}.j2$ is the unweighted total mean of the phobic, anorectic, and obsessional clients ($n = 84$) on list j at admission; $\bar{X}pj2$ is the mean score of the phobic and anorectic clients ($n = 40$) on questionnaire j at admission; and $\bar{X}oj2$ is the mean score of the obsessional clients ($n = 44$) on questionnaire j at admission.

The second parameter, the standard deviation, is calculated in analogy of the total mean score:

$$SD.j2 = \sqrt{\frac{(SDpj2^2 + SDoj2^2)}{2}}$$

2. These evaluations were conducted in close collaboration with Hugo J. Duivenvoorden, MD.

3. Most neurotic manifestations include such disorders as phobias, obsessions, depression, conversion, anorexia, and other psychosomatic dysfunctions.

where $SD.j2$ is the unweighted pooled standard deviation of phobic, anorectic, and obsessional clients on list j at admission; $SDpj2$ is the standard deviation of the phobic and anorectic clients on questionnaire j at admission; and $SDoj2$ is the standard deviation of the obsessional clients on questionnaire j at admission.

By applying this procedure it becomes possible to compare the changes within the individual with regard to the mean score and the standard deviation. Supposing that the distribution is normal, 95% of the clients fall within the interval of 30–70.

All scores are coded or recorded in the same direction, in such a way that high scores have a negative meaning and low scores have a positive meaning. In order to be able to interpret the scores, the theoretical highest feasible score range (the transformed maximum and minimum values) are calculated (see Table 8-4).

The scores of Anny and Bill are plotted in Figure 8-2, where one can see that for both clients there is a general tendency of improvement. In the case of Anny there is some evidence that there was a decrease in scores for assertiveness (about 5 points), introversion (5–10 points), complaints (20–25 points), and rationality (about 15 points). As the theoretical minimum score range value on complaints is 20 (see Table 8-4), her level of 25 means that Anny was almost "symptom" free at that time. Data on psychophysiologic arousal are lacking after the second measurement. Two measures suggest that there is a worsening trend for this scale as well as for rationality, complaints, and assertiveness. Her stay in a neighboring mental hospital, during 3 months before her admission for multimodal residential therapy, did not seem to have had any important effect on the target variables. The results have a long-lasting character in view of the fact that the scores are stable at discharge and at follow-up for all variables. The introversion scale shows a prolonged improvement of 5 points.

TABLE 8-4. Theoretical Score Range of Transformed Maximum and Minimum Values on the Target Variables

Variables	Theoretical transformed scores	
	Minimum	Maximum
"Neurotic" complaints	20	96
Introversion (trait)	13	67
Rational ideation	19	81
Assertive behavior	14	77
Physiologic arousal	19	84

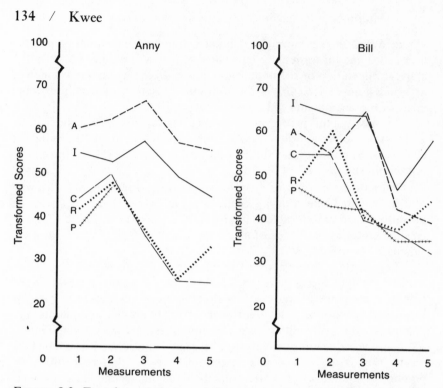

FIGURE 8-2. Transformed scores with a mean value of 50 and a standard deviation of 10, on the variables Complaints (C), Introversion (I), Rationality (R), Assertiveness (A), and Psychophysiologic arousal (P) over five measurements at (1) intake, (2) admission, (3) in-between, (4) discharge, and (5) follow-up in the cases of Anny (left) and Bill (right).

In the case of Bill there was a significant drop (about 15 points) in the introversion scale at discharge in comparison with the scores on the previous measurements. However, one can see an important relapse at follow-up of about 10 points. Considering that 67 is the theoretical maximum score range value for introversion (see Table 8-4), Bill's extreme score on this scale at the beginning was at least attenuated. In the area of assertiveness, Bill improved at admission (5 points) but worsened after 12 weeks of his stay (10 points) to improve again at discharge and at follow-up (25 points). He improved importantly in his complaints with 15 points after 12 weeks at discharge to more than 20 points at follow-up. While there is a worsening trend in rationality in the beginning (more than 10 points), there is an improvement after 12 weeks and at discharge (more than 20 points), and a relapse at follow-up (15 points). Thus, finally the improvement is 5 points, if compared with the first measurement, and more than 15 points, if compared with the second measurement. The level

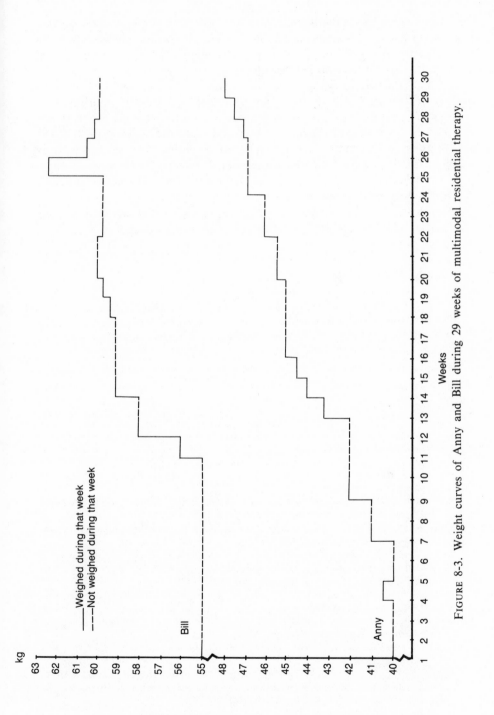

FIGURE 8-3. Weight curves of Anny and Bill during 29 weeks of multimodal residential therapy.

135

of arousal shows a consequent drop of more than 10 points over the five measurements. The relapses on introversion and rationality seem to be an indication that Bill must be careful, and keep practicing the newly learned cognitive and behavioral skills intensively.

In conclusion, Anny's and Bill's process of weight gain is shown in Figure 8-3. One can see that Anny progressed constantly according to a strict operant program that was offered to her, whereas Bill was not pushed to weigh, nor to work on his weight increase. During the first 10–12 weeks Bill's treatment was directed to overcome the grief problems by grief therapy as described by Ramsay (1979). Verbal follow-up checks 3 years after treatment revealed that the results were substantial, durable, and stable: Anny weighed more than 50 kg and Bill weighed nearly 70 kg. His eating attacks disappeared. Both felt happier and adjusted in their marriages, and were fully functioning in their daily lives.

ACKNOWLEDGMENTS

I wish to express my gratitude to Dr. J. H. Thiel, Professor of Psychotherapy at Erasmus University, Rotterdam, The Netherlands, and his coworkers, Drs. R. W. Trijsburg and H. J. Duivenvoorden, for their assistance and helpful comments on an earlier draft of this chapter.

REFERENCES

Agras, S., & Werne, J. (1977). Behavior modification in anorexia nervosa: Research foundations. In R. A. Vigersky (Ed.), *Anorexia nervosa.* New York: Raven Press.

American Psychiatric Association. (1980). *Diagnostic and statistical manual of mental disorders* (3rd ed.). Washington, DC: Author.

Bandura, A. (1976). Self-reinforcement: Theoretical and methodological considerations. *Behaviorism, 4,* 135–155.

Beck, A. T. (1976). *Cognitive therapy and the emotional disorders.* New York: International Universities Press.

Bemis, K. M. (1978). Current approaches to the etiology and treatment of anorexia nervosa. *Psychological Bulletin, 85,* 593–617.

Ben-Tovim, D. I., Hunter, M., & Crisp, A. H. (1977). Discrimination and evaluation of shape and size in anorexia nervosa: An exploratory study. *Research Communications in Psychology, Psychiatry and Behaviour,2,* 241–257.

Bergin, A. E., & Strupp, H. H. (1972). *Changing frontiers in the science of psychotherapy.* Chicago: Aldine-Atherton.

Brownell, K. D. (1981). Assessment of eating disorders. In D. H. Barlow (Ed.), *Behavioral assessment of adult disorders.* New York: Guilford.

Bruch, H. (1973). *Eating disorders: Obesity, anorexia nervosa, and the person within.* New York: Basic Books.

Brunell, L. F. (1982). The multimodal approach: An appraisal. In L. F. Brunell & W. T. Young (Eds.), *Multimodal handbook for a mental hospital: Designing specific treatment for specific problems.* New York: Springer.

Casper, R. C., Halmi, K. A., Goldberg, S. C., Eckert, E. D., & Davis, J. M. (1979). Disturbances in body image estimation as related to other characteristics and outcome in anorexia nervosa. *British Journal of Psychiatry, 134,* 60–66.

Chassan, J. B., & Bellack, L. B. (1966). An introduction to intensive design in the evaluation of drug efficacy during psychotherapy. In L. A. Gottschalk & A. H. Auerbach (Eds.), *Methods of research in psychotherapy.* New York: Appleton-Century-Crofts.

Crisp, A. H. (1980). *Anorexia nervosa: Let me be.* New York: Academic Press.

Crisp, A. H., Harding, B., & McGuiness, B. (1974). Anorexia nervosa psychoneurotic characteristic of parents: relationship to prognosis. A quantitative study. *Journal of Psychosomatic Research, 18,* 167–173.

Crisp, A. H., & Kalucy, R. S. (1974). Aspects of the perceptual disorder in anorexia nervosa. *British Journal of Medical Psychology, 47,* 349–361.

Dally, P., & Gomez, J. (1979). *Anorexia nervosa.* London: Heinemann.

Eckert, E., Goldberg, S. C., Halmi, K. A., Casper, R., & Davis, J. M. (1979). Behavior therapy in anorexia nervosa. *British Journal of Psychiatry, 134,* 55–59.

Ellis, A. (1962). *Reason and emotion in psychotherapy.* New York: Lyle Stuart.

Endler, N. S., Hunt, J. McV., & Rosenstein, A. J. (1962). An S-R inventory of anxiousness. *Psychological Monographs, 76* (Serial No. 17).

Erwin, W. J. (1977). A 16-year follow-up of a case of severe anorexia treated by behavior therapy. *Journal of Behavior Therapy and Experimental Psychiatry, 8,* 157–160.

Feighner, J. P., Robins, E., Guze, S. B., Woodruff, R. A., Winokur, G., & Muñoz, R. (1972). Diagnostic criteria for use in psychiatric research. *Archives of General Psychiatry, 26,* 57–63.

Frank, J. D. (1959). Problems of controls in psychotherapy as exemplified by the psychotherapy research project of the Phipps Psychiatric Clinic. In *Research in psychotherapy.* Washington, DC: American Psychological Association.

Garner, D. M., & Bemis, K. M. (1982). A cognitive-behavioral approach to anorexia nervosa. *Cognitive Therapy and Research, 6,* 123–150.

Garner, D. M., & Garfinkel, P. E. (1981). Body image in anorexia nervosa: Measurement, theory and clinical implications. *International Journal of Psychiatry in Medicine, 11,* 263–284.

Hallsten, E. A. (1965). Adolescent anorexia nervosa treated by desensitization. *Behaviour Research and Therapy, 3,* 87–91.

Halmi, K. A. (1980). Anorexia nervosa. In A. M. Freedman, H. I. Kaplan, & B. J. Sadock (Eds.), *Comprehensive textbook of psychiatry* (Vol. 3). Baltimore: Williams & Wilkins.

Hautzinger, M. (1980). Anorexia nervosa: A behavior-analytical model. *Behaviour Analysis and Modification, 4,* 210–223.

Jacob, R. G., Nordlund, O., & Schwieler, G. H. (1975). Treatment of anorexia in early infancy—some behavioral approaches. In J. C. Breugelmann (Ed.), *Progress in behaviour therapy.* Berlin: Springer Verlag.

Kiesler, D. J. (1966). Some myths of psychotherapy research and the search for a paradigm. *Psychological Bulletin, 65,* 110–136.

Kwee, M. G. T. (1981). Towards the clinical art and science of multimodal psychotherapy. *Current Psychological Reviews, 1,* 55–68.

Kwee, M. G. T. (1982a). Psychotherapy and the practice of general semantics. *Methodology and Science, 15* (3).

Kwee, M. G. T. (1982b). Rationeel-emotieve therapie in praktijk. In H. M. van der Ploeg (Ed.), *Psychotherapie.* Alphen a/d Rijn: Stafleu.

Lazarus, A. A. (1971). *Behavior therapy and beyond.* New York: McGraw-Hill.

Lazarus, A. A. (1978). *In the mind's eye.* New York: Rawson. (Reissued 1984, Guilford.)

Lazarus, A. A. (1981). *The practice of multimodal therapy.* New York: McGraw-Hill.

Lazarus, A. A., & Davison, G. C. (1971). Clinical innovation in research and practice. In A. E. Bergin & S. L. Garfield (Eds.), *Handbook of psychotherapy and behavior change: An empirical analysis.* New York: Wiley.

Lazarus, A. A., & Fay, A. (1982). Resistance or rationalization? A cognitive behavioral perspective. In P. L. Wachtel (Ed.), *Resistance: Psychodynamic and behavioral approaches.* New York: Plenum.

Lazarus, A. A., & Wilson, G. T. (1976). Behavior modification: Clinical and experimental perspectives. In B. B. Wolman (Ed.), *The therapist's handbook: Treatment methods of mental disorders.* New York: Van Nostrand Reinhold.

Liebman, R., Minuchin, S., & Baker, L. (1974). An integrated treatment program for anorexia nervosa. *American Journal of Psychiatry, 131,* 432–436.

Luteyn, F., & Kingma, L. (1978). Een Nieuwe Verkorte MMPI. R. U. Groningen: Heymans Bulletins.

Luteyn, F., Kok, A. R., Hamel, L. F., & Poiesz, A. (1979). Enige Ervaringen met een Klachtenlijst (de HSCL). *Nederlands Tijdschrift voor de Psychologie, 34,* 167–179.

Maultsby, M. C. (1978). *A million dollars for your hangover.* Lexington, KY: Rational Self-Help Books.

Mavissakalian, M. (1982). Anorexia nervosa treated with response prevention and prolonged exposure. *Behaviour Research and Therapy, 20,* 27–31.

Minuchin, S., Rosman, B. L., & Baker, L. (1978). *Psychosomatic families: Anorexia nervosa in context.* Cambridge, MA: Harvard University Press.

Rathus, S. A. (1973). A 30-item schedule for assessing assertive behavior. *Behavior Therapy, 4,* 398–406.

Russell, G. F. M. (1970). Anorexia nervosa: Its identity as an illness and its treatment. In J. H. Price (Ed.), *Modern trends in psychological medicine: II.* New York: Appleton-Century-Crofts.

Schnurer, A. T., Rubin, R. R., & Roy, A. (1973). Systematic desensitization of anorexia nervosa seen as a weight phobia. *Journal of Behavior Therapy and Experimental Psychiatry, 4,* 149–153.

Selvini-Palazzoli, M. (1978). *Self-starvation: From individual to family therapy in the treatment of anorexia nervosa* (rev. ed.). New York: Jason Aronson.

Slade, P. D., & Russell, G. F. M. (1973). Awareness of body dimensions in anorexia nervosa: Cross-sectional and longitudinal studies. *Psychological Medicine, 3,* 188–199.

Strupp, H. H., Hadley, S. W., & Gomes-Schwartz, B. (1977). *Psychotherapy for better or worse: The problem of negative effects.* New York: Jason Aronson.

Van de Loo, K. J. M. (1981). Anorexia Nervosa: Belichaamde levensonmacht. In K. J. M. van de Loo (Ed.), *Anorexia Nervosa: Diagnostiek, behandeling en onderzoek.* Nijmegen: Dekker & van de Vegt.

Vandereycken, W. (1980). Anorexia nervosa. In J. W. G. Orlemans (Ed.), *Handboek voor Gedragstherapie.* Deventer: Van Loghum Slaterus.

Wolpe, J., & Lazarus, A. A. (1966). *Behavior therapy techniques.* New York: Pergamon.

Wright, W. S., Manwell, M. K. C., & Merrett, J. D. (1969). Anorexia nervosa: A discriminant functional analysis. *British Journal of Psychiatry, 115,* 827–831.

Yager, J. (1982). Family issues in the pathogenesis of anorexia nervosa. *Psychosomatic Medicine, 44,* 43–59.

9

A Multimodal Approach for the Counselor/Consultant: A Case Study

EDWIN R. GERLER, JR.

It is well known that many clients enter therapy with "calling cards"— face-saving pretexts that enable them to determine whether it is likely to be safe and productive to state their real concerns. The manner in which Edwin Gerler dealt with his client's initial defensiveness opened the door to more basic revelations. Thereafter, by employing the multimodal framework, Gerler was able to delineate the full range of the client's interactive problems, and then to select appropriate treatment tactics. It is noteworthy that a "psuh-button" panacea approach was avoided; some clinicians might have concluded that the client was depressed and therefore in need of antidepressant medication. Certainly, this would have been indicated had the client failed to respond immediately to Gerler's other interventions. Again, this case shows that a unitary approach would have led to incomplete treatment.

INTRODUCTION

The professional literature for counselors is filled with notions about why and how counselors can best help children by consulting with the adults in children's lives. Ritchie (1982) and Purkey and Schmidt (1982), for example, suggested reasons and methods for counselor consultation with parents and other adults. Johnston and Fields (1981) discussed a consultation model involving teachers in establishing a kind of "classroom family" to promote learning and psychosocial development in children. Childress (1982) proposed consultation with middle school teachers "to promote the development of positive learning environments for students" (p. 127). As Male (1982) noted, counselors who consult with the important adults in children's lives "play important roles in creating positive change and facilitating the growth and development of the clients they serve" (p. 31).

THE CASE OF MARSHALL

It was in my work as a consultant with Marshall, a 40-year-old, un-married, sixth-grade teacher, that I fully realized that the role of con-sultant sometimes involves helping a teacher overcome some personal difficulties to improve the classroom environment created by the teacher. My first professional contact with Marshall came when I discovered the following poem scribbled on the outside of a crumpled envelope sitting in my office mailbox:

> *Little Paine*
> I waived goodbye to Paine,
> Forever,
> When his image
> Strangled thoughts behind my eyes,
>   And
> I could not bear to see his little grasping,
> Always,
> For older hands
> Filled with big work to do.

Stapled to the envelope was a note which read, "How do you like this? May I come and talk with you?"

When Marshall came to my office, it was obvious from the beginning that he wanted more than my evaluation of his poem. The first few lines of our initial conversation indicate Marshall's broad concerns about himself and about the children he served:

Marshall: How did you like my poem?

Counselor: I enjoyed it—though I'm not sure I understand it alto-gether. Perhaps you could tell me about it?

Marshall: Poems are to be experienced, not understood.

Counselor: You might help me experience your poem if you told me something about it.

Marshall: A poem stands or falls—without explanation.

Counselor: Maybe then you might tell me how you came to write the poem. How about it?

Marshall: I've been sleeping poorly recently and decided to try my hand at poetry late at night instead of eating midnight snacks and watching television. I've needed to find somehow to relax at night and get some sleep. My teaching is suffering from my lack of sleep and the kids are letting me know it.

Counselor: You haven't been sleeping well lately?

Marshall: That's only about half the problem. My drinking has increased—not to the point that I'm a drunk—and I can barely drag myself out of bed to go to work. In fact, sometimes I don't get out of bed on weekends.

Counselor: Anything else?

Marshall: I don't want to teach kids anymore. I'm tired of kids. They bother me.

Counselor: Little Paine?

Marshall: I guess the poem expresses some of my frustrations. I need some creative outlets other than teaching to stimulate myself. What can I do?

At the end of the first session I suggested that Marshall continue to write poems and that he bring these to our next couple of sessions. I intimated that I might get to know him and his concerns better through discussing his poetry. He agreed.

At our second session he brought in the following poem:

> *Ineffectual*
> I glanced up just in time
> To see
> A puff of smoke floating upward
> Past a "no smoking" sign
> Mounted on the wall
> Beneath a silent smoke alarm.

Our discussion began:

Counselor: How did this poem come to be?

Marshall: Same as before. Couldn't sleep. Wrote it instead of eating, watching TV late at night.

Counselor: How did the words come to your mind?

Marshall: I don't know exactly, but they remind me of me.

Counselor: How so?

Marshall: Children in my class pay about as much attention to me lately as some people pay to "no smoking" signs.

Counselor: Let's talk about this feeling you have about yourself and the way children respond to you.

With my invitation Marshall seemed to explode with information about the problems and concerns he experienced. Over the next couple of sessions he seemed to get most of his concerns aired. Table 9-1 outlines the concerns Marshall expressed. Marshall's concerns are outlined and were eventually treated using the multimodal approach (see Lazarus, 1981). I chose this approach because I have found it effective in counseling

TABLE 9-1. Marshall's Multimodal Profile

Modality	Problem
Behavior	He could not organize his time for work.
	He had trouble sleeping.
	He ate and drank too much.
	He sometimes did not get out of bed on weekends.
Affect	He felt angry about his being ineffectual.
	He felt guilty about his lack of caring for the children he taught.
	He felt restless and wanted to do something other than teaching.
	He feared that he might be fired.
Sensation	He craved sensory stimulation from producing and consuming artistic products such as music and poetry.
Imagery	He was preoccupied with artistic imagery and was unable to concentrate on the everyday duties of his teaching job.
Cognition	He had irrational thoughts about how he would be fired from his job if he did not concentrate more energy on his work. These thoughts detracted him from doing what he needed to improve his teaching and from getting the help he needed to improve.
	He had trouble disciplining his thinking.
Interpersonal relationships	His relations with children in the classroom were often tense.
Drugs/biology	He gained weight as a result of excessive eating and drinking.
	He had increasing difficulty maintaining a regular exercise program.
	He experienced fitful sleep.

with children and in consulting with the adults in children's lives. My views about the usefulness of multimodal counseling and consulting are explained in detail in the book *Counseling the Young Learner* (Gerler, 1982). Simply stated, I chose to use the multimodal approach with Marshall because "we are biological beings who move, feel, sense, imagine, think, and relate to one another" and "each of these dimensions requires our attention when problems emerge" (Lazarus, 1978, p. 8).

PROCEDURES USED TO RESOLVE MARSHALL'S CONCERNS

Behavior and Physiology

Marshall's apparent ineffectiveness as a teacher was rooted, in part, to behavioral and physical problems (see Table 9-1). His overeating and occasional excessive drinking contributed to his gaining weight and inability to sleep. The weight gain and inability to sleep, in turn, reduced Marshall's willingness and ability to exercise regularly and thus reduced his energy for teaching. It is noteworthy that just a year or so before seeking help Marshall had been an avid runner, averaging 40–50 miles of running each week. During his third session with me, he explained that his running had diminished to under 10 miles each week and that a medical examination had uncovered no physical problems to account for the lack of energy for and dedication to running.

To begin to alleviate Marshall's overeating and excessive drinking I asked Marshall to monitor his eating and drinking patterns. Self-monitoring has sometimes been used successfully to change behaviors of this kind. McFall (1970), for instance, noted the effects of self-monitoring on smoking behavior. Marshall seemed faithfully to record the times of his eating and drinking, but the procedure did not reduce Marshall's excesses. The record did, however, provide better information about the extent of his poor habits.

As an alternative method to self-monitoring, Marshall and I worked out a behavior contract that designated specific times and places for Marshall to eat and drink. One facet of the agreement was that Marshall could eat food and drink alcoholic beverages at only one place in his home, namely, at the kitchen table. He had previously found many other places at home to eat and drink, particularly, in his recreation room while watching television.

The behavior contract paid off. He organized his eating and drinking to the extent that he no longer had snack foods and alcoholic drinks available to him during late night television watching. His sleep improved. Further counseling about sleep problems also convinced Marshall that he needed less sleep than he had once thought. He tried going to bed about 1½ hours later than normal, which resulted in his being tired and in his usually getting to sleep within 15 minutes of going to bed. On his own he decided not to stay in bed if he was unable to get to sleep quickly. His new approach was to leave bed, read or watch television for about 30 minutes, and then return to bed. This change initiated by Marshall added to quality sleep.

The benefits of better sleep and reduced eating and drinking increased Marshall's energy somewhat, and he was able to exercise more regularly. His running improved, but instead of concerning himself about mileage, Marshall settled on running 20–30 minutes for 5 days each week. He was thus less compulsive about increasing his weekly mileage and seemed more energetic. Coincidentally, he reported feeling much less tired while teaching during the last hour or so of the school day. In summary, improved physical habits had personal benefits for Marshall which also undoubtedly had positive effects on the children with whom he worked in the classroom.

Affect, Interpersonal Relations, and Cognition

Marshall seemed to suffer at times from a kind of "delusion of uniqueness" (Sullivan, 1947) in regard to his feelings about teaching; that is, he talked almost as though no one else in teaching felt as guilty, angry, and restless about professional inadequacies as he did. To ease this situation I arranged for him to join a teacher effectiveness group wherein teachers discussed not only their work in the classroom but also their feelings about the work. I knew the leader to be group-centered and an empathic listener. I also knew that the group consisted mainly of teachers who had expressed feelings of "teacher burnout" and that the group would provide a better than average chance for Marshall to overcome his apparent feelings of being alone with his problems.

Somewhat reluctantly, Marshall agreed to join the group. He commented while agreeing to join that he really did not need "another meeting in his life." He stayed with the group for only three sessions, remarking that the people in the group simply wanted "to shoot the breeze for a couple of hours" and that he did not have the time for such a group. We discussed his feelings about the group and finally decided not to pursue membership in a counseling group.

What seemed to help Marshall more than anything else in dealing with his feelings about teaching was our discussion of irrational thinking. I recommended that he read Chapter 3, "Irrational Ideas Which Cause and Sustain Emotional Disturbances," from *Reason and Emotion in Psychotherapy* (Ellis, 1962). He especially benefited from our discussing the following irrational ideas explained in the Ellis book:

> The idea that one should be thoroughly competent, adequate, and achieving in all possible respects if one is to consider oneself worthwhile. (p. 63)

> The idea that it is awful and catastrophic when things are not the way one would very much like them to be. (p. 69)

> The idea that if something is or may be dangerous or fearsome one should be terribly concerned about it and should keep dwelling on the possibility of its occurring. (p. 75)

The latter idea, in particular, intrigued Marshall. He disclosed during our discussions that he secretly feared being fired for not "teaching energetically." The notion that dwelling on this possibility would do nothing but increase the chances of its occurring made sense to Marshall. After much consideration of irrational thinking, his fear seemed to diminish as evidenced by his more relaxed demeanor. Some of the children in his classroom, incidentally, commented to him about the easing of tension in the classroom.

Sensation and Imagery

Marshall was consumed with a desire to experience artistic sensations and images. He was distracted from his everyday work in the classroom by listening to music and, most especially, by trying to write poetry. After several counseling sessions, we agreed that his interest in poetry was positive. (In fact, he showed some promise as a poet, having had poetry published in several respected publications.) We agreed further that writing poetry would be of little benefit to him if writing it caused him to feel guilty about incompetent teaching and caused him to fear losing his livelihood in teaching.

I recommended that he set a time limit (perhaps 2–3 hours a day) wherein he would write poetry exclusively. I also recommended that he think of ways to share some of his own enjoyment of artistic imagery and sensation with the children in his classroom. Thereafter, he set aside about 30 minutes near the end of each school day for himself and his students to engage in artistic, creative expression. At times, the students showed him their work, and he disclosed some of his as well. He reported, however, that the time became mostly a private time for everyone in the classroom.

CONCLUSION

Marshall's concerns centered on his inadequacies as a teacher. The concerns grew from many parts of his life and hence needed to be treated from a multimodal perspective. As a counselor/consultant, I used the multimodal approach to alleviate some of his personal concerns and in so doing to increase his effectiveness in the classroom.

REFERENCES

Childress, N. W. (1982). Group consultation with middle school teachers. *School Counselor, 30*, 127–132.
Ellis, A. (1962). *Reason and emotion in psychotherapy.* New York: Lyle Stuart.
Gerler, E. R. (1982). *Counseling the young learner.* Englewood Cliffs, NJ: Prentice-Hall.
Johnston, J. C., & Fields, P. A. (1981). School consultation with the "classroom family." *School Counselor, 29*, 140–146.
Lazarus, A. A. (1978). What is multimodal therapy? A brief overview. *Elementary School Guidance and Counseling, 13*, 6–11.
Lazarus, A. A. (1981). *The practice of multimodal therapy.* New York: McGraw-Hill.
Male, R. A. (1982). Consultation as an intervention strategy for school counselors. *School Counselor, 30*, 25–31.

McFall, R. M. (1970). Effects of self-monitoring on normal smoking behavior. *Journal of Consulting and Clinical Psychology, 35*, 135-142.

Purkey, W. W., & Schmidt, J. J. (1982). Ways to be an inviting parent: Suggestions for the counselor-consultant. *Elementary School Guidance and Counseling, 17*, 94-99.

Ritchie, M. H. (1982). Parental consultation: Practical considerations. *School Counselor, 29*, 402-410.

Sullivan, H. S. (1947). *Conceptions of modern psychiatry*. Washington, DC: William Alanson White Psychiatric Foundation.

10

Multimodal Therapy in a Case of Somatization Disorder

MICHEL R. H. M. ROBORGH

MAURITS G. T. KWEE

As can be seen from Chapters 8 and 10 in this book, our colleagues in The Netherlands have not been afraid to treat cases that others have considered hopeless. Difficult cases call for diligent, systematic, and hard work! Michel Roborgh and Maurits Kwee show how the multimodal assessment–therapy connection provides a clear-cut rationale for the implementation of cost-effective techniques. By examining the "firing order" of the specific modalities that tended to elicit and sustain their client's major problems, logical treatments could be selected. As this chapter indicates, the use of different methods in the multimodal fashion is indeed comprehensive, but critics who have accused us of using a random "shotgun" approach are incorrect. The choice of techniques follows logically and scientifically from the diagnostic data. Students frequently ask how, after drawing up a Modality Profile, the therapist decides where to intervene and which methods to use. This chapter should provide some significant answers to these (and other) questions.

The case to be described fits most of the criteria for the diagnosis of a "somatization disorder" according to the *Diagnostic and Statistical Manual* (DSM-III) of the American Psychiatric Association (1980).

CASE DESCRIPTION

The client was a middle-aged married woman with a chronic astasia-abasia (motor incoordination for standing; inability to walk; no organic basis), which confined her to a wheelchair and caused her pain. She wanted to learn to walk so that her husband, a heart and hernia patient, would no longer have to push her wheelchair.

At 40 years of age the client developed pains in her back and neck. At that time she was working in an office as a bookkeeper. The complaints increased despite physiotherapeutic treatment. Some years later, she was

147

declared medically unfit for her job as a result of pain complaints in her left arm. Shortly afterwards, she began to have difficulty in walking, and 2 years later was no longer able to walk without aids. At the same time pain complaints developed in the left hip, groin, and upper leg. The client was examined by an orthopedic surgeon, who was unable to find any abnormalities; neurologic abnormalities also were not found. In the ensuing years she experienced increasing difficulty in walking, and there were periods when she frequently fell without apparent reason. Eventually, because of increasing pain in her left hip, groin, and leg, she could do no more than hobble for about 10 minutes. When she was almost 50 years old, she became paralyzed overnight and had to be carried by her husband. She was given a walker, a wheelchair and (via a pain clinic) a transcutaneous electrical nerve stimulator to combat the pains (eight electrodes attached to back and lower left leg). At the beginning of the treatment, she sat in the wheelchair and the nerve stimulator was attached to her.

Previously, during her teens, shortly after her parental home had been bombed, she had an "attack" and was unable to walk for about a month after seeing a woman at her choral society suffer what was probably an epileptic attack. Since then she had experienced numerous treatments, hospitalizations, and operations. The patient received the following treatments, which are listed chronologically; a psychiatric consultation in connection with abasia; an inguinal hernia operation; 4 weeks of psychiatric hospitalization as a result of her father's death and a miscarriage; a tonsillectomy; an umbilical hernia operation; diagnosis of a disorder of the large intestine; physiotherapeutic treatment for back and neck complaints; treatment by a neurologist for depression and anxiety complaints that arose after the death of her mother and a second miscarriage; examination by an orthopedic surgeon in connection with pain complaints in left hip, groin, and upper leg (no neurologic abnormalities were found); prolapse of the uterus; nose septum correction in connection with migrain complaints; internal examination for suspected diverticula; neurologic examination again failing to reveal abnormalities; uterus extirpation; admission for 9 weeks to a rehabilitation department, followed by a year and a half of outpatient rehabilitation without result. Outpatient internal examination in connection with pain in the left side of the hypogastrium and with diarrhea again failed to reveal somatic abnormalities. A transcutaneous electrical nerve stimulator was provided by a pain clinic for the pains in the back and the left leg. Meanwhile, the client had also spent 4 months in a Roman Catholic monastery to cure herself of her love for a neighbor. After a year of partner–relationship therapy, she was referred for multimodal treatment.

From the anamnesis it was learned that the client was the second of four children. She had an elder brother and a younger sister and brother. Her father, an office worker, had died of tuberculosis shortly after an attempted suicide (he was a "nerve patient") when the client was 28 years old. Her mother, a housewife, died of lung cancer when the client was 42 years old. Both were Roman Catholic. The client got on well with her father, whom she described as a "very caring, conscientious, religious, and strict man." She got on less well with her mother, whom she described as follows: "strong character, stubborn, sometimes very hard, but she could also be pleasant and warmhearted." The client had been somewhat anxious in early childhood. She had had diphtheria as a child. In adolescence and early adulthood the client suffered from "fits of nerves and disturbances of equilibrium." At that time her hobbies were sports, clubs, singing, gymnastics, and dancing. She was also interested in monastic life. Prior to her marriage she worked as a shorthand typist–secretary. She again worked for 12 years after her marriage, as a shorthand typist–secretary and then as a bookkeeper. She was declared medically unfit for work because of her paralysis.

Her marriage produced four children (boys), one of whom died at the age of 10 months, probably as a result of convulsions. The client also had three miscarriages at 5 months and one premature birth at almost 7 months. Her husband had originally been an office worker; for the past 12 years he had been a wage clerk for a firm of contractors. Three years previously he had been admitted to a hospital with heart complaints. During one of her visits he suffered an infarction; the shock was so great that the client was scarcely able to move and had to be pushed out of the room. Half a year after this event she became totally unable to walk. Because her complaints gave her a limited radius of action, her husband obtained a driving license after his infarction. He went to a great deal of trouble for her, and this irritated the client. For a long time he had been doing the shopping and taking her out either in the car or pushing her wheelchair.

MODALITY PROFILE

A Modality Profile, or topographical macroanalysis, was made with the help of the Life History Questionnaire (Lazarus, 1981) and is given in Table 10-1.

FUNCTIONAL MACROANALYSIS

With the help of the Modality Profile, a functional macroanalysis was drawn up (see Figure 10-1). This maps the factors and psychological mechanisms that are thought to have given rise to and maintained the emotional problem and complaint behavior, in this case astasia–abasia. The hypothetical factors are arranged in accordance with the BASIC I.D.

TABLE 10-1. Modality Profile

Modality	Problem
Behavior	Astasia–abasia
	Remains in wheelchair: does not walk or stand
	Requests support in standing up and walking
	Avoids contact with people
	Complains of pain and fatique
	Goes to talk to priests and others who provide help
Affect	Anxious when in contact with people
	Depression
	Guilt feeling toward father's death
	Guilt feeling toward husband
	Incapable of expressing emotions
	Anxiety-laden pictures of future death of husband
	Strong need for warmth and affection
Sensation	Pain sensations in back, joints, extremities, stomach, genital region, neck, and chest
	Hypersensitivity toward sexuality
	General tenseness, finding expression in: swallowing complaints, vomiting tendencies, aphonia, hazy vision, fainting tendencies, loss of consciousness, nausea, shortness of breath, heart palpitations, dizziness
	Fatigue
	Weak feeling in muscles
	Insomnia
Imagery	Images of future misery and suffering
	Absolutist and perfectionist images
	Images of others studying and judging her
	Images of being guilty of all misery and having to prevent it
	Negative self-image
Cognition	Guilt thoughts about misery and suffering of others
	Thinks she would look silly if she could walk again
	Negative self-talk
	Thoughts of being punished by God
	Thinks that people disapprove of her
	Thinks she is coming down with a physical disease
Interpersonal relationships	Lives in social isolation
	Conflictual relationship with husband, children, and many others, including those who help her
	Stuck in marital relationship
	Dominating attitude in relationships
	Independent posture
Drugs	Medication: Natuvit, Dalmadorm 15 mg, Voltaren 50 mg, Tranxene 10 mg, Lasix 20 mg, Primperan 10 mg, Thiamine 50 mg, Prominol 50 mg, vitamin B complex, Muthesa complex, Trianal ointment, and Solkoseryl ampules

TABLE 10-1. (*Continued*)

Modality	Problem
	Physical complaints: paralyses, frequent urination or urine retention, attacks, diarrhea, irregular menstruation, excessive blood loss
	Electrical subcutaneous nerve stimulator for pain complaints
	Wheelchair to move about in

The hypothetical psychological mechanisms are in the form of vicious cycles that connect the different factors/modalities with one another.

Cycle 1 (S-I-C-A) shows that an anxiety reaction (A) was produced by the absolutist and perfectionist ideation images (I) and thoughts (C) arising from a disturbed perception (S) of traumatic and interpersonal relationships. This anxiety was caused by the client's inability to satisfy the norm of being able to spare other people misery and suffering. When she saw misery and suffering, therefore, she believed that she personally had failed, which resulted in guilt and anxiety. This is in accordance with the ABC model of Ellis and Grieger (1977).

Cycle 2 (B-S-D.-A) shows the intrinsic loss. Undesired feelings—anxiety—were avoided symbolically by the client's ceasing to be able to stand or walk on her own (B). She thereby avoided her own responsibility for supposedly causing misery in others. The anxiety resulted in astasia–abasia. The intrinsic loss was the result of the fact that the astasia–abasia (B) gave rise to sensations of physical pain and fatigue, depression and insomnia (S), a state of affairs which led in the long run to a form of atrophy of the muscles, confinement to a wheelchair (D.), and finally to guilt and depression (A). The client's handicaps also gave rise to feelings of anxiety based on thoughts of "coming down with some serious physical disease" and "being punished by God."

Cycle 3 (B-I.-S-A) is that of the extrinsic loss. We have already seen that the client's anxiety was avoided by means of the conversion complaint astasia–abasia (B). The extrinsic loss resulted from the fact that, because she was unable to stand or walk on her own (B), she was dependent on other people for her mobility. On the other hand, because of her strongly internalized parental norm of independence and self-reliance, she did not have the inclination to seek help, and this resulted in further social isolation (I.). This isolation caused the client loss of contact, loss of face, and a form of sensory deprivation (S), in which she lost her job and was heavily dependent on her husband, which lead to an increase in depression, guilt, and anxiety (A).

Cycle 4 (B-S-I/C-A) is that of the intrinsic gain. The conversion reaction of astasia–abasia (B) resulted in a reduction of tension (S),

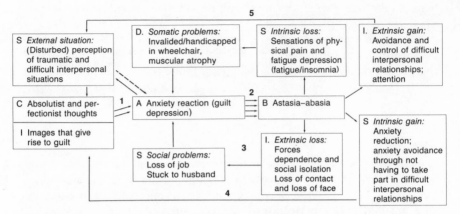

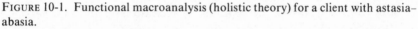

FIGURE 10-1. Functional macroanalysis (holistic theory) for a client with astasia-abasia.

because the client did not have to engage in interpersonal relationships. Again, the experiencing of pain partly prevented the experiencing of anxiety. Initially, being able to keep her anxiety under control gave her a good feeling (gain) and this confirmed or reinforced her absolutist and perfectionist thoughts and images (I/C). Later, however, these thoughts and images again gave rise to feelings of anxiety (A), because she found that she was unable to prevent misery and suffering in other people.

Cycle 5 (B-I.-S-A) is that of the extrinsic gain. Because of her astasia-abasia (B), the client did not need to engage in interpersonal relationships. She therefore experienced a sense of control (gain) over interpersonal relationships (I.). Moreover, her complaining attracted attention from her environment (gain). However, because of her norms of independence and responsibility and the fact that the attention attracted by her complaints was often negative, conflicts arose in her interpersonal relationships, which she again perceived in an "erroneous" manner (S), thus giving rise to anxiety (A) because of absolutist and perfectionist thoughts and images, which had become "automatic."

The astasia-abasia had become chronic, which meant that the client could no longer allow herself to stand or walk unsupported in the presence of other people because of the risk of losing face. The problem of possible loss of face was more acute as she became increasingly convinced that her complaint could have been the result of mental and relational problems.

The prolonged conflict between the client and her parents can be identified as an antecedent factor in her decompensation with neurotic complaints. During adolescence a power struggle took place with her parents, who exerted strong pressure on her to be independent. Because her attitude was one of dependence and a need for attention and she was not skillful in expressing emotions, she was unable to comply. As a result, unresolvable feelings of guilt and anxiety developed. She became demoralized and sought refuge in complaint behavior, which manifested itself in the form of astasia–abasia. Precipitating events were the bombing of the parental home and the witnessing of an insultus suffered by a woman.

TREATMENT[1]

The Modality Profile and the functional analysis were used to draw up an efficient treatment plan. It was ensured that interventions would be made in each modality (see Table 10-2). The motivation for the choice of techniques and the order in which they were applied will be discussed in the following sections.

DIFFERENTIAL ATTENTION TECHNIQUE

As the astasia–abasia problem was most problematic and concrete, and as it occupied a central place in the functional analysis, it was decided with the client that the treatment would be directed first at this conversion complaint. The client herself clearly indicated that she had come for walking therapy and was therefore motivated for it.

Astasia–abasia is a conversion phenomenon and can be translated as role behavior that is reinforced both by the patient and by his or her environment. Unpleasant situations are avoided and, at the same time, attention is secured. The attention secured can be wholly positive, but it is often mixed with irritation and/or doubt. The latter fact makes it more difficult for the client to relinquish his or her symptoms because, aside from having to face certain painful or frightening things, he or she runs the risk of being exposed as someone who is "putting it on" (loss of face).

The main objective, then, was that the client should regain the ability to stand and walk on her own. In this context, the following subobjectives were formulated:

1. Learning to stand and walk on her own while supporting herself with both hands against the wall.
2. Learning to stand and walk on her own while supporting herself with one hand against the wall.

---

1. The terms taken from learning theory should be interpreted metaphorically here (see Lazarus, 1981).

TABLE 10-2. Treatment Techniques Aimed at the Diagnosed Modalities

Modality	Problem	Technique
Behavior	Astasia–abasia	Differential attention technique (walking exercises)
Affect	Anxiety	Self-hypnosis
	Depression	Mourning therapy
Sensation	Pain	Self-hypnosis
	"Loss of face"	Self-hypnosis
Imagery	Absolutist and perfectionist images	Rational–emotive imagery
Cognition	Absolutist and perfectionist thoughts	Cognitive therapy
	Guilt thoughts	
Interpersonal relationships	Social anxiety: avoidance of interpersonal relationships, forced dependence, and social isolation	Systematic desensitization with regard to activities and social contacts
		Relationship therapy
Drugs/biology	Atrophy	Physiotherapy and medication

3. Learning to stand and walk without support.
4. Learning to stand and walk unsupported without being prompted.

In addition to the therapeutic walking program, the realization of these objectives also required that the client's mildly atrophied muscles, and particularly those of the legs, should be kept supple and in adequate condition. The method chosen was regular physiotherapy, restricted to massage and vibration. This procedure afforded a means of sparing the client loss of face. Another requirement was that the electrical nerve stimulator should be dispensed with beforehand, because it was an added burden in walking. It was decided that the apparatus would be phased out in two stages and, if necessary, pain-killing medication would be provided as a substitute. The client could also request pain-killing medication to reduce any pains she might experience while walking.

The procedure was as follows. A psychological assistant visited the client twice a day during each phase of the treatment. During these visits she talked to the client for about 10 minutes about subjects that were unrelated to the client's complaints and problems. At the end of this conversation, the client was given the instruction, "Try to walk as far as you can." The client could then walk along the cleared wall of the dormitory, to which no one else had access during the assistant's visits. If the client refused to walk, the visit was terminated.

The phases of the program accorded with the ABAB design and were as follows:

- Phase 1 (1st week): Instructions only in accordance with the above procedure. No verbal reinforcement for walking behavior or attempts to walk.
- Phase 2 (2nd week): Instructions and social reinforcement. The same procedure as in phase 1 except that, walking attempts and actual walking behavior, met with social reinforcement in the form of verbal rewards ("Good," "Fantastic," "You're doing very well," etc.) accompanied by positive nonverbal attention responses such as looking and laughing.
- Phase 3 (3rd week): Again, instructions only, as in phase 1.
- Phase 4 (4th week): Again, instructions and social reinforcement, as in phase 2.

During this 1-month treatment program, all those involved, including the client's husband, were instructed either to ignore her walking behavior (1st and 3rd week) or to reward it verbally (2nd and 4th week). Every request for a painkiller by the client was complied with. To prevent the client's taking too many painkillers as a result of increased pain during the walking program, she was alternately given a painkiller and a placebo, which were visually indistinguishable.

The assistant received careful instructions before the treatment program began. While the program was in progress, regular evaluation and feedback discussions took place. Prior to commencement the client was told on which day the program would start, that it would last for 4 weeks, and the two fixed times at which the assistant would visit her every day. The client was told nothing about the contents of the program except that it was a "walking program with which fantastic results have been achieved." She was also told that a start would be made on the partner–relationship therapy she had requested if the therapist considered the results to be satisfactory at the end of the walking program. After this 1-month program everybody concerned was to reward the client's walking behavior continuously by means of verbal praise, and the assistant would continue to visit her for some weeks in order to increase the walking distance further by means of instruction and social reinforcement.

Explicit use was made of *instruction*, aimed at walking behavior (continuously for the 1st month during the assistant's visits); *social reinforcement* in the form of verbal praise contingent on walking behavior (continuously during the 2nd and 4th weeks and subsequently during the assistant's visits and during the day from others concerned); and *positive reinforcement* in the form of partner–relationship therapy at the end of the walking program. It could be assumed that expectation, self-reinforcement, and social reinforcement from people not involved in the treatment would be implicitly operative if the client was denied explicit social reinforcement in the 1st and 3rd weeks of the program.

Measurements made by the assistant during her visits[2] included the number of steps taken (because of the client's tendency to drag her feet, the foot had to leave the ground completely for it to count as a step); the total distance walked (as the client walked back and forth along a marked wall, this was the number of times multiplied by the marked distance, plus the last stretch of wall up to where she had stopped); the number of times the client lost her balance; the number of requests for painkillers during all phases of the program; and the number of painkillers and placebo tablets given per day during all phases of the program.

SELF-HYPNOSIS

Self-hypnosis was chosen as a therapeutic technique to combat the pain complaints as well as anxiety and tenseness.

Melzack and Wall (1965) formulated a neurophysiologic theory of pain, "the gate control theory," which was placed in a wider context by Fordyce (1967). According to this theory, there is a pain gate mechanism, which lets pain stimuli through or holds them back partly or wholly as they enter the central nervous system. This pain gate is influenced on the one hand by peripheral nerve fibers (e.g., scratching closes the gate, causing the itch to disappear) and on the other by higher brain centers (attention and anxiety open the gate for pain stimuli). People with chronic pain complaints are often preoccupied with pain and other signals from the body. This preoccupation can in itself increase the pain, in the sense that more pain is felt than the physical pain stimuli indicate. It is therefore important to investigate to what extent pain is caused by physical pain stimuli and to what extent it is reinforced by the consequences. Attention, for example, tends to increase pain, whereas diversion diminishes it. Anxiety, depression, and hypochondriacal thoughts can lead to an intensification of the pain. As tension can intensify the experiencing of pain, according to this theory, obviously the antagonist of tension, relaxation, can reduce it. Through deep relaxation a client experiences pain as less distressing. A relative insensitivity to pain can be achieved by teaching a self-hypnosis technique.

As this client complained not only about pain in the hip and legs while standing and walking but also occasionally about pain in the neck,

2. An initial visit with the nonspecific instruction, "Let's see if you can walk along this wall," without feedback or social reinforcement, served as a baseline measurement.

back, and stomach, *pain reduction* was set as one objective of the therapy. As mentioned earlier, the electrical nerve stimulator (with electrodes on the back, hip, and legs) was to be gradually phased out prior to the commencement of the walking program. The pain reduction treatment would not be started until the walking program had been completed, because the latter would be hard enough for the client on her own. Moreover, she was still heavily dependent on medication and would be particularly dependent on painkilling medication when the electrical nerve stimulator was dispensed with.

The subobjectives selected for pain reduction were reducing the subjective experience of pain by reducing muscle tension and thereby reducing the use of painkilling medication. To obtain these objectives, hypnosis was proposed to the client. She was given the opportunity to pour out all her views, prejudices, and questions on hypnosis and was given the necessary information and answers. She was explicitly reassured that hypnotherapy worked well with all pain complaints, irrespective of their cause. Hypnotherapy commenced only when the client agreed to it.

A hypnotic state was induced through eye fixation, first during the therapy session and later during practice sessions at home. If the results were satisfactory eye fixation was used again, followed by deepening exercises involving the counting of exhalations; specifically, "You musn't make a mistake . . . keep on counting . . . relax more and more . . . deeper and deeper in a trance . . . keep on counting . . . less and less pain . . . when you consider the pain is far enough away, stop counting and remember the last number . . . count backward from the last number to one . . . as you breathe in . . . and you're fresh and clear-headed again." The expectation was then expressed that the client would reach the same point of experiencing no pain even more quickly (at an even lower number). If this progressed satisfactorily through practice at home, the next step was hypnotic induction through eye fixation, followed by a deepening exercise involving the counting of exhalations with the therapist suggesting pleasant experiences. The client also practiced this at home.

Hypnotherapy included the following behavioral techniques: During eye fixation suggestibility was increased, which was associated with re-laxation, suggestion, and an altered state of consciousness, by (1) clearly presenting the situation to the client as hypnosis and (2) bringing about more positive attitudes, motivations, and expectations concerning the hypnotic procedures, as well as a related willingness to think along with the suggestion. Hypnosuggestive techniques consisted of direct suggestions of relaxation and pain reduction. The experiencing of ever deeper muscle relaxation is linked to an increasing disappearance of pain. The term "relaxation" can be used here instead of "hypnosis" and "instructions" instead of "suggestions"; one can speak, therefore, of deep relaxation by means of instructions. Finally, pleasant experiences were suggested; the therapist verbalized images of agreeable situations which produce relaxation.

The measurements used were the number of exhalations in the deepening procedure (direct) and the daily consumption of painkillers recorded by the client (indirect).

SYSTEMATIC DESENSITIZATION

Anxiety was the central feature in the functional macroanalysis of the client. Anxiety triggered the first and subsequent conversion phenomena, and also reinforced the client's pain and depression and gave rise to hyperventilation. Anxiety about loss of face was the reason that the client dared not entirely relinquish her conversion complaint and, hence, remained socially isolated. This was the motive for treating the client's social anxieties; it was hoped that, if these anxieties diminished, she would be able to generalize her partly re-acquired walking behavior. An obvious course would perhaps be to deal with the anxiety over loss of face by means of a cognitively oriented therapy. As cognitions play an important role in the maintenance of anxiety, rational–emotive therapy (Ellis & Grieger, 1977) or cognitive therapy (Beck, 1976) could provide a solution. However, as the client had already learned self-hypnosis for combatting pain, and as an indirect approach often has distinct advantages (particularly for conversion complaints), it was decided, in consultation with the client, to use systematic desensitization employing self-hypnosis. The aim was to reduce anxiety for possible loss of face resulting from the disappearance of her astasia–abasia complaints. To achieve this, the following subobjectives were formulated: the ability to imagine, without anxiety, situations in which loss of face is possible and the ability to actually appear in situations in which loss of face is possible. These were situations in which the client had regularly appeared in her wheelchair and in which she now had to appear on foot.

Regarding the desensitization procedure, Rothman, Carroll, and Rothman (1976) described a combined approach consisting of hypnosis, self-hypnosis (or relaxation), and conditioning with homework steps. The steps begin with a neutral, unthreatening picture and gradually move toward those situations in which the client experiences strong anxiety. The process we used, therefore, is a form of systematic desensitization (Wolpe & Lazarus, 1966) combined with the technique of Cautela (1970), in which learning principles are applied internally. The client is advised to gradually replace self-humiliating, negative brooding with self-hypnosis and positive self-imagination and visualization, and, where possible, constructive action is encouraged. The client makes daily reports on homework, including the number of self-hypnotic visualization exercises, how far he or she has got in the hierarchy, and what *in vivo* attempts he or she has made. Reinforcement is provided for successful homework steps.

Together with the client, a hierarchy was drawn up of social situations about which she felt anxiety over loss of face if she were to appear in them. In addition to these, there was one situation in which the client felt most relaxed. During the therapy sessions and the twice-daily exercises at home, the client had to imagine, under hypnosis, that she appeared in a difficult situation, starting with the least difficult. Each time she succeeded in this she pictured herself in the pleasant (anxiety-free) situation as an immediate reward.

She was instructed as follows:

1. Pick the situation from the list on which you are going to work.
2. Use self-hypnotic induction by means of eye fixation.
3. Picture the difficult situation.
4. If successful, picture the reward situation.
5. If unsuccessful, go back one step in the hierarchy, and if that succeeds try the unsuccessful step again.
6. Try to do in reality those exercises that have succeeded in your imagining. If successful, reward yourself with pleasant activity; if unsuccessful, practice again first by imagining.
7. Do not begin on the next step until the previous one has been mastered.

The following techniques were employed: (1) hypnotic induction by means of eye fixation; (2) systematic desensitization *in vitro* and *in vivo*; (3) covert and overt reinforcement. The following measurements were made by the client: (1) number of self-hypnotic visualization exercises; (2) number of successful and unsuccessful *in vitro* steps; (3) number of successful and unsuccessful *in vivo* steps.

MOURNING GUIDANCE

As the client's husband died at the end of the fourth-phase program (in the 33rd year of their marriage, as she had predicted!), attention was also paid in the therapy sessions to guiding her mourning, the aim being to help her to work through her emotions and thereby prevent the mourning process from taking a "pathologic" course (as in the past). The client was invited to tell about the death in detail and reacted with violent emotions, all of this in accordance with Ramsay (1978). The following features of her husband's death are worthy of note. Two years previously the client had had a vision that her husband would die in the 33rd year of their marriage. She recounted that she had seen 33 red roses and 1 white orchid as a symbol of the purity of marriage. The vision came true: Her husband died of a myocardial infarction on the first day of their 33rd year of marriage during a visit to the client and after reading in her presence a letter from her regarding their 33rd wedding anniversary. The letter included the following lines (in verse):

> . . . then tomorrow your hands too will start to tremble, then tomorrow perhaps you will already be very old, and the day is coming when you too will die, when I must get through the winter alone . . .

This seemed to be a case of a self-fulfilling prophecy because, according to the eldest son, the husband knew about her vision of the 33 roses and the white orchid. By discussing her husband's demise, visualizing salient aspects of their relationship, and encouraging the client to experience the full impact of her loss, the process of mourning was permitted to take its course.

COGNITIVE THERAPY

The feelings of anxiety and depression resulting from guilt thoughts and the client's absolutist and perfectionist thinking were combatted with cognitive techniques, including the three-column technique of Beck (1976). To combat anxiety and depression resulting from absolutist and perfectionist images, use was made of the technique of rational–emotive imagery (Ellis & Grieger, 1977). Through these techniques the client learned to convert irrational thoughts and images into rational thoughts and images, thus bringing about a decrease in feelings of anxiety and depression. A reduction of negative affect was achieved, particularly of her extreme guilt feelings. In applying these techniques, no systematic measurements were made.

THERAPY EVALUATION

Figure 10-2a gives the results of the four-phase program regarding the quantitative changes in the client's walking behavior. The total distance walked each day is given in meters and represents the sum of the results of the assistant's two daily visits. The first notable feature is the rapid increase in the distance walked in phase 1 (instruction only). Whereas the client was still not able to take a single step herself at the time of the baseline measurement, by the end of this first phase she had reached a distance of 300 meters. This conflicts with the findings of Turner and Hersen (1975) and Mumford and Paz (1978) that no change in walking

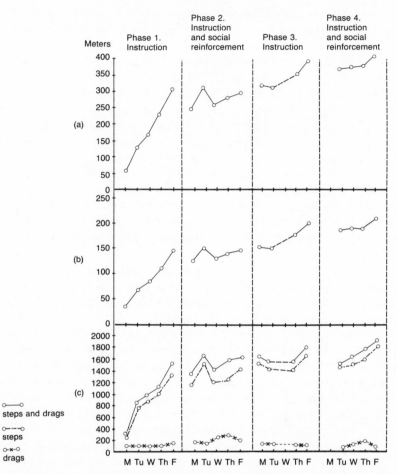

FIGURE 10-2. (a) Total distance walked per day during the two visits. (b) Average distance walked per visit. (c) Total number of steps (foot leaves ground completely) and "drags" (foot does not leave ground completely).

behavior takes place in the first phase (instruction only). This continuous rise can be attributable to instruction only, to expectancy and/or to strong motivation in the client. In phase 2 (instruction and social reinforcement) a small initial drop (possibly due to the absence of walking exercises during the previous weekend) was followed by stabilization, with the client not exceeding 300 meters. This too conflicts with previous studies (Agras, Leitenberg, Barlow, & Thomson, 1969; Hersen, Gullick, Matherne, & Harbert, 1972; Kallman, Hersen, & Hemphill-O'Toole, 1975; Turner & Hersen, 1975; Mumford & Paz, 1978), according to which social reinforcement had a stronger effect than instructions; the second phase should exhibit a very large increase in walking distance. Not only is this not the case here, but in comparison with the results of phase 1 it seems that instruction alone had a powerful effect, while the addition of social reinforcement yielded no cumulative or further increase in the walking distance. In phase 3 (instruction only) a gradual further increase in walking distance is seen. At the end of this phase, the client walked almost 400 meters. In accordance with previous studies, no decline took place as a result of the withdrawal of social reinforcement (extinction); Agras *et al.* (1969) see this as the result of the instructions. In this case, however, the instructions in phase 3 did not only prevent the occurrence of extinction phenomena; they also brought about a further increase in the distance walked. In phase 4 (instruction and social reinforcement), as in phase 2, stabilization occurred, and there was no further increase in walking distance. This again points to the action of instructions and the absence of any superimposed effect produced by social reinforcement.

Figure 10-2b shows the average distance walked per visit in meters during the four-phase program. There were two visits a day during this program, one in the morning and one in the afternoon. The results of the afternoon visits exceeded those of the morning visits, which may indicate that performance improved as the day progressed. During the continuation of the visits (three times a week, with instruction and social reinforcement) for 10 weeks after the four-phase program, the overall average walking distance was roughly 200 meters per visit, with troughs as low as 100 meters and peaks of 275–300 meters. The peaks were well in excess of the maximum distances achieved in the four-phase program. On average, though, no further increase in walking distance took place.

The greater distances walked in the afternoons than in the mornings suggest that walking became easier in the course of the day, rather than that a deterioration occurred as a result of fatigue. In the longer term no further increase in the walking distance took place through instruction and social reinforcement. There were, however, incidental increases up to a total of 300 meters per visit.

Figure 10-2c shows the total number of true steps per day (two visits), the total number of all steps, including "drags" (steps in which the foot did not entirely leave the ground), and the total number of drags. Dragging, or sometimes twisting of the foot, occurred chiefly at the end of each visit and was a clear sign of fatigue. This explains the almost constant number of drags each day; that is, at the end the client began to drag her feet from fatigue to such an extent that she finally stopped walking. This means that the quality of walking did not improve in the course of the four-phase program; there was no sustained decline in the number of drags. In phase 2, and to a lesser extent in phase 4, (the phases with social reinforcement), the number of drags in relation to the number of steps was higher than in the phases with instruction only. This may point to the effect of social reinforcement. For example, it is possible that feedback in the form of social reinforcement for steps and its absence in the case of drags, made the client more conscious of the fact that she dragged her feet, and her attempts to eliminate or reduce dragging actually may have reinforced this behavior. Better results may have been achieved if there had been specific instructions for walking quality ("Heel off the ground, foot off the ground, leg forward, and foot on the ground again").

The quality of the client's walking, then, did not change: The more tired she grew, the more she dragged her feet until she could go no further. Social reinforcement may have had a negative effect on walking quality (by fixing the client's attention on the poor quality of her walking), and it is suggested that specific instructions for good walking behavior might have improved the quality and possibly also the distance walked.

Figure 10-3 gives the results obtained from self-hypnosis for combatting pain complaints. The number of exhalations needed in the deepening exercise to become free of pain is shown in the form of a graph (the client practiced self-hypnosis 152 times in the course of the treatment, achieving a pain-free result on 98 occasions).

The figure also contains a histogram of the number of painkillers used by the client per day, which is an indirect measure of the effect of self-hypnosis.

FIGURE 10-3. Number of counted exhalations needed per hypnosis exercise and number of painkillers per day.

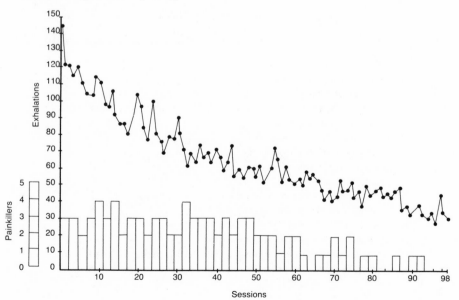

The results show that the number of exhalations needed to become pain free declined very gradually (from 144 to about 35). The number of exhalations needed also became more consistent, more stable over time. Similarly, there was a gradual decline in the use of painkillers when applying the self-hypnosis exercises (from 3 to 1). The decline in the use of painkillers (not until halfway through the period) occurred later than the sharpest decline in the number of exhalations (chiefly the first third of the period). The reason for this may be that the client did not start refraining from the use of painkillers until she had acquired sufficient confidence in self-hypnosis.

The client succeeded in attaining a pain-free state in 65% of her self-hypnosis exercises and reduced the time needed to a quarter of what she had required initially. The chief reasons for the failures were being disturbed, developing headaches, and falling asleep. The client herself was very pleased with the self-hypnosis, which she described as "giving your unconscious orders," and she often experienced spontaneous positive experiences in her trance (e.g., peace, freedom, orgasm). Self-hypnosis also finally proved to be an adequate substitute for the painkillers.

The hierarchy relating to social anxiety, which was drawn up with the client, is given in Table 10-3. The client pictured these situations during hypnosis when she had finished counting exhalations and, thus, was pain free; she pictured herself walking unaided, without a stick. She was encouraged to put herself in reality (*in vivo*) in situations that she had successfully imagined *in vitro*.

TABLE 10-3. Social Anxiety Hierarchy

	Anxiety level
1. Doing jobs on outside of house	10
2. Going on a boat trip as guide	10
3. Visiting a cemetery	20
4. Singing in the church choir again	20
5. Doing her own shopping	20
6. Swimming in swimming pool	30
7. Walking on beach with children	30
8. Going to hairdresser/beauty specialist	30
9. Buying clothes	40
10. Social work with sick or old people	40
11. Visiting office where she formerly worked	50
12. Taking driving lessons	60
13. Visiting friends and acquaintances by train	70
14. Going to a women's union meeting/competition by train	70
15. Visiting husband's grave	90

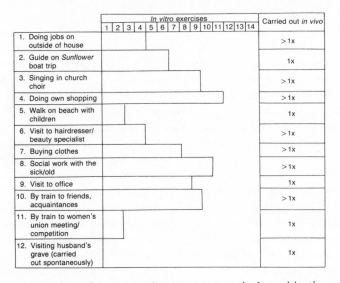

FIGURE 10-4. Number of *in vitro* and *in vivo* systematic desensitization exercises per situation.

Figure 10-4 depicts the number of *in vitro* and *in vivo* exercises carried out by the client per situation. Swimming and taking driving lessons were omitted by the client, because she decided later to postpone them. Visiting her husband's grave was the most anxiety provoking; its degree of difficulty for the client was found to be 90%. The results show that she was able to put herself in all the situations *in vivo* after she had done so a number of times *in vitro*.

Thus, by means of systematic desensitization the client was able to overcome her most oppressive and restrictive social anxieties *in vitro* and *in vivo*.

A follow-up assessment 2 years after treatment showed that a generalization of the results had taken place. This was apparent especially from the increased number of activities in which she engaged, the increase in her social contacts, and also from a further decline in the use of painkillers. The quantity and quality of her walking behavior appeared not to have been generalized, though they had been stabilized; that is, the maximum distance she could walk at a stretch had remained virtually the same, and she still walked with a crutch outdoors. This use of a crutch probably reveals a remnant of anxiety for loss of face, although in view of the constancy of the client's maximum walking distance (followed by fatigue and exhaustion), muscular atrophy is also a plausible explanation.

DISCUSSION

This case study concerns a client with chronic astasia–abasia who had already undergone numerous treatments and was considered hopeless. A defect of the previous treatments seems to have been that they were all "unimodal." It is, at any rate, a fact that multimodal therapy worked with this client. This involved a thorough assessment in the form of the Modality Profile and a holistic theory, and interventions that were an outgrowth of that assessment. It was ensured that the treatment was geared to each of the modalities, completeness being strived for in order to prevent a relapse in the future. Specific techniques were applied to the specific complaints and problems presented by the client.

As regards the effectiveness of specific techniques, this case study showed that "instructions" were a highly effective therapeutic strategy. In contrast to previous studies (Agras et al., 1969; Hersen et al., 1972; Kallman et al., 1975; Turner & Hersen, 1975; Mumford & Paz, 1978), instructions rather than social reinforcement were found to be the effective factor in the differential attention technique applied to astasia–abasia complaints. It was noted that in these previous studies, no relapse took place when social reinforcement was withdrawn. Agras et al. (1972) attributes this to the effects of instructions. Remarkably, however, Agras and the other authors demonstrated that instructions alone were not effective! The obvious explanation on the basis of the present case study is that instructions themselves can be a highly effective technique. Instructions, including self-instructions, were also the effective factors in the self-hypnosis and systematic desensitization for pain and social anxiety complaints. It is possible that appropriate instructions would also have improved the quality (and thereby the quantity) of the client's walking behaviors (e.g., "Heel off the ground, foot off the ground, leg forward and heel and foot on the ground again"). The reinforcement of the quality of walking without differentiation may have reinforced the dragging of feet; this persisted and impeded better walking behavior. Undifferentiated social reinforcement of walking behavior and atrophy of the leg muscles had a limiting effect on the results of the treatment. Probably, too, they were responsible for the continuing physical pain. It is noteworthy that no difference existed between the effect of the pain-killers and the placebos on the client's pain behaviors. This was one of the reasons for using hypnotherapy, or relaxation.

Kallman et al. (1975) previously used social reinforcement in a case of chronic astasia–abasia. A relapse to baseline behavior occurred in his client during treatment. The treatment results remained stable over time, however, after a second course of therapy in which the family and social system was also included and informed about ignoring undesired behavior and socially reinforcing desired walking behavior. In our case the system was informed and instructed prior to the commencement of the treatment.

The death of the client's husband may have been therapeutically effective in the context of extrinsic gain, in that he drove her about, brought her everywhere, did the housework—in short, looked after her completely.

Anxiety over loss of face (intrinsic gain) proved to be a motive for the client's not relinquishing her "symptoms." The follow-up showed that she was still searching for a medical explanation for her symptoms in order to prove that she was not "putting it on."

We agree with Turner and Hersen (1975) that "once all medical and laboratory tests have been completed and a differential diagnosis has been established, the traditional medical model should be discontinued for the astasia–abasia patient" (p. 612).

REFERENCES

Agras, W. S. D., Leitenberg, H., Barlow, D. H., & Thomson, L. E. (1969). Instruction and reinforcement in the modification of neurotic behavior. *American Journal of Psychiatry, 125,* 1435–1439.

American Psychiatric Association. (1980). *Diagnostic and statistical manual of mental disorders* (3rd. ed.). Washington, D.C: Author.

Beck, A. T. (1976). *Cognitive therapy and the emotional disorders.* New York: Meridian Book.

Cautela, J. R. (1970). Covert negative reinforcement. *Journal of Behavior Therapy and Experimental Psychiatry, 1,* 273–278.

Ellis, A., & Grieger, R. (1977). *Handbook of rational-emotive therapy.* New York: Springer.

Fordyce, W. E. (1967). *Behavioral methods for chronic pain and illness.* St. Louis: Mosby.

Hersen, M., Gullick, E. L., Matherne, P. M., & Harbert, T. L. (1972). Instructions and reinforcement in the modification of a conversion reaction. *Psychological Reports, 31,* 719–722.

Lazarus, A. A. (1981). *The practice of multimodal therapy.* New York: McGraw-Hill.

Kallman, W. M., Hersen, M., & Hemphill-O'Toole, D. (1975). The use of social reinforcement in a case of conversion reaction. *Behavior Therapy, 6,* 411–413.

Melzack, R., & Wall, P. D. (1965). Pain mechanism: A new theory. *Science, 150,* 971–989.

Mumford, P. R., & Paz, G. (1978). Differential attention in the treatment of astasia–abasia. *Journal of Behavior Therapy and Experimental Psychiatry, 9,* 369–371.

Ramsay, R. (1978). Rouwtherapie. In J. W. G. Orlemans, W. Brinkman, W. P. Haayman, & E. J. Zwaan (Eds.), *Handboek voor gedragstherapie* (Vol. 1). Deventer: Van Loghum Slaterus.

Rothman, I., Carroll, J. L., & Rothman, F. D. (1976). Homework and self-hypnosis: The conditioning therapies in clinical practice. In E. Dengrove (Ed.), *Hypnosis and behavior therapy.* Springfield, IL: Charles C Thomas.

Turner, S. M., & Hersen, M. (1975). Instructions and reinforcement in modification of a case of astasia–abasia. *Psychological Reports, 36,* 607–612.

Wolpe, J., & Lazarus, A. A. (1966). Behavior therapy techniques. New York: Pergamon.

11

The Case of Joan:
The "Bipolar" Agoraphobic

ALLEN P. BLASUCCI

Here is the case of a woman who had responded marginally to drug therapy, electroconvulsive therapy (ECT), psychotherapy, and milieu therapy. Similarly, attempts by a behavior therapist and later by a family therapist produced little, if any, constructive change. Allen Blasucci shows how, by employing certain procedures that are unique to the multimodal perspective, he was able to gain access to the client's main areas of disturbance. The overlap between multimodal therapy and cognitive–behavior therapy is quite clear in this chapter, but the discerning reader will discover subtle but crucial points of difference. Indeed, it would appear that these slight but significant differences were responsible for the clinically favorable outcome.

INTRODUCTION

Comprehensive, effective, and durable psychotherapeutic results are sought after by most clinicians. Unfortunately the behavior therapy literature often describes the use of one or two specific techniques (be that graded exposure, systematic desensitization, assertiveness training, etc.) for the treatment of what most practicing clinicians find to be complicated, multifaceted problems. It is not surprising then that the unimodal assessment of problems leads to singularity in treatment with questionable results. Franks, Wilson, Kendall, and Brownell (1982) assert that any good clinician will ferret out all four maintaining variables in a complete assessment, be they interpersonally, behaviorally, imaginally, or cognitively based, in order to assure completeness of treatment. Unfortunately, they offer no clear-cut assessment plan or system to accomplish this goal. The multimodal framework has been suggesting such a comprehensive schema for more than 10 years (Lazarus, 1973). It is this comprehensiveness in treatment, both on the assessment and intervention levels, that separates multimodal therapy from cognitively based behavior therapy and gives the practitioner a practical problem-oriented "map" to follow in providing complete psychotherapy.

As will be exemplified in the following case history, various techniques derived from assorted theoretical perspectives were used following the principle of "technical eclecticism." As any good clinician can attest, not all clients will respond favorably to one specific technique, irrespective of its proven efficacy or theoretical rationale. The art of psychotherapy in these cases is to apply other scientifically proven interventions to correct specific problems. What becomes of paramount importance, therefore, is not necessarily the intervention chosen from the various strategies available, but the proper and complete problem assessment in the application of treatment interventions. Multimodal therapy, as stated previously, is the one clearly defined framework available to the practitioner to assure this thoroughness in assessment and treatment.

As stated elsewhere (Lazarus 1973, 1976, 1981), multimodal therapy uses an assessment system where individual problem areas are assessed over seven discrete yet interactive modalities: Behavior, Affect, Sensation, Imagery, Cognition, Interpersonal relationships, and Drugs/biology (BASIC I.D.). It is the thoroughness of this assessment procedure that fosters the completeness of treatment, which is positively correlated with maintenance of gains (Chambless & Goldstein, 1982). Indeed, recent research has moved away from the single intervention strategy method in the treatment of anxiety and panic states to a multidimensional model where interactional theory, behavior therapy, and drug therapy are combined to more fully ensure thorough treatment. Chambless and Goldstein in their eclectic model have identified three primary target areas in the assessment–interaction process: (1) person variables where hypersensitivity to aloneness–separation experiences, style of dealing with stress, and ability to deal with stress and panic are seen as a symptom clusters; (2) onset variables idiosyncratic to that individual; and (3) classically conditioned fear-of-fear or anticipatory anxiety responses. Goldstein (1982) further reports that "the synergistic effect of combinations of treatment modalities . . . leads me to a conclusion that there is a clear interactive effect among the modalities herein combined" (pp. 183–187). We cannot agree more strongly with Goldstein, but would argue that his interaction–synergistic model is in need of a more individualistic and thorough assessment–intervention system to ensure completeness.

Lastly, by following the multimodal model, the client and the clinician can often pick and choose exactly where to begin and where to bridge out of any system cluster. In other words, the treatment program can be modified and reorganized depending upon the idiosyncratic conditions of a particular client, without forcing the client into an area for which he or she is not prepared, or is unwilling to enter. The model will help to assure, however, that all potential and overt problems are addressed in order to prevent relapse.

CASE HISTORY

Joan, a 45-year-old married mother of two children (aged 13 and 10 years), had been suffering from anxiety and panic attacks for 7 years. Initially, she had been an inpatient for 3 months in a major university hospital where chemotherapy, ECT, psychotherapy, and milieu therapy had been marginally successful in partially remitting some of her symptoms. She had been diagnosed as suffering from a bipolar depressive disorder. She and her husband were told to expect no major changes in her condition, and that they should learn to live with and to adjust to a more restrictive life style.

In the ensuing 7 years, Joan had received continual psychiatric treatment (tricyclic antidepressants and tranquilizers), as well as attempts at behavior therapy and family therapy with little or no relief of her symptoms. When she entered multimodal therapy, she was taking tricyclic antidepressants prescribed by her psychiatrist who had referred her for treatment, and had become completely housebound, except for occasional outside trips accompanied by her husband. For the past 18 months, her condition had worsened to the point where she could not stay alone without experiencing debilitating panic attacks, necessitating one of her children remaining home from school for support and frequent telephone contacts with her husband. She was generally fearful, exhibiting extreme anxiety symptoms in nearly all interpersonal situations (no matter how insignificant) to the point where she would refuse to answer the door and became increasingly reluctant to respond to the telephone. She saw her condition as hopeless and she was somewhat reluctant to reenter therapy.

ASSESSMENT AND TREATMENT

Following the initial visit and her completion of the Multimodal Life History Questionnaire, the Multimodal Profile shown in Table 11-1 was developed.

In order to establish a working relationship where Joan was to develop an ongoing responsibility for her own treatment, the BASIC I.D. Profile was thoroughly shared and explained to her. She was taught the basics of reinforcement and extinction procedures, and how her solution to the panic (withdrawal) was actually reinforcing the problem. Secondly, she was given a clearer understanding of the physiological process involved in panic attacks, and made to see how her strong physical reaction was actually an extension of a normal process set off by both conditioned and cognitively based factors. She took well to this educational process and then seemed better equipped to reenter the first steps of treatment.

TABLE 11-1. Joan's Modality Profile

Modality	Problem
Behavior	Withdrawal and avoidance
	Social immobility
Affect	Anxiety and panic attacks
	Depression/guilt
	Temper outbursts
Sensation	Heart palpitations
	Excessive perspiring
	Tightening of throat
	Loss of appetite
	Stomach tension with related gastrointestinal complaints
	Sexual disinterest
	Fitful sleep
Imagery	Self-image of helpless and hopeless
	Seeing self as losing control and "going crazy"
	Burden on the family
Cognition	"I will go crazy and/or have a nervous breakdown."
	Negative and catastrophic thinking
Interpersonal relationships	Dependence on husband and children
	Few social contacts
	Underassertive marital communication
Drugs/biology	Possible hypoglycemia
	Excessive alcohol intake

Since so many of her difficulties and fears were associated with the strong sensory responses, initial treatment steps were directed toward this modality. Treatment involved a four-step procedure at that point.

SENSORY TREATMENT

Sensory treatment included relaxation training, via an audiotape made by the therapist for the patient's home use at least twice daily, and biofeedback training using electromyography (EMG). Specifically, Joan was trained in sensory- and imagery-oriented relaxation methods to pave the way for entry into other modalities. (See "bridging" and "firing order" below.) A relaxation sequence was selected wherein a sensory development of calmness and heaviness was achieved. The corroborative use of EMG feedback was added so that she could actually "see" the results of her training as well as develop deeper levels of muscle relaxation.

A second benefit of relaxation training was for Joan to experience her own capacity to control the panic through this method. The therapist strongly reinforced this new cognitive attribution whereby she saw herself in better control, thus maximizing other cognitive restructuring efforts that were simultaneously employed.

IMAGERY EXERCISES

Imagery exercises were specifically developed to assist in graded exposure, where she was given the instruction to image herself in a specific situation while feeling reasonably calm and relaxed. She and I developed increasingly complex imagery rehearsal exercises to be employed following a relaxation training session (once again, at least twice daily at home). In the most simple of these, she was to see herself sitting or standing on the front porch, or walking to the mailbox at the foot of the driveway to her house. These exercises were then increased to more difficult situations (walking to a nearby park, shopping with her husband while he was in the next aisle, etc.) as she progressed.

BEHAVIORAL TREATMENT

Graded exposure exercises were developed in incrementally difficult steps. The technique used in this graded exposure does not differ substantially from the *in vivo* tactics typically employed by behavior therapists. Basically, she was instructed to image the exposure situation in her mind's eye prior to the actual event. She was also to practice relaxation prior to the event, and while in the situation itself, she was instructed to give herself positive self-statements as well as to practice deep breathing.

COGNITIVE RESTRUCTURING

Cognitive restructuring was implemented on two different levels. First, she was to repeat to herself the physiological process she was experiencing, thereby giving the fear a more rational and less catastrophic attribution. Second, a number of irrational cognitions were treated using Ellis's (Ellis & Grieger, 1977) ABC approach; Joan was taught to identify her own irrational thoughts and then to dispute them with more rational ones. She became quite adept at this procedure and found it helpful to do this rational disputation with paper and pencil rather than simply in her head.

It is noteworthy at this point to recognize the "firing order" principle, which Lazarus (1981) introduced to account for individual differences in problem development. In this case a strong sensory–affective component was followed by negative imagery and cognition, resulting in behavioral dysfunction and interpersonal demands (S/A→I/C→B→I.) The intervention strategies employed adhered to this paradigm as much as possible and accomplished two major therapeutic goals:

1. It treated those problems most important to the patient.
2. It provided an understanding of the patient's problems that could be demonstrated to her in a manner where expectational characteristics were maximized by pinpointing their effects.

The second major concept illustrated here is "bridging" (Lazarus, 1981). Bridging can be best defined as movement from one modality to another in an understandable and rational transition for both the patient and therapist. Here again, the patient becomes increasingly sophisticated and educated in his or her own idiosyncratic style of problem development so that change can occur earlier in the negative response chain. In Joan's case assessment revealed that the cognitive and interpersonal factors maintained much of her problem. But to first intervene on this level appeared to be fruitless without giving her the ability to control her sensory dysfunctions. In this regard, it was not surprising that an earlier course of family therapy was neither understood nor appreciated by Joan and her family, and thus proved ineffective in terms of its therapeutic impact.

The bridging and firing order principles developed through the multimodal assessment led again to a logical, pragmatic, and scientifically proven set of interventions *specific to this patient*. The relaxation training method chosen was imagery-based so as to maximize the later use of imagery rehearsal in preparing her for graded *in vivo* exposure. The specific assignments in the graded exposure were built around those interpersonal situations where she felt the most comfort (i.e., at home, with her family, shopping with her husband) so as to build on a position of some strength in decreasing the dependency on her family. Lastly, this process resulted in a change in cognitive attributions of herself and her problem, so that she could now view herself as an effective and competent person, in place of the highly negative and catastrophic thought processes that were maintaining the problem areas.

Following 8 weeks of therapy conducted as described above, she was staying home alone, taking short walks around the neighborhood, and generally feeling in control of this limited environment without experiencing anxiety attacks.

Since Joan was highly dependent on her husband to transport and to "protect" her in all other ventures away from the home, he was then brought into therapy as a means of training him as a behavioral assistant.

It became readily apparent, however, that Joan felt controlled by her husband, partly as a function of her dependency on him, and also as a function of her generally nonassertive style. Assertiveness training and marital therapy were initiated at this juncture, covering a full range of marital unhappiness as assessed through the Marital Satisfaction Questionnaire (Lazarus, 1981). Concurrently, her husband assisted in a desensitization program using the graded exposure method, *vis-à-vis* driving, shopping, and socializing, with good results.

The marital therapy and assertiveness training were crucial for achieving total problem resolution for major reasons:

1. Interpersonal conflict invariably resulted in a heightened affective state that then triggered or maximized the probability of a panic attack.
2. Joan felt responsible for the marital difficulties. She viewed herself as a burden on the family, which often resulted in depression and guilt, which then had the same affective consequence as described in 1.

One unfortunate side effect of her previous therapy is noteworthy. She had been told that her illness was due to her husband's controlling style, and that he was in fact invested in maintaining her illness for fear that if she improved, she would end the marriage. This belief system resulted in anger and further marital discord. It took a good deal of time and reeducation to correct what was, I believe, an unfortunate iatrogenic error.

Following 6 months of therapy, Joan was discharged from treatment, experiencing no anxiety attacks and reporting a general sense of control and a much improved marital situation. She had taken a job in a department store and was in need of no medication.

RELAPSE

Although the thorough treatment across all modalities seemed to have resulted in a complete remission, I received a telephone call some 15 months later in which Joan complained of a complete "relapse." Upon assessment, Joan noted many of her previous symptoms (although they were less severe) and she expressed a hopeless feeling of "being back at square one." No specific events or maintaining variables could be identified, and she was placed back on the previous treatment program with good and quick results. She appeared more depressed than she had been previously, and upon much questioning by the therapist, she finally admitted to experiencing a great amount of guilt surrounding the birth of an illegitimate child, whom she had given up for adoption. This had taken place many years ago, but was an event she had never told anyone about. It was around the anniversary date of the child's birth that the depression and the return of her panic had commenced. Rational–emotive therapy proved helpful here as well as her involvement in Adoptee Liberty Movement Association (ALMA, an adoptees organization). After 3 months of bimonthly therapy, she was again discharged.

SUMMARY

This case exemplifies a number of important variables in Multimodal Therapy: (1) comprehensiveness in assessment; (2) comprehensiveness in treatment; (3) logical movement across modalities to be treated with interventions developed according to bridging and tracking principles.

In addition, however, this case shows how even the most careful assessment–intervention program can be sabotaged by unknown variables that cannot be assured other than through the client's honesty and candor. In this case I believe my persistent questions around the issue of why relapse had occurred, together with the shared assessment and treatment plan strategies and the openness of our relationship, facilitated her important disclosure. Trust, although a nonspecific factor in all good therapy, appeared to be maximized in this case by a thorough understanding on both the patient and the therapist's part of the specifics of her anxiety disorder. Without this understanding of the process of therapy on her part, I doubt if the disclosure of the guilt which had led to her depression and relapse would have been made. In essence, this case shows how multimodal therapy combines both art and science in the remediation of problems that other orientations may find intractable.

REFERENCES

Chambless, D. L., & Goldstein, A. J. (Eds.). (1982). *Agoraphobia: Multiple perspectives on theory and treatment.* New York: Wiley.
Ellis, A., & Greiger, R. (1977). *Handbook of rational–emotive therapy.* New York: Springer.
Franks, C. M., Wilson, G. T., Kendall, P. C., & Brownell, K. D. (1982). *Annual review of behavior therapy* (Vol. 8). New York: Guilford Press.
Goldstein, A. J. (1982). Agoraphobia: Treatment successes, treatment failures, and theoretical implications. In D. L. Chambless & A. J. Goldstein (Eds.), *Agoraphobia: Multiple perspectives on theory and treatment.* New York: Wiley.
Lazarus, A. A. (1973). *Multimodal behavior therapy: Treating the BASIC I.D. Journal of Nervous and Mental Disease, 156,* 404–411.
Lazarus, A. A. (1976). *Multimodal behavior therapy.* New York: Springer.
Lazarus, A. A. (1981). *The practice of multimodal therapy.* New York: McGraw-Hill.

12

The Multimodal Approach: A Case Study

LUIS R. NIEVES

Multimodal assessment and therapy emphasize the need to ferret out highly specific antecedent and maintaining factors, whereupon each problem area receives clearly focused interventions. In this chapter, Luis Nieves outlines the specific details that point to the principal target areas for effective treatment. He shows how multimodal methods encompass (1) specification of goals and problems; (2) specification of treatment techniques to achieve these goals and remedy these problems; and (3) systematic measurement of the relative success of these interventions. When describing "Norma" and her problems, it is clear that the multimodal framework provides an integrative therapy plan that considers the whole person without sacrificing precision. It is also evident that the multimodal approach (as some critics have alleged) is not a fragmented or mechanistic barrage of techniques. Nieves shows how the procedures follow logically and blend smoothly into meaningful interventions.

PRELIMINARY INFORMATION

Client: "Norma" (this name is for identification only)
Age: 25 years
Education: MA, Performing Arts, recent graduate
Referred: by previous client
Present occupational activity: unemployed
Living arrangement: single, living with parents
Physical characteristics: visible weight problem, short, facially attractive
Financial status: 100% dependent on parents
Other relevant information: At the time of the initiation of therapy, Norma had returned to her childhood home after 6 years of undergraduate and graduate training at a private institution in a neighboring state. Her parents expected that she would find employment and generally follow the regular developmental stages of marriage, children, and so on.

Norma's older brother (aged 30 years) was married and lived away from the parents' home. She expressed strong resentment and hatred for her brother. Norma's family was middle class.

PRESENTING PROBLEM

CLIENT'S VIEW

Norma described her major problems as "irrational fears, low self-image, overweight, psychosomatic symptoms in the forms of attacks (hyperventilating), periods of prolonged and constant fear." She expanded her description to include regular and severe headaches, insomnia, shaking fits, and an array of additional somatic problems including stomach and chest pains. Norma described her symptoms as "moderately severe" although she was experiencing the hyperventilation attacks daily (four to five times a day).

Since the inception of the physical shaking, 4 weeks previously, Norma had been unable to sleep in her own bed and was now sleeping regularly with one of her parents. She described any attempt to sleep in her own bed as resulting in an overpowering fear of dying if she fell asleep. Norma's daily routine was marred by the fear that an "attack" would overpower her at any moment, so she refrained from leaving the house. Norma reported some relief from these symptoms when she did not go out of the house, and at these times was more successful in sleeping alone in her room.

In the initial interview Norma stressed her strong ties with the past; these were closely associated with her present home, in which she also grew up. The survival of childish gestures as "wriggling her nose," and her self-image "I've been fat all my life" seemed to support her behaviors and fears. Norma articulated her immediate concerns as a dislike for the unstructured postgraduate world, fear of job hunting, fear of rejection (job hunt and social life). She mourned the "good friends" and the structured world she left behind at school and described a pervasive feeling of being alone. She expressed being very conscious of her dependency on her parents and the fact that dating was avoided because it frightened her. Men characteristically had responded to her as a "buddy" but not, she complained, as the girl you would take to a dance. Norma reported that she had the opportunity and considered the possibility of joining a "gay" crowd as an alternative to dating, but concluded that she hated that lifestyle and was now emphatic about "making it in the straight world."

During the next phase of the initial interview, Norma described her brother as "big," "rough," "unaffectionate." She said that she was unloved by her brother and was the constant target of his verbal abuse. He was perceived as smart and witty, and used these attributes to criticize her. In describing the family matrix Norma reported that she was close to her father and was, in fact, like him; her mother, like her brother, was perceived as a powerhouse. She said her father was "disintegrating," a result of the normal aging process, and that she would probably have to stand alone against the traditional mother–son alliance.

At this point in the initial interview, Norma experienced one of her attacks, with muscle spasms, and collapsed. This episode subsided immediately after Norma breathed into a paper bag, confirming the hypothesis that she was hyperventilating. She became calm and was able to resume normal discussion.

THERAPIST'S VIEW

On first impression the following hypotheses and patterns were organized to direct future sessions:

1. Norma's accustomed structure had now been disrupted by her graduation, and she lacked the behavioral skills to define a structure for herself. Another way to put this is that Norma had no familiar script to follow and was now behaving in a confused manner, unable to define priorities and develop a plan of action. Old scripts as child, comedienne, buddy, dependent student, and so on, were now inappropriate. There were no comparable or understandable scripts to play.

2. Norma felt confused without a script, very frightened at the new and unfamiliar expectations she now perceived, and obligated to fulfill these expectations, yet at the same time, incabable of doing so. Confusion, fear of failure, fear of being unable to live up to the next set of expectations, fear of being rejected, and so on, dominated and pervaded a large part of her daily living. Norma also felt anger, specifically directed toward her brother because he was so capable; by contrast, she felt inadequate and incompetent. This anger was only heightened when her brother tormented her by pointing out her weaknesses and predicting failure for her. She felt her father, her strong ally, was losing his ability to protect her.

3. Norma felt unsure of her sexuality. Threatened by the implications of her traditional "buddy" role with men substituting for the preferred feminine role, she flirted with a gay lifestyle but ultimately rejected it. Lacking the confidence for an easy acceptance to sexuality, she rejected interpersonal opportunities and guarded against easy exploration and development in this area.

4. Norma had a very oppressive self-image. Being significantly overweight dominated her self-perceptions. She saw herself as sexually un-

attractive and "physically disgusting." Perceptions of future doom, failure, and death dominated her reveries and daydreams.

5. Norma had many rules and imperatives, which were frequently contradictory, and which she felt compelled to follow, but was unsuccessful in her attempts. These included expectations that she would be a good homemaker, daughter, and a professional success; must always be amusing to others; must not be boring; should enjoy and be good at sex; must be thin in order to be attractive and worthwhile; must find a job; must be independent; and overall must meet the expectations of others.

6. For Norma, relationships seemed to require structure in order for her to successfully handle them. Thus, her role as student, friend, and performer were all successful. Less effective for her were roles as lover, daughter to mother, and sister to brother. She was positively frightened of adult roles as employee, independent single (living in her own apartment), and generally having responsibility for herself.

7. Norma had very poor health and dieting habits. She was a compulsive eater, had no exercise, used aspirin and painkillers, and relied heavily on mild tranquilizers (Serax) to sleep and cope with stress.

A variety of observations assisted the writer in developing hypotheses about the course of the problem and the factors maintaining it, and also suggested treatment directions. Most helpful was the multimodal analysis, which generally suggested that Norma had a narrow behavioral repertoire appropriate only to a limited setting and specific conditions which no longer existed; that she was reacting with extreme anxiety over the changes in her life; and that historically Norma lacked sensory awareness and consequently could not call on traditional sensory strengths to combat the anxiety, which expressed itself through somatic symptoms. There was, for Norma, a highly active imagination focused into the tragedies, traumas, and pitfalls that lay ahead. These images of failure and disaster exacerbated the anxiety reaction. The thought pattern consisting of her negative self-image and statements of incompetence also served to underscore the behavioral and affective defeat patterns.

All of these patterns seemed to form together in an interpersonal style that was rigid and prescribed by familiar surroundings and expectations. New situations did not elicit any behavioral, affective, and cognitive repertoire, which supported Norma's compulsion to comply with perceived expectations of success and competence. Instead, these deficiencies underscored expectations of failure and incompetence. The current reliance on tranquilizers and overeating as coping mechanisms were serving to block new developments in Norma's coping armamentarium.

There was, indeed, in Norma's story, a listing of underlying conflict, anger, and frustration. Her identification with her father as the weak, sensitive one, contrasted with her description of her mother and brother as "powerhouses" of success and efficiency.

Norma's motivation for therapy seemed very strong. She was seeking help on her own volition and had previously undertaken professional help.

HISTORY OF THE PROBLEM

The presenting psychophysiological problems, including severe headaches, insomnia, heart palpitations, chest pains, muscle spasms, and general weakness, began 4 weeks before the initial contact. No single precipitating event could be identified; rather, general life situations seemed to precipitate the symptoms. The more pervasive adjustment problems had an insidious onset beginning in late childhood and early adolescence. Various symptoms, including nervous tics and compulsive finger snapping, were characteristic of Norma's development since adolescence.

No significant medical problems were reported other than the typical childhood diseases. There was no known history of emotional disorder on either side of the family.

Interpersonal problems with men had characterized Norma's college and graduate school experience. Doubts about her self-worth and fear of death, rejection, ridicule, failure, and of never losing weight always had a dominant role in Norma's life. They were particularly strong forces in blocking appropriate heterosexual behavior. Norma nevertheless functioned well in the school environment by substituting group membership for individual heterosexual relationships (the latter being preferred but unattainable).

Norma's middle-class upbringing by high-achieving and high-aspiring parents was generally stressful. She judged herself the least worthy, most needy and most overshadowed by an assertive mother and brother, as well as a warm but weak father. Patterns of self-doubt emerged early in Norma's development, coupled with anxious striving for approval. None of Norma's anxious reactions had ever reached the level of severity characterizing the present psychophysiological and phobic symptoms representing her problem.

PREVIOUS TREATMENT HISTORY

Norma had received 3 years of psychotherapy in the college counseling center as an undergraduate student. The problems then were overeating and general anxiety reactions, as well as fears that she would be unable to cope with college life. In addition, and during an overlapping period, Norma underwent 3 years of psychoanalysis. She reported that both treatment experiences had been helpful, assisting her to cope with day-to-day events. Norma's current problem ostensibly had no connection with previous problems. She attributed this new problem to more complex life forces that therefore required a different kind of help. She was not aware that for each new stage of her life she had acquired a symptomatology that required psychological treatment.

ASSESSMENT AND TREATMENT

A multimodal assessment was conducted and maintained throughout the course of treatment. The questions and answers generated by the assessment were as follows:

Behavior
1. What were the antecedents and consequences of the attacks?
2. What possible secondary gains were there for the attacks?
3. Can competing responses be identified?
4. Which behaviors contribute to the problem?
5. Which behaviors can relieve the problem?

Affect
1. What are the dominant feeling states?
2. What factors (behavior, events, or thoughts) control and maintain the dominant feeling?
3. What factors control positive feelings?

Sensation
1. What are the familiar sensory pleasures?
2. How is this modality related to the problem?
3. How can sensory awareness contribute to the alleviation of the problem?

Imagery
1. Are there identifiable pervasive negative images?
2. How do images contribute to the main problem?
3. What are some positive images?

Cognition
1. What is the belief set contributing to the feeling of inferiority?
2. What are the dominant imperatives? Values?
3. How are the imperatives used to maintain the main problem?

Interpersonal relationships
1. What are the dominant interpersonal styles? Under what circumstances?
2. How is interpersonal behavior affected by the behavioral, affective, and cognitive dimensions of the problem?

Drugs/biology
1. What are the main causes of Norma's overweight condition?
2. How do eating and exercise habits contribute to the problem?
3. How does the drug and alcohol use contribute to the problem?

These questions represent the preliminary questions, which were used to guide the assessment. Assessment and intervention were reciprocally utilized throughout the treatment program. Many more questions than those outlined above proved to be important as treatment proceeded, guided by the multimodal assessment strategy. These only represent an initial set, which served to guide the inquiry and define intervention points.

The problem was redescribed as the assessment proceeded. Norma had a dominant thought that she would be inadequate and incapable of fulfilling parental, social, and personal expectations as a postgraduate adult. She was, in a way, certain that she would fail, and further, that this failure would be traumatic and had to be avoided at all costs. Should she fail, she thought, she would then prove herself unworthy of membership in her family.

These beliefs about the need to succeed supported a network of fears related to failure and the consequences of failure. Feeling like a failure was paralleled by feeling unloved and unworthy. Being unworthy was judged to be the ultimate sin or worse possible condition. Thus, beliefs about achievement and the necessity for achievement created the groundwork for a set of fears about failure and the consequences of not measuring up.

Psychosomatic symptoms, as opposed to other symptoms, seemed to have a logic after Norma explained that what she had done well all her life was to be a "child." As a dependent person relying on the structure of parental rules or school rules, Norma was relatively happy and functional. In these conditions she escaped from demanding situations by being "sick." When Norma was sick at school, she was allowed to come home, make up work later, and so on. When she was sick at home, she was excused from many obligations. It could be said that this pattern was continuing in that a new set of obligations (seeking a job) was perceived by Norma, and, fearing failure, she found an excuse which was accepted. Thus, cognitions about what was a legitimate excuse might have directed the symptoms (medical reports had shown no organic etiology).

An exploration of dominant images revealed that Norma had recurring pictures of being rejected at interviews, and of being rejected and ostracized by peers and men because she was obese. Very little of Norma's use of imagery ever focused on coping, success, or positive areas. This pattern supported the fear of failure and influenced the value judgment placed on the consequences of failure.

The high values for a contribution to society, keeping the family tradition of excellence, and being good at things, were a natural set of values resulting from Norma's family life. She had always been expected to "do well" at school and socially, in order to compete favorably with neighborhood children. These patterns helped to develop a strong belief that she must do well in all things at all times; failure was inexcusable. These beliefs helped support another debilitating belief that Norma had: She had to please everybody all the time or have a good excuse for failing to do so.

These beliefs and their related impact on Norma's fears and imagined failure may have been the foundation for Norma's neurotic symptomatology. Her developing agoraphobia protected her from fulfilling personal obligations and expectations. Behaviorally, then, she was becoming housebound, afraid to go out because she might have an attack at any time. Thus, she restricted her interpersonal interaction and any external activity; this kept her at home and away from the demanding situations.

Finally, the high state of generalized anxiety was occasionally relieved by extraordinary quantities of sweets and large servings of other foods at meals. Smoking marijuana and cigarettes and drinking liquor were strategies of relief, used differently depending on the situation. Marijuana and liquor were used on social occasions; cigarettes were relied upon when she was alone.

This assessment suggested that a broad-spectrum psychoeducational program might prove to be most beneficial as a beginning point. Norma had already undergone 3 years of psychoanalytic therapy. What was now needed was a practical life-skills program that encouraged adult functioning and provided for the development of adult skills and the confidence to engage in the adult world. It would be beneficial to start with such an intervention while searching for opportunities to develop different strategies with the momentum of high motivation. The broad-spectrum approach might offer early and more immediate relief from the debilitating effects of the symptom constellation.

The Multimodal Profile presented in Table 12-1 lists the problem areas and a treatment regimen. The course of the treatment required different modalities to receive attention at different times. For example, it was important to demonstrate that Norma could control the hyperventilation attacks by breathing into a paper bag (inhalation exercise). This was done in the first session when Norma experienced one of her attacks.

TABLE 12-1. Norma's Multimodal Profile

Modality	Problem	Treatment
Behavior	Early agoraphobia, failure to assert with men	Self-control training, reinforcement management and controlling antecedents, positive activity exercises
Affect	General anxiety related to fear of failure, low self-esteem, feeling inferior to brother and other members of her family; occasional depression mixed with manic episodes	Densensitization, role rehearsal, time projection
Sensation	Hyperventilation, muscle strain, secondary orgasmic dysfunction, difficulty sleeping	Inhalation exercise, relaxation training, sensate focus
Imagery	Rejection on employment interviews, being snubbed because she is obese	Positive imagery exercises
Cognition	Belief that one must meet expectations of others, succeed at all endeavors, and generally be an achieving person	Rational–emotive therapy, disputation and self-talk, bibliotherapy, cognitive restructuring
Interpersonal relationships	Role as entertainer, the funny one (clown), unassertive with others, performing for the approval of others	Assertiveness training
Drugs/biology	Overeating, lack of exercise, over-dependence on Valium and Serax	Weight-control program, exercise program

This was followed by a process designed to identify and clarify the characteristics of the person she wanted to be. Norma was asked to write scripts of the "adult Norma." Emphasis was placed on the need for Norma to disengage from the need to comply with her parents' expectations and provide maximum emphasis on her wishes and preferences.

Rational–emotive therapy was woven into every session from the start. By the fourth session the hyperventilation symptoms had disappeared, although for some time after that Norma continued to carry the paper bag. Reinforcing adult behavior through cognitive restructuring characterized the next two sessions before the introduction of behavioral self-control techniques. The control of behavior and thoughts was thoroughly discussed as a way of influencing feeling states. A self-control program, coupled with relaxation training, concluded the sixth session. In the seventh session Norma reported that almost all the symptoms had abated.

In an additional six sessions, while no symptoms were reported, a multimodal self-assessment and self-control program was discussed in a psychoeducational context. This included self-assessment exercises (descriptions of deficits and excesses). Relaxation training was continued in the eighth session, coupled with imagery specifically directed at her sleeping difficulty.

The cognitive restructuring effort was having a definable result, and Norma was now expressing her views more frankly with her parents when her opinions differed from theirs. Independence activities at home were assigned and encouraged; these were designed to help Norma become functionally independent. All of these efforts were showing results, so that from sessions 4–10, steady progress was made.

At the 10th session the weight problem was directly addressed, coupled with an assertiveness training regimen utilizing dating, and more mature ways of communicating with her parents. The weight-control program and assertiveness training interacted to accelerate the progress. Norma, during the 12th–16th sessions, was losing weight gradually and steadily, and expressing more confidence with men, as well as showing signs of positive feelings of self-worth.

Beginning in the 15th session, specific problem solving dominated the sessions, coupled with a general review of progress in each of the modalities. All the elements of the treatment plan had now been instituted except a direct effort to overcome the sexual dysfunction.

This part of the program was initiated in the 16th session and was developed together with an interpersonal skills program on dating and relating to men. At the 20th weekly session, rehearsal for job interviews and related information discussions were initiated.

By the 22nd session, Norma had a job as a theater arts teacher; she was going out with several men and was having sexual relations with one of them. Although Norma was still nonorgasmic during penetration, she reported feeling more comfortable and experiencing orgasms from manual and oral stimulation.

Termination discussions began at the 24th session. Norma had now lost 28 pounds and was having no trouble maintaining the weight-control program (intake control coupled with exercise). Norma was now working and enjoying better interactions with her parents. Her feelings of hostility toward her brother had subsided, and she now was experiencing more filial interactions and emotions.

Termination occurred after the 26th session. Norma had found an apartment and her move was imminent. Norma was seen for the last time 3 months after her termination interview for a specific problem-solving session, but at the time, none of her symptoms had returned and she characterized herself as "coping admirably."

SUMMARY AND CONCLUDING STATEMENT

The case of Norma was presented within the multimodal treatment approach (Lazarus, 1973, 1976, 1981). This approach draws heavily from the social learning theory (Bandura, 1969). Norma's learning history seemed to be the foundation for the behavioral and affective patterns that proved maladaptive for her in her functioning in the adult world.

The treatment, then, focused on teaching new behavioral and adaptive patterns that were functional under different environmental conditions. Rational–emotive therapy (Ellis, 1962) was the treatment of choice to change the cognitive assumptions that supported the maladaptive behavior patterns. Relaxation training and self-management (Thoresen & Mahoney, 1974) were directed at overeating and problems of behavioral excesses. Assertiveness training (Alberti & Emmons, 1974; Lange & Jakubowski, 1976) was the treatment of choice for interpersonal deficits.

A broad range of techniques were employed to carefully offer support within the multimodal approach (Lazarus, 1981). Under this approach it is theorized that a complete therapy must direct treatment interventions to seven different personality modalities: Behavior, Affect, Sensation, Imagery, Cognition, Interpersonal relationships, and Drugs/biology (Lazarus, 1973).

REFERENCES

Alberti, R. E., & Emmons, M. L. (1974). *Your perfect right: A guide to assertive behavior* (2nd ed.). San Luis Obispo, CA: Impact Press.

Bandura, A. (1969). *Principles of behavior modification.* New York: Holt, Rinehart & Winston.

Ellis, A. (1962). *Reason and emotion in psychotherapy.* New York: Lyle Stuart.

Lange, A. J., & Jakubowski, P. (1976). *Responsible assertive behavior: Cognitive behavioral procedures for trainers.* Champaign, IL: Research Press.

Lazarus, A. A. (1973). Multimodal behavior therapy: Treating the BASIC I.D. *Journal of Nervous and Mental Disease, 156,* 404–441.

Lazarus, A. A. (1976). *Multimodal behavior therapy.* New York: Springer.

Lazarus, A. A. (1981). *The practice of multimodal therapy.* New York: McGraw-Hill.

Thoresen, C. E., & Mahoney, M. J. (1974). *Behavioral self-control.* New York: Holt, Rinehart & Winston.

13

The Case of Sally: Heuristic Questions, Speculative Answers

MARTIN YANIS

It needs to be understood that while all multimodal therapists are eclectic, all eclectic therapists are not multimodal therapists. Current psychotherapy is characterized by multidimensional, multidisciplinary, and multifaceted interventions. Many therapists embrace multifactorial and multiform assessment and treatment procedures. The foregoing approaches are not synonymous with "multimodal therapy." To underscore this point, when Martin Yanis showed me the write-up of "The Case of Sally," which exemplified a thorough and skillful psychotherapeutic handling by a competent eclectic clinician, I asked him if he would care to speculate as to important differences that may have arisen had he used multimodal assessment and therapy. I found his chapter most illuminating, and I trust that the reader will agree that Yanis's exposition provides nourishing food for thought.

HOW THIS CHAPTER CAME ABOUT

The reporter on this case came to multimodal therapy in midcareer. While I had heard of the type of systematic eclecticism advocated by Arnold A. Lazarus, and while I had read about prescriptive eclecticism published by Dimond, Havens, and Jones (1978), I had rarely found it necessary to prefix any adjective to the Yanis brand of eclecticism. The exception could occur in conversations with colleagues known to adhere (or "suspected" of adhering) to a particular doctrine of therapy (or to the doctrine that one comprehensive and exclusive therapy doctrine is necessary), and perhaps known to be judgmental about others of a different persuasion. For such dialogues I would, if necessary, hoist my banner and "show the flag" by identifying myself as an unapologetic eclectic. Such "chutzpa" would on occasion evoke in the listener the very combativeness it was supposed to avoid, but that's another story.

The occasion of settling in the geographic area close to this volume Editor's base of teaching, research, and practice provided the opportunity for me to show him a report of therapy I recently concluded with a 43-year-old woman given the name Sally. Since the multichannel approach used in this case seems to have had favorable results, and since the founder of multimodal therapy has an understandable interest in the possible net-effect differences between "unsystematic eclecticism" (Lazarus, 1981, p. 4) and multimodal therapy, we decided I would design and carry out an independent thought experiment. One immediate purpose would be to communicate to others a retrospective analysis, by one practitioner, of one case that gave him professional satisfaction—said analysis being carried out under the self-discipline imposed by an itemized agenda of "What if I had used multimodal therapy?"

The present report begins with an abstract of the therapy as it was actually done, then moves on to a comparison of what took place with what would have or might have taken place under the hypothetical condition of the same therapist's having been a practitioner of multimodal therapy. Samenesses are duly noted; differences are sniffed out and held up to the light. Contrasts are what we are looking for. Finally, I try to draw some conclusions.

TREATMENT COMPLETED: AN ABSTRACT

It was in a suburban independent-practice setting that Sally consulted me at the urging of her 22-year-old daughter, a college student. The client, a 43-year-old married white mother of three, employed in an office, asked this daughter to attend the entire first session. Presenting complaints included perceived severe marital dysfunction punctuated by her fear of repeating a dimly recalled physical attack on her husband, anxieties and depressions over numerous past and future events, unhappiness in her job, and clashes and concerns with respect to her children. Implicit problems and complaints included inappropriate use of alcoholic beverages, ambivalences in almost every area of living, and an apparently long-standing cognitive–affective style that seemed to confine her and drive her along a submissive, duty-bound track in life and to stand in the way of enjoyment.

The course of progress in treatment seems to have been almost uninterruptedly upward, starting with the palpably reduced worry over her potential for violence that was evident by session 2, up to and including posttermination reports (after 22 weekly sessions) of improved relationships with her husband and children and a somewhat more tranquil outlook on life-cycle events in her family.

Assessment in this case began with the two telephone conversations that preceded Session 1. Assessment continued through semistructured interviewing, through formal and quasi-formal procedures—such as the

Millon Clinical Multiaxial Inventory (1976) (MCMI), Female Assertiveness Inventory,[1] diary keeping, and episode-analysis assignments—and through some completely informal clinical "tests" based on experience. Interventions stemmed from two kinds of sources, the reactive and the proactive. In other words, in some instances an intervention would flow from a client question of the type "How can I solve the problem of . . . ?" In other instances, the therapist provided the impetus. I would have identified some aspect of the client's outlook, personality stimulus value, behavior repertoire, or imminent or future life situation in which improvement or planning was indicated. Or I would want to do some exploring. Any therapeutic goals so derived could still be decided jointly.

Unlike those humanistic psychologists who suggest the clients always know best, I believe we owe it to our clients to apprise them, sooner or later, of anything that our assessment art and science tell us makes them different with implications for their self-understanding and their self-guidance. Accordingly, I use so-called personality inventories not because I accept all the tenets of the trait theorists, but because their products can be useful in putting vital personal issues on the table. Following is the way I implemented the aforementioned proactive policy with Sally. The MCMI asks the client to answer "true" or "false" to 175 printed statements describing "your feelings and attitudes." Based on both empiric and *a priori* keying, the scoring program then prints out a histogram of trait scores, followed by verbal statements derived from these scores that are addressed to the five axes of DSM-III.

Relying mostly on the scale scores (and partly on what the client has told me about himself or herself and his or her problems), I try to weave a spoken personality analysis or "character sketch" for the client to listen to while he or she looks at the histogram and I point out the relevant "long bars" and "short bars." What the client presumably hears is an objective account of what this neutral nonjudgmental measuring instrument says about how he or she compares on many human qualities with others in his or her group. The client also hears how an interpreter and synthesizer of such chunks of data would put them all together into a unified and sympathetic portrait of a coping and still developing human being. As for the inferential verbal statements that are derived from the scale scores, I select not more than a dozen of them and copy them individually on separate 2" × 2" cards for client reading and sorting. The yield from this assignment is from one to five stacks of statements placed in one or more of the five solid squares in Figure 13-1.

The client's participation may have been largely passive in the "character sketch" undertaking, but it has to be quite active in the sorting assignment. Several benefits seem to flow from this combination of

1. This was an unstandardized, informal measure printed in a women's magazine.

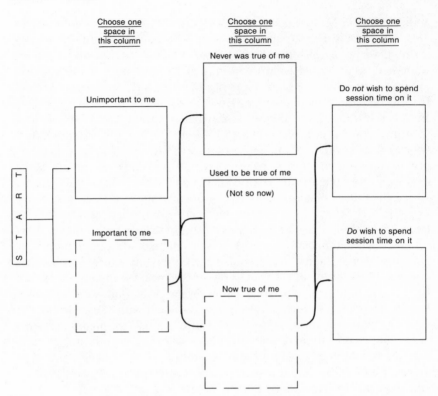

FIGURE 13-1. Sort of MCMI statements. Client "walks" each statement through from left to right.

passive followed by active. One is that the contemplation of what a supposed expert says makes the client tick is followed soon after by an invitation to the client to make judgments of his or her own. These judgments are forced choice, to be sure, but in this social context I think they come across as free and democratic in flavor. Another benefit is that, as the client's judgments are asked for and obtained, the accompanying discussion sets the stage for a consideration of possibly additional treatment goals that may be broader and deeper than surface complaints or initially presented problems. In the case of Sally my expectations for the above MCMI procedure were borne out rather well. Her penchants for data and for direction were displayed at this juncture. She took notes during this session and continued to take occasional notes (with carbon copies for our dossier) at most sessions thereafter. The sort assignment turned out to be a bit of a strain for her, but the effort seems to have paid dividends. I believe the process of her becoming aware of the variety of ways to resolve the dilemma of emerging from a life-long submissive role got started here. Another dividend was to strengthen our understanding of the source and maintenance factors in her particular depressive syndrome.

A list of the discrete and nameable therapeutic tactics I used might give a theoretical purist indigestion. Their heterogeneity stems from a desire on my part to fit therapeutic interventions to the client's particular need and to the particular stage of client recovery. The tactics used follow:

1. Reassurance based on empathy, reasoned analysis, and an early use of telephone support.
2. Moderately structured anamnesis and opportunities for ventilation.
3. Analysis and discussion of assessment instrument findings.
4. Review of diary for perspective on her satisfactions and dissatisfactions and for leads to purpose-in-living types of discussion.
5. Teaching on the origins of personality traits.
6. Assertion training coupled with instruction on self and other behavior shaping.
7. A number of maneuvers scattered throughout the course of therapy intended to strengthen self-esteem. For example, an assignment to "list your strengths and assets"; this led to extensive analysis, discussion, and cognitive reframing during sessions 11 and 12.
8. Discussions of the availability of natural relaxation techniques and of biofeedback approaches to greater self-control, but no formal training in either.

As reflected in posttermination correspondence and calls, Sally improved in all the major areas she had brought to my attention, with the possible exceptions of adjustment to her elderly father's decline and to the mortality of humankind in general. (Termination of therapy, somewhat too soon due to my change in residence, precluded coming to grips with this enduring issue.) In addition I would like to think that some progress was made in reworking certain mental sets and expectancies that seemed maladaptive to likely future life challenges.

THE THOUGHT EXPERIMENT

I turn now with trepidation to the task of reporting private imaginings in a public milieu. It was during my attendance of an advanced workshop on multimodal therapy that I started to wonder about ways to begin assimilating some of the procedures I was finding both cogent and compatible with my earlier strongly held eclectic ways.

As explained in Chapter 1, the usual way to get multimodal therapy started in earnest is to give the client the 12-page Multimodal Life History Questionnaire (MMLHQ) to fill out between sessions 1 and 2. The client's answers to its 390 wide-ranging items are then used by the therapist to prepare the seven-part Modality Profile. This is a fractional distillation and resynthesis of symptoms, complaints, and problems from the vast material in the MMLHQ and from the interviews up to that point. Usually the Modality Profile then serves as a basis for discussion and treatment planning with the client.

One variant of this procedure is to entrust the preparation of the Modality Profile directly to the client by giving him or her the much shorter three-page form, Personality Profile (PP). This form asks the client to focus on his or her own Actions, Affect, Images, Thoughts, Relationships, and Physical Health. The client is to recall as much as possible, and write in the scratch space provided for each of these seven modalities the negatives he or she has experienced in each. Then, in the Columnar Summary on the last page of PP, the client transcribes in condensed form only that which he or she wants to increase and that which he or she wants to decrease in each of the seven modalities. Thus, the Columnar Summary represents a telescoping by the client in do-it-yourself fashion of the more extensive diagnostic process that customarily begins with the 12-page MMLHQ and requires a substantial amount of therapist time for clinical processing.

Phase 1 of this thought experiment consists of challenging myself to see how well I knew Sally. How closely could my filling out the PP approximate the way she would have filled it out? While a fully quantitative answer might not be possible, the attempt could be instructive. My first step was to try it without session notes or other written cues, simply answering the questions printed on the PP: "What would you like to start DOING? . . . stop DOING? Write down your unwanted EMOTIONS. Make a list of any negative SENSATIONS. . . . (And so on.)" The yield from this was ample for Physical Health, Images, Thoughts, and Relationships; sparse for Sensations; and moderate for Actions and Affect. (The next step would have been to look in the written record for clues to more PP entires, but it is my duty to report that the self-challenge for this line of effort dwindled, and my response potential dropped below the threshold of overt expression. In other words, I didn't do this next step.)

What are we to make of the paucity of my recall of her verbalized Sensations and the plethora in my recall of her responses in Physical Health, Images, Thoughts, and Relationships? These differences could tell us how much the client talked about, and was troubled with, the respective modalities. These differences could also tell us how much the therapist facilitated talk about these modalities. Phase 2 of the thought experiment came later when this volume was under way, and I was asked to redirect my attention to the larger question of how this case would have turned out if I had been a user of multimodal therapy from the start. This is a problem in postdiction of a sort that, unlike certain others in the literature, cannot ever be settled. Moreover, a bit of reflection suggests that contained within this large question, "How would this case have turned out if I had been a multimodal therapist?," are at least three component, stepwise subquestions, namely:

1. What would I, the therapist, have done? (Call this *Operational postdiction.*)

    Then, assuming my answer to Subquestion 1 is OK . . .
2. What would Sally's overt and covert, immediate and delayed responses have been? (Call this *Client response postdiction.*)

    Then, assuming my answer to Subquestion 2 is OK . . .
3. What would have been the net therapeutic effect, and when? (Call this *Effects postdiction.*)

Associated with all data, including objective and quantitative data, is the uncertainty principle. In a book of case reports, data can also be drawn from sources that are subjective and qualitative. The three-stage procedure just described includes such data. Since each stage builds on the preceding, the logic of this situation requires that we acknowledge the cumulativeness of uncertainty in the heuristic question and its answer at the latter two stages.

Let us look now at some specific "what-if's." What differences would there have been in session 1 if I had been a practitioner of multimodal therapy?

Operational postdiction: Assuming that early in the session the client and I seemed to be moving toward continuation of services beyond session 1, I would have had the MMLHQ in mind to give her near the end of session 1. Accordingly, instead of using my two-sided Couple Intake blank as a checklist for significant dimensions of people's lives and as a collector of vital biographic information, I would at the outset have asked for permission to record the session and probably slanted the discussion toward maximum utilization of the opportunity afforded by the daughter's presence. Thus I would have been sparser in my writing (customarily I take unstructured notes on a blank sheet of ruled paper, as well as structured notes on the intake form) and more of a catalyst toward self-expression by, and between, the mother and daughter.

Client response postdiction: Clients differ appreciably. Some clients feel more comfortable during their first session, others, less comfortable, in proportion to the amount of attentive writing being done by their new helper. (The junctures in dialogue at which the pen-in-hand starts to move is also a determinant of client comfort, and the reader is asked to hold that parameter constant while considering this generalization.) My guess is that Sally, a dutiful homemaker and a highly principled person, very unsure of herself in the emotionally charged new situation that therapy presented, derived real comfort from seeing some of her key words being written down. I believe that the pacing helped her collect her thoughts and that the attention strengthened her battered self-esteem. By contrast, tape-recording, if authorized, and immediate talk focusing on her filial (and other?) problems might have put her "on display" and made her uncomfortable. What then?

Effects postdiction: In the short term I think the dynamics-oriented dialogue or trialogue might have shaken her hunch and hope that coming for psychological help would be good for her. It might have exacerbated, or at least highlighted, the mother–daughter tensions that they seemed to have shelved in view of "Mom . . . [being] . . . on the verge of a divorce." The therapy undertaking might have started to look unproven and controversial early in the session. In the long run, however, I postdict no difference in effects. Therapist radar would have sensed what issues were in greatest need of attention to save the client for the full helping process she seemed to be tentatively trying out. Most likely the therapist would have set the occasion for enough client expression of her worst fears such as to permit the requisite anxiety reduction to take place (as in the actual case), thereby reinforcing the client's incipient decision to come back for more professional help. Finally, the delivery of the MMLHQ into Sally's hands as an assignment to be completed for session 2 would have had a salutary effect. Throughout treatment she welcomed detailed and thorough analytical approaches to her problems. In actuality, I gave her the MCMI to fill out at home, along with the usual comment, "This is to help me get to know you better sooner; give quick first-thought answers; we'll go over the results together." (She responded with one of the neatest answer sheets I've ever seen, including just two barely detectable erasures.) Either instrument would have enhanced rapport.

Session 2 was exactly 1 week later. About midway during the week, I had telephoned Sally according to our plan made at session 1. The purpose was to give her a chance to report on her greatest fear, that is, repeating anything like a recent episode in which she had been disarmed of a kitchen knife she was brandishing at her husband one night while she was under the influence of alcohol. No overt violence recurred during the week, nor has any since. However, in an infrequently recurring nightmare, Sally later reported she would dream of violence between her husband and herself.

Session 2 (with daughter absent then and thenceforth) covered much ground. Leads opened in session 1 were followed, and anamnestic history was pursued in moderation, with Sally displaying considerable fluency.

Among our conclusions was that she start a daily diary consisting of "Things I Did" and "Other Events of My Day."

Resuming the postdictive thought experiment, I ask what would have been different in session 2 under multimodal therapy.

Operational postdiction: Assuming Sally returned the complete MMLHQ, Modality Profile construction might have started before the end of session 2. More likely, the reading of this richly yielding factual and projective document would have occasioned immediate, relatively focused examination and discussion, filling the entire session.

Client response postdiction: The imagery section is my guess as to where the emphasis in dialogue would have fallen. Predominating would have been memories of her mother dying of cancer, scenes of her two visits to the "old country" in Europe, and pictures of idiosyncratic associations in her mental life (e.g., I am like King Lear in my fatal imperfections).

Effects postdiction: My guess is that earlier and more explicit attention would have been accorded Sally's covert life. Sensations and affect, for example, would have been topics, but I have little basis for estimating how big. To illustrate, while she had in actuality described a minidynamic of how her weekday tensions at the office would often culminate in evening bouts, both with the bottle and with the unreachable clod she was married to, I'm not as clear as I would have become with multimodal therapy as to what part her taste buds or other sensations and feelings (outrage, chemically induced relaxation, synthetic courage?) might have played in the interpersonal arena. Multimodal therapy directs the practitioner toward such "firing order" investigations.

Here is another illustration of how the availability of MMLHQ's 390 written responses would almost certainly have provided quicker entrees to more aspects of Sally's life possibly pertinent to assessment and therapy. In actuality, her affectional life was brought into explicit verbal focus in session 13. This timing was governed chiefly by client readiness and client religious background. If, however, all of MMLHQ's questions had been completed, I would have had a number of options for earlier timing. These options materialize by virtue of an objective and thoroughly professional printed questionnaire, which, in four or five places, provides opportunities to broach topics related to one's sensual, sexual, and affectional life. (When marital dysfunction or marital therapy is the major focus of a referral, I usually use one or more special instruments designed specifically for this subject area.)

I have applied the three-step postdictive process to session 1 and to session 2. Therapy does indeed consist of a series of numbered sessions spaced in time. But therapy also consists of verbal and gestural interactions between two people working on certain problems. I now spell out my postdictions of what differences multimodal therapy would have made in certain processes my client and I underwent.

History taking occupies a position of importance in most therapy systems. (The few systems that downplay it did not arise in private practice, open-marketplace settings wherein early rapport and prompt confidence building are absolute requirements.) If thorough, history taking enhances assessment of the person and his or her problems. If done sensitively, history taking *per se* can serve a therapeutic function even before formal interventions are undertaken.

Operational postdiction: With multimodal therapy sooner or later I would have administered at least the MMLHQ, the Structural Profile, several second-order BASIC I.D.s, and the Deserted Island technique.

Client response postdiction: Sally would have eaten all this up. She liked structure in our sessions, and I rather doubt that I fully satisfied her appetite for structured approaches. Telling about herself was an urge; the techniques we did use facilitated that urge. The four additional techniques mentioned above would have amplified that inner voice so long suppressed. A second-order BASIC I.D. on topics such as her mother's death and her fear of repeating the conjugal attack would have elicited highly motivated participation. Thanks to all modalities' being on our scorecard, the anamnestic process would likely have been intensified.

Effects postdiction: Over the short term, therapeutic change is not likely to have been measurably better. But we would have been busier. In actuality, certain portions of some sessions were, in retrospect, like coasting (it's not necessarily bad if part of a session is not highly goal directed). With multimodal therapy my guess is that a variety of interventions would have always been on tap, tending to make each session eventful. Accordingly, over the coming years, I think she would have a larger store of dramatic recollections to draw on. Take for example the image of Mother dying. Systematic desensitization did not seem strongly indicated, but in the spirit of multimodal therapy, it likely would have been tried.

Let's look at another process. The first process we looked at, "history taking" we called it, is an early (and often continuing) process in which the aim is to get to know the client in as many aspects and nuances as possible, with the hope that we will learn what we need to know in order to be of benefit. A later process Sally and I underwent in the course of this helping–teaching–evolving–maturing relationship resided in how we handled her anxieties and grievances regarding her marriage of 24 years' duration. Scarcely any of the 22 sessions went by without one of us, usually Sally, bringing up Jason, her husband. He was either in the forefront of her mind or in the background in many of the session segments nominally dealing with other problems. It might be no exaggeration to postdict that she would not have consulted a psychologist had it not been for her self-styled "indignation" at the treatment that her husband was meting out to her and their children. Clearly, to her the state of the marriage was pivotal in her troubles.

As her therapist, I inwardly counted on her husband's eventual participation, inasmuch as he was reportedly tolerating her weekly sessions, intimating early that he would be available if she insisted, and allowing very occasionally as how he thought she (!) was "improving." Outwardly, I concentrated on her as a complete person with great potential for self-reliance, who would be well-advised to shoulder the responsibility for her own happiness. I taught her some rudimentary operant shaping applications and also brought to bear some of the more traditional psychological lore that has helped submissive, depressed wives to become "liberated" without necessarily sacrificing their marriages. In writings about the treatment of dyadic relationships, Peter Martin (1976), for example, classifies and analyzes the various approaches relative to who-treats-whom and what to do when one spouse shows reluctance toward any participation. In the case of Sally I attribute our success in helping her to achieve equanimity without the radical surgery of family break-up to Sally's initial open-mindedness toward the idea of "I could be doing better regardless of who is the 'real' culprit." The eclecticism I practiced at that time, albeit somewhat "unsystematized," was suited to such a client because its underlying tenets included "One need not tear down before starting to rebuild," and because it did not sneer at developing remedies for specific problems of daily living. The result approximately 1 year after termination was a greatly improved state of marital well-being.

What if my eclecticism had been multimodal therapy?

Operational postdiction: In addition to discussions with Sally of her feelings and actions toward her nonattending husband, I would have had at my disposal her written answers to 19 printed questions on marital topics in the interpersonal relationships section of the MMLHQ, plus whatever connotative spillover there might have been from such topics into the sections devoted to the other six modalities. In all likelihood, these would have prompted somewhat earlier connections being made between her answers to "Describe your spouse's personality. In what areas are you compatible? . . . incompatible?" and her many unwanted actions, feelings, images, and thoughts.

Client response postdiction: My guess is that Sally would have felt a greater early affinity for psychological treatment, as a function of the MMLHQ's encompassing such problem areas. I retrospectively posit, on her part, feeling tempted to show the questions and her answers to her husband but not doing it. I further posit, but with less confidence, her asking me later in therapy for a blank questionnaire for her to offer to Jason.

Effects postdiction: No significant difference in outcomes. Possibly Sally would have realized the following more quickly and/or more certainly:

1. Her professorial, perfectionist, socially immature, and intellectually mighty husband was limited by personal history and by his preset course of choices.
2. He was doing what he thought was right according to his lights.
3. She would increase her own satisfaction in living by getting together with herself and expanding her horizons with or without Jason.

My guess is that the second-order BASIC I.D. would have accelerated and firmed up these developments.

SUMMARY IMPRESSIONS

A thought experiment of this type could go on forever, but this report must not. There is almost no limit to the number of *post hoc* "what if's" that could be analyzed by the three-step approach used here. The analyses reported are only a subset of those undertaken.

The data assembled in the chapter to this point suggest that a successful case would not have turned out differently in any radical way had the therapist been an adherent to published multimodal procedures. The data also indicate that the therapist wishes he would have had in his armamentarium these same multimodal procedures. His reasons for having this wish seem to have been as follows:

1. Less chance of "missing something" in the assessment.
2. Possibility of picking up some keys to more rapid progress in treatment.
3. Having another well-documented procedure for constructing multidimensional "maps" of clients and their problems, thus possibly supplying an aid to planning the course of therapy.
4. The belief that this particular client would have reacted with enthusiasm to this additional structuring of her sessions.

"Structuring" is also the nub of this reporter's expressed reservations. Over the years he developed his own implicit algorithms for (1) how to involve various kinds of clients in the constructive work of relieving symptoms, solving problems, and enhancing personal development, and (2) what to do if the client–therapist fit seems to be in doubt. (Beyond these algorithms were, of course, the unformalized, semi-intuitive re-

sponses to unique or unforeseen client needs). Since the tangible cornerstone of multimodal therapy is the MMLHQ (I will mention another
cornerstone in a moment), most of the reservations expressed so far
revolve around the introduction of this rather formidable instrument
before we begin to capitalize on its benefits. After its introduction some
questions can be raised from the cost-efficiency standpoint; in other words:
Do the added advantages justify the extra time and effort expended? To
summarize, the possibility of being bound to a procedure is the crux of
this eclectic's reservations. Some of these reservations would be dissipated
by arranging for either MMLHQ or PP to be completed by the client
before he or she arrives, perhaps as a prerequisite for session 1.

A word about the conceptual cornerstone of multimodal therapy. As
I see it, it is "flexibility and versatility in meeting the idiosyncratic needs
of diverse individuals" (Lazarus, 1981, p. 166). Multimodal therapy
operationalizes a principle to which most therapists give lip service. At
least, few would ever explicitly contest it. But how do we know if, in our
allegiance to this principle, we are picking up all that we need to know?
Multimodal therapy provides a tool. The tool has both conceptual roots
and procedural adaptations. Taken together, they offer a great deal to
those of the eclectic persuasions.

REFERENCES

Dimond, R. E., Havens, R. A., & Jones, A. C. (1978). A conceptual framework for the
practice of prescriptive eclecticism in psychotherapy. *American Psychologist, 33*,
239–248.
Lazarus, A. A. (1981). *The practice of multimodal therapy.* New York: McGraw-Hill.
Martin, P. A. (1976). *A marital therapy manual.* New York: Brunner/Mazel.
Millon, T. (1976). *Millon clinical multiaxial inventory.* Minneapolis: National Computer
Systems.

14

The Specificity Factor in Psychotherapy

ARNOLD A. LAZARUS

This chapter looks at the major emphasis of the multimodal orientation, and therefore I thought that it would serve a useful function as the final chapter of this Casebook. The case of Ms. WR underscores the precise multimodal assessment–therapy procedures that separate this approach from most other orientations. This brief overview also stresses the need to determine when and when not to involve families. It goes beyond mere technique selection by listing specific questions that must be asked when a particular method (e.g., relaxation) has been selected. I regard this chapter as one of the most important statements vis-à-vis efficient and effective therapy that I have written.

It is well known that systems, methods, and techniques of psychotherapy continue to proliferate at an astonishing rate. Herink's (1980) potpourri of more than 250 therapies purports to represent only a fraction of extant treatment approaches. Perusal of this bewildering array of psychic nostrums reveals what may be termed a *generalization fallacy*. Instead of providing remedies or strategies for overcoming specific problems, the majority claim to have the answer for all victims of "neurotic suffering," or "emotional disturbance," or other global dysfunctions. Thus, Holden (1980), a primal therapist, states that only the full reexperience of childhood pain "is the way to reverse neurosis." Mowrer (1980) offers "integrity groups," a type of secular confessional, as another all-encompassing solution. Rogerian counselors provide all comers with identical sets of "facilitative conditions." Which particular treatment the consumer receives appears to depend mainly on whose consulting room he or she happens to enter, whether or not this is what he or she requires.

If the same mode of dispensing services pertained to the practice of medicine (psychiatry excluded), we might picture the following scenario: A woman with a sore throat consults a physician whose name she picks out of the telephone book. The MD into whose consulting room she is

From *Psychotherapy in Private Practice*, 1984, *2*, 43–48. Copyright 1984 by the Haworth Press, Inc. Reprinted by permission.

ushered turns out to be a gynecologist. Consequently, the patient undergoes a routine pelvic examination during which a mild infection is discovered. An antibiotic is prescribed resulting in the serendipitous remission of her throat ailment. This felicitous result might lead the patient to seek gynecologic assistance for all future throat ailments. To analogize further from the field of psychotherapy, we would then have a doctor who would insist that the pelvis was the royal road to the pharynx.

In an attempt to avoid the manifold traps of overgeneralization, I have developed a carefully structured set of multimodal assessment procedures (Lazarus, 1981). A brief case presentation will illustrate how multimodal tactics focus on personalistic variables.

Ms. WR, a 32-year-old woman, complained of "panic attacks" that she attributed to her divorce 4 years earlier. At least twice a month, she would experience mounting anxiety for no apparent reason. Occasionally, if sufficiently distracted at the time, she would calm down; if not, her anxiety would escalate into what she termed "a panic attack" replete with intense tachycardia, dizziness, shortness of breath, and nausea. She first consulted her family doctor, who diagnosed her condition as "episodic, acute hyperventilation" and advised her to breathe into a paper bag before her symptoms reached panic proportions. When this proved ineffective, he referred her to a psychiatrist who prescribed a tricyclic antidepressant and, later, a monoamine oxidase inhibitor. This lessened the intensity of her panic attacks but not their frequency. Her next consultant, a psychodynamic psychotherapist, intimated that it was necessary to understand the underlying causes of her anxiety and panic, but indicated that this might take several years, with no guarantees. Instead, she joined a biofeedback clinic and received training in electromyography (EMG), galvanic skin response (GSR), and thermal control, with little benefit.

I was her fourth mental health consultant. She was referred to me by a former client who said that I "dabbled in hypnosis." Instead of "dabbling" with her, or "hypnotizing" her, I conducted a fairly typical initial interview and asked her to complete and mail back by Multimodal Life History Questionnaire (Lazarus, 1981). By the end of our second meeting, two significant findings were apparent:

1. Her divorce was but one of several antecedent factors. Three events that predated her divorce were the death of a close friend, job insecurity due to nonpromotion, and a bout with pneumonia and pleurisy that left her physically debilitated for several months after being hospitalized for more than 2 weeks.

2. Close questioning of Ms. WR revealed that her anxiety and panic followed a fairly distinctive pattern: Something would bring her dead friend to mind and/or her thoughts would drift back to her own spell of physical debilitation. If these thoughts lingered, her mind would immediately flash back to scenes of her friend's funeral and her own hospitalization. If not interrupted at this juncture, she tended to focus on real or imagined negative sensations, which would finally culminate in panic, especially if she got in touch with physical reactions that predominated during her illness and convalescence.

In multimodal terms (Lazarus, 1981) her modality "firing order" usually occurred in the following sequence: Negative *c*ognitions were followed by distressing mental *i*mages, which in turn elicited unpleasant physical *s*ensations, culminating in an *a*ffective anxiety response. We would term this a C-I-S-A pattern (cognition–imagery–sensation–affect). Our experience is that such a patient would respond better to an initial cognitive intervention. Had she followed, say, an S-C-I-A pattern—in which the *sensory mode* initiated the sequence—biofeedback would probably have seen an effective initial treatment. But in this case, where the sensory modality follows cognition and imagery, a predominantly sensory intervention such as biofeedback would not be expected to prove especially helpful until her dysfunctional cognitions and aversive images were brought under control. Please note the treatment specificity that is being addressed here.

First, the client's insight into her own "firing order" enabled her to realize that her "panic attacks" were precipitated by predictable events. Secondly, she learned that to ward off future episodes it was essential to disrupt her negative thoughts and replace them with positive self-statements. Next, her gloomy images were to be deliberately counterposed by scenes that evoked *joie de vivre*. Finally, she was to cultivate subjectively pleasant sensory responses that yielded calm and tranquil emotions (e.g., relaxation, diaphragmatic breathing, and autogenic warmth, heaviness, and peace). These specific objectives were achieved in four sessions. Ms. WR had not suffered a panic attack for almost 4 years. (She has since enrolled in an EdD program in counseling psychology.)

Gordon Paul (1967) was the first to underscore the specificity factor. He asked, "*What* treatment, by *whom*, is most effective for *this* individual with *that* specific problem, and under *which* set of circumstances?" (p. 111). Studies have indicated that patients with identical psychiatric diagnoses fare better when treatment is tailored to individual response patterns. For example, phobic patients may be divided into two broad categories, behavioral reactors and physiological reactors. Clients with social phobias who are "behavioral reactors" responded better to social skills training than to applied relaxation, whereas the latter proved more effective with "physiological reactors." Claustrophobic patients were more responsive to relaxation than to exposure if they were "physiological reactors" whereas "behavioral reactors" found exposure significantly more effective (Öst, Jerrelmalm, & Johansson, 1981; Öst, Johansson, & Jerrelmalm, 1982).

The specificity factor is clearly exemplified by some of the latest findings in the treatment of obsessive–compulsive disorders. *In vivo* exposure is almost a *sine qua non* of effective outcomes (Marks, Hodgson, & Rachman, 1975; Rachman & Hodgson, 1980; Steketee, Foa, & Grayson, 1982). Severely incapacitated patients often require supervision in a psychiatric setting where trained personnel apply *response prevention* (i.e., they ensure that the patients refrain from carrying out their rituals). Three specific findings have emerged:

1. The actual exposure component tends to reduce anxiety.
2. Response prevention reduces the ritualistic behaviors.
3. *Imagined* exposure facilitates the maintenance of therapeutic gains.

(See Foa, Steketee, & Milby, 1980; Foa, Steketee, & Turner, 1980.)

Basically, the specificity factor is concerned with the age-old dictum of finding appropriate treatments for particular patients, instead of performing procrustean maneuvers that force one and all into the same preconceived system. In theory, nearly all therapists appear to be in agreement with the need for flexibility and respectful attention to individual differences. In practice, they often tend to violate the specificity factor. For example, Haley (1976) eloquently stresses that "any standardized method of therapy, no matter how effective with certain problems, cannot deal successfully with the wide range that is typically offered to a therapist. . . . A skillful therapist will approach each new person with the idea that a unique procedure might be necessary for this particular person and social situation" (pp. 9–10). In direct contradiction to the foregoing, Haley then states: "Today it is assumed that to begin therapy by interviewing one person is to begin with a handicap" (p. 10).

I recently interviewed a 24-year-old man who, in his quest for psychotherapy, had telephoned a well-known treatment center for an appointment. He was referred to an "intake receptionist" who ascertained that he was living at home with his parents and younger sister, and insisted that the entire family be present. Unbeknownst to the client, he had called a family therapy center that presumably wished to avoid "beginning therapy with a handicap." For reasons that I will not go into here, in my opinion it would have been a grave mistake for this young man to be seen in family therapy.

The specificity factor goes far beyond attempts to match clients to the best (individually compatible) therapy and therapist. Let us assume that a therapist, fully cognizant of specificity, has asked and affirmatively answered each of the following questions: Am I well-suited to this person? Do we appear to have established rapport? Would it not be in the client's best interests to be referred elsewhere? Do I feel confident that my ministrations will prove effective? Have I deduced what type of treatment style, form, speed, and cadence to adopt? Have we agreed upon the initial frequency and duration of the treatment sessions? Given positive responses to each of the foregoing, the therapist now deduces that the client will derive benefit from relaxation training. A new set of questions arise. Some of the more obvious ones are: Which of the many types of relaxation training programs is this particular client likely to respond to most favorably? How frequently, and for what length of time, should the client practice the selected relaxation sequence? Will compliance be augmented or attenuated by the supplementary use of cassettes for home use?

These types of questions are generally not pondered by Freudians, Jungians, Adlerians, Sullivanians, Rogerians, and most other psychotherapeutic disciplines. In my view, this omission has given rise to the omnibus theories, overgeneralizations, and the many fads that characterize the field. In this age of accountability, with new demands for cost-effective and cost–benefit analyses being foisted on the profession by outside agencies, our survival may depend on our ability to arrive at specific answers to highly specific questions.

Most of my own professional endeavors have focused on attempts to develop an assessment structure that would permit clinicians to ask the right questions in order to reach the most plausible solutions. While artistry and clinical intuition remain indispensible, a worthwhile goal is to have sufficient "checkpoints" and "markers" to minimize reliance on subjective factors. As long as the field of psychotherapy continues to spawn systems, schools, and other nonspecific and all-embracing orientations, there is little hope of achieving far-reaching scientific respectability. The need for greater specificity cannot be overstated.

SUMMARY

In theory, most clinicians agree that every client is a unique person, and treatment has to be tailored to his or her specific problems. In practice, the consumer all too often is fitted to preconceived treatment modes, whether or not this is what he or she requires. As a result, overgeneralizations and many fads characterize the field of psychotherapy. The present chapter cites research evidence in favor of specificity, and presents new clinical strategies for arriving at "custom-made" treatment choices.

REFERENCES

Foa, E. B., Steketee, G., & Milby, J. B. (1980). Differential effects of exposure and response prevention in obsessive–compulsive washers. *Journal of Consulting and Clinical Psychology, 48*, 71–79.

Foa, E. B., Steketee, G., & Turner, R. M. (1980). Effects of imaginal exposure to feared disasters in obsessive–compulsive checkers. *Behaviour Research and Therapy, 18*, 449–455.

Haley, J. (1976). *Problem solving therapy*. San Francisco: Jossey-Bass.

Herink, R. (1980). *The psychotherapy handbook*. New York: New American Library.

Holden, E. M. (1980). Primal therapy. In R. Herink (Ed.), *The psychotherapy handbook* (pp. 494 496). New York: New American Library.

Lazarus, A. A. (1981). *The practice of multimodal therapy*. New York: McGraw-Hill.

Marks, I. M., Hodgson, R., & Rachman, S. (1975). Treatment of chronic obsessive-compulsive neurosis by in vivo exposure. A two-year follow-up and issues in treatment. *British Journal of Psychiatry, 127*, 349 364.

Mowrer, O. H. (1980). Integrity groups. In R. Herink (Ed.), *The psychotherapy handbook* (pp. 313 315). New York: New American Library.

Öst, L.-G., Jerrelmalm, A., & Johansson, J. (1981). Individual response patterns and the effects of different behavioral methods in the treatment of social phobia. *Behaviour Research and Therapy, 19*, 1 16.

Öst, L.-G., Johansson, J., & Jerrelmalm, A. (1982). Individual response patterns and the effects of different behavioral methods in the treatment of claustrophobia. *Behaviour Research and Therapy, 20*, 445 460.

Paul, G. L. (1967). Strategy of outcome research in psychotherapy. *Journal of Consulting Psychology, 31*, 109 118.

Rachman, S., & Hodgson, R. (1980). *Obsessions and compulsions*. Englewood Cliffs, NJ: Prentice-Hall.

Steketee, G., Foa, E. B., & Grayson, J. B. (1982). Recent advances in the behavioral treatment of obsessive-compulsives. *Archives of General Psychiatry, 39*, 1365 1371.

AUTHOR INDEX

206

SUBJECT INDEX

Page numbers in italics indicate material in tables and figures.

ABC approach, 172
Adoptee Liberty Movement Association, 175
"Adult body weight phobia," 117
Affect
 agoraphobia, *40, 171, 184*
 alcohol dependence, *4*
 anorexia nervosa, 118–120, *130, 131*
 and BASIC I.D., 1, 2
 and cognitive dissonance, *110, 113*
 depression and obesity, *54*
 enuretic child, *72,* 78
 "ghetto clients," *85, 86, 96*
 Modality Profile construction, 7
 posttraumatic stress disorder, *102, 103*
 school teacher, consultation, *142,* 144
 somatization disorder, *150,* 151–153, *154*
 tension headache, *110*
 and therapy specificity, 202
 "typical" client, 20, *32*
Aggression, children, 70
Agoraphobia
 assessment and treatment plan, 39–48, 181,
  182
 family factors, 37–39
 "ghetto client," 84, *85*
 in vivo exposure, 6
 multimodal approach, 35–49, 168–186
Alcohol dependence, 3–6, 88
 Modality Profile, *4*
Anorexia nervosa, 116–138
 definition, 116, 117
 functional analysis, 117–120
 residential therapy, 120–127
Anxiety (*see also* Agoraphobia)
 in anorexia nervosa, 118–120
 autogenic therapy, 44
Arousal, anorexia nervosa, 132–134
Assertive Training for Women (Osborn &
  Harris), 66
Assertiveness Inventory, 82, 84, 87, *92, 93,* 95,
  100, 101, 102
Assertiveness schedule, 132–134
Assertiveness training
 agoraphobia, 174
 alcohol abuse case, 5, 6
 anorexia nervosa, 126, 132–134

depression/obesity case, 57–59, 66
 "typical" client, 30, 31
Assessment (*see* Multimodal assessment)
Astasia–abasia, 147–167
Attributions, agoraphobia, 42
Autogenic training, 126, 127
Aversive imagery, 5

BASIC I.D. (*see also specific modalities*)
 in agoraphobia, 35–49
 anorexia nervosa, 118–120, 122
 depression and obesity, 50–69
 description of, 1, 2
 Modality Profile construction, 7–11
 posttraumatic stress disorder, 99–107
 somatization disorder, 140, *150, 151*
 Structural Profiles, 13, 14
 and therapeutic activities, inpatients, *121*
BASIC I.D. Structural Profiles, 11, 12
Behavior
 agoraphobia, *40, 171, 172, 184*
 alcohol dependence, *4*
 anorexia nervosa, 118–120, *130, 131*
 and BASIC I.D., 1, 2
 and cognitive dissonance, *110, 113*
 depression and obesity, *54*
 enuretic child, *72,* 78
 "ghetto clients," *85, 96*
 Modality Profile construction, 7
 posttraumatic stress disorder, *102*
 school teacher, consultation, 142, *142,* 143
 somatization disorder, *150,* 151–153, *154*
 tension headache, *110*
 "typical" client, 20, *32*
 weight-loss program, 61–64
Behavior contracts
 anorexia nervosa, 122
 enuretic child, 75
Behavioral medicine, 108–115
Behavioral shaping, 27
Biofeedback, 109–112, 171 (*see also* Relaxation
  training)
Biology (*see* Drugs/biology)
Bipolar disorder, 168–175
Body image, 123

209